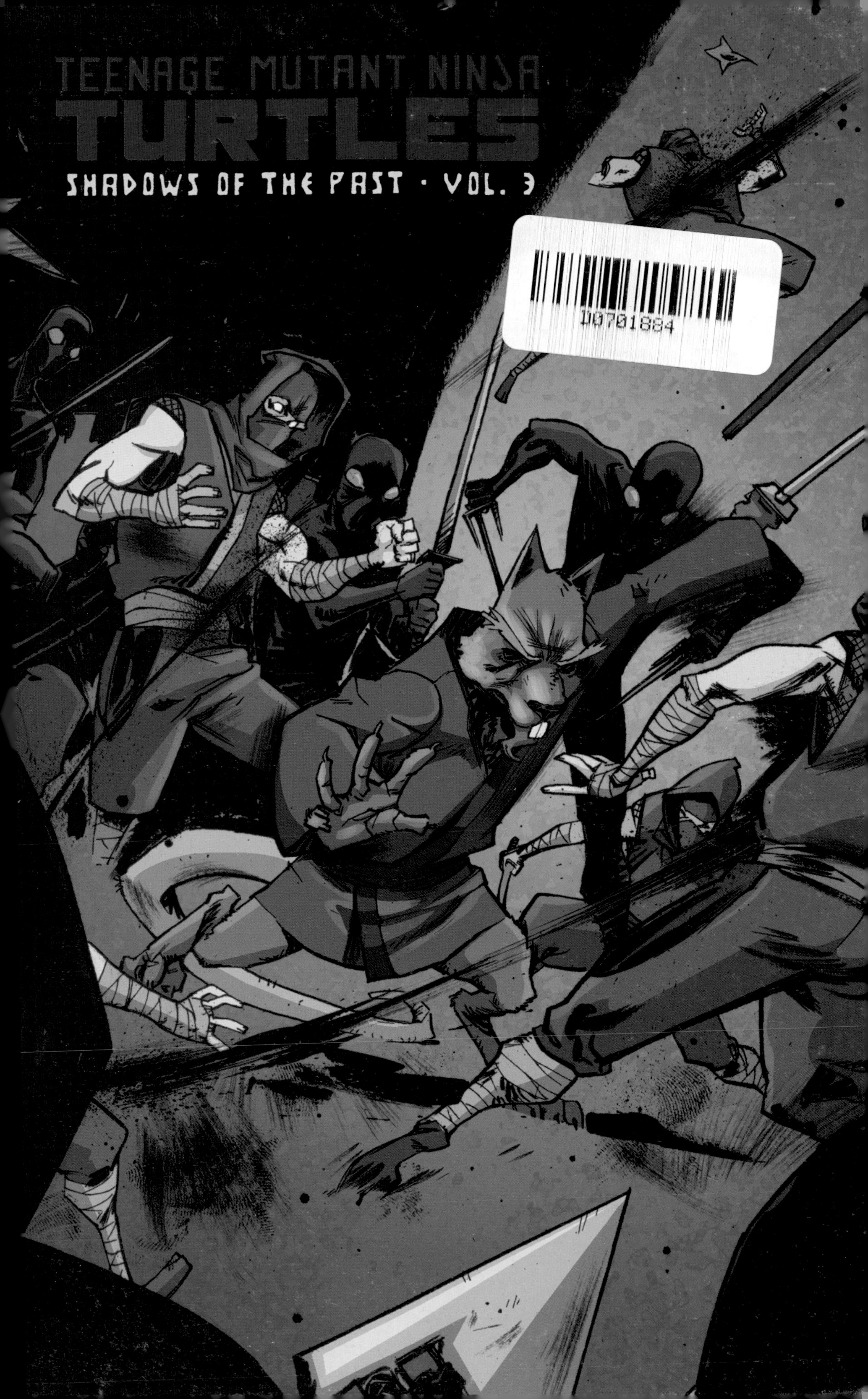
TEENAGE MUTANT NINJA
TURTLES
SHADOWS OF THE PAST · VOL. 3

Story by Kevin Eastman & Tom Waltz · Script by Tom Waltz
Art by Dan Duncan

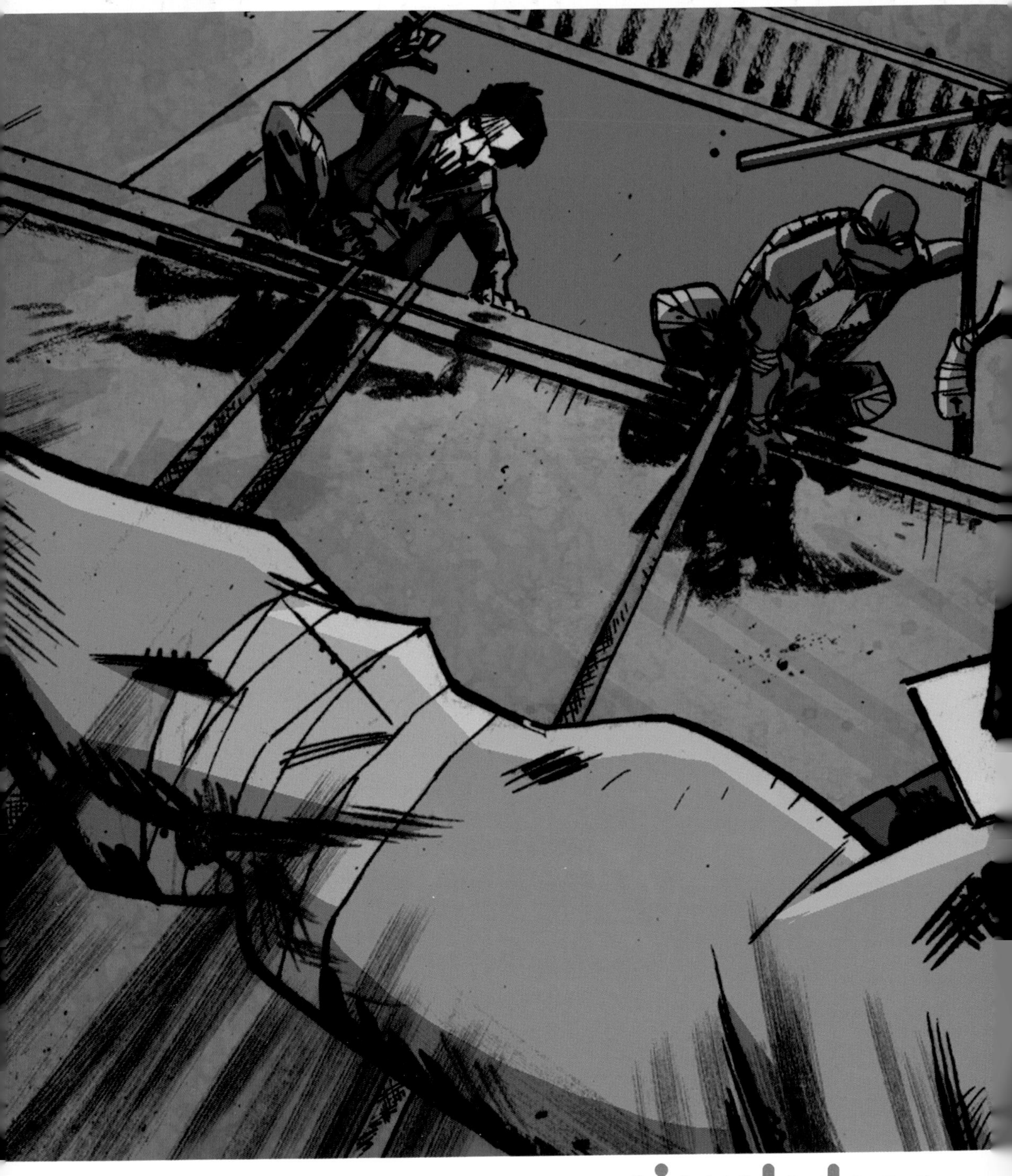

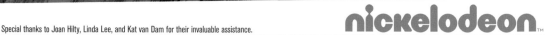

Special thanks to Joan Hilty, Linda Lee, and Kat van Dam for their invaluable assistance.

IDW founded by Ted Adams, Alex Garner, Kris Oprisko, and Robbie Robbins

ISBN: 978-1-61377-405-2

17 16 15 14   4 5 6 7

IDW

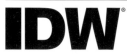

Ted Adams, CEO & Publisher
Greg Goldstein, President & COO
Robbie Robbins, EVP/Sr. Graphic Artist
Chris Ryall, Chief Creative Officer/Editor-in-Chief
Matthew Ruzicka, CPA, Chief Financial Officer
Alan Payne, VP of Sales
Dirk Wood, VP of Marketing
Lorelei Bunjes, VP of Digital Services

Originally published as TEENAGE MUTANT NINJA TURTLES Issues #9–12.

Colors by Ronda Pattison • Letters by Shawn Lee & Chris Mowry

Series Edits by Bobby Curnow

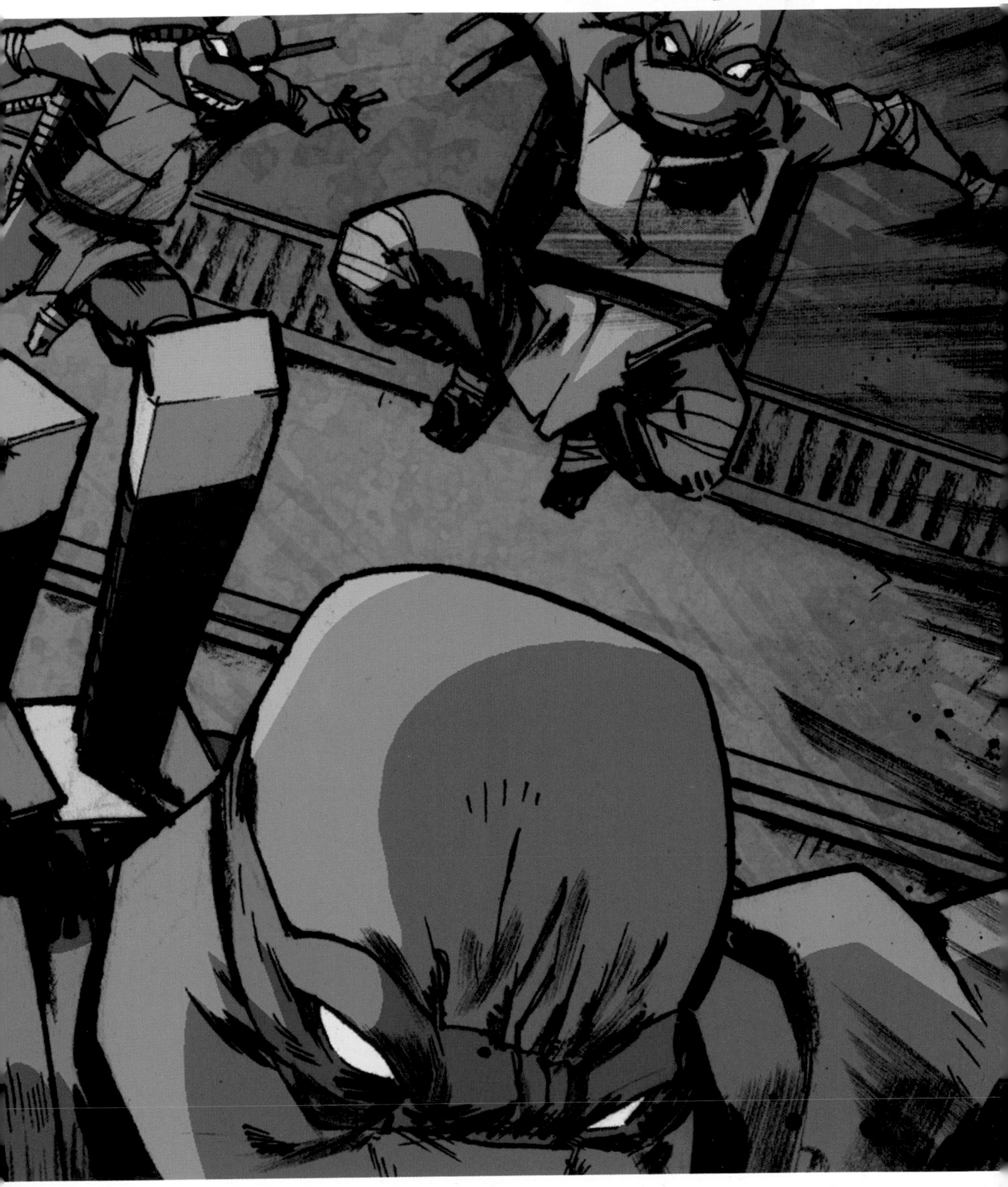

Collection Edits by Justin Eisinger & Alonzo Simon

Collection Design by Robbie Robbins • Cover by Dan Duncan • Cover Colors by Ronda Pattison

Based on characters created by Peter Laird and Kevin Eastman

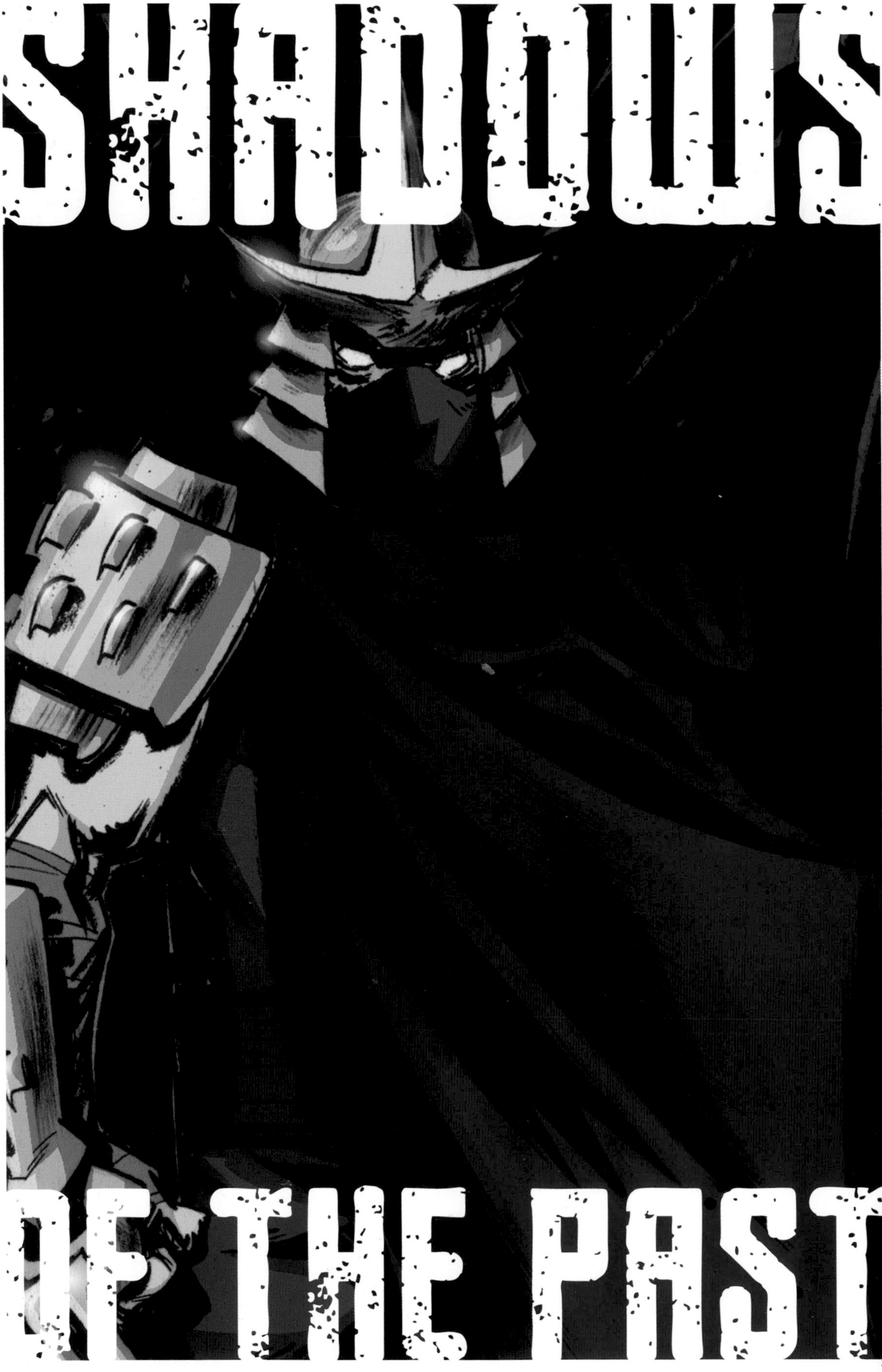
SHADOWS
OF THE PAST

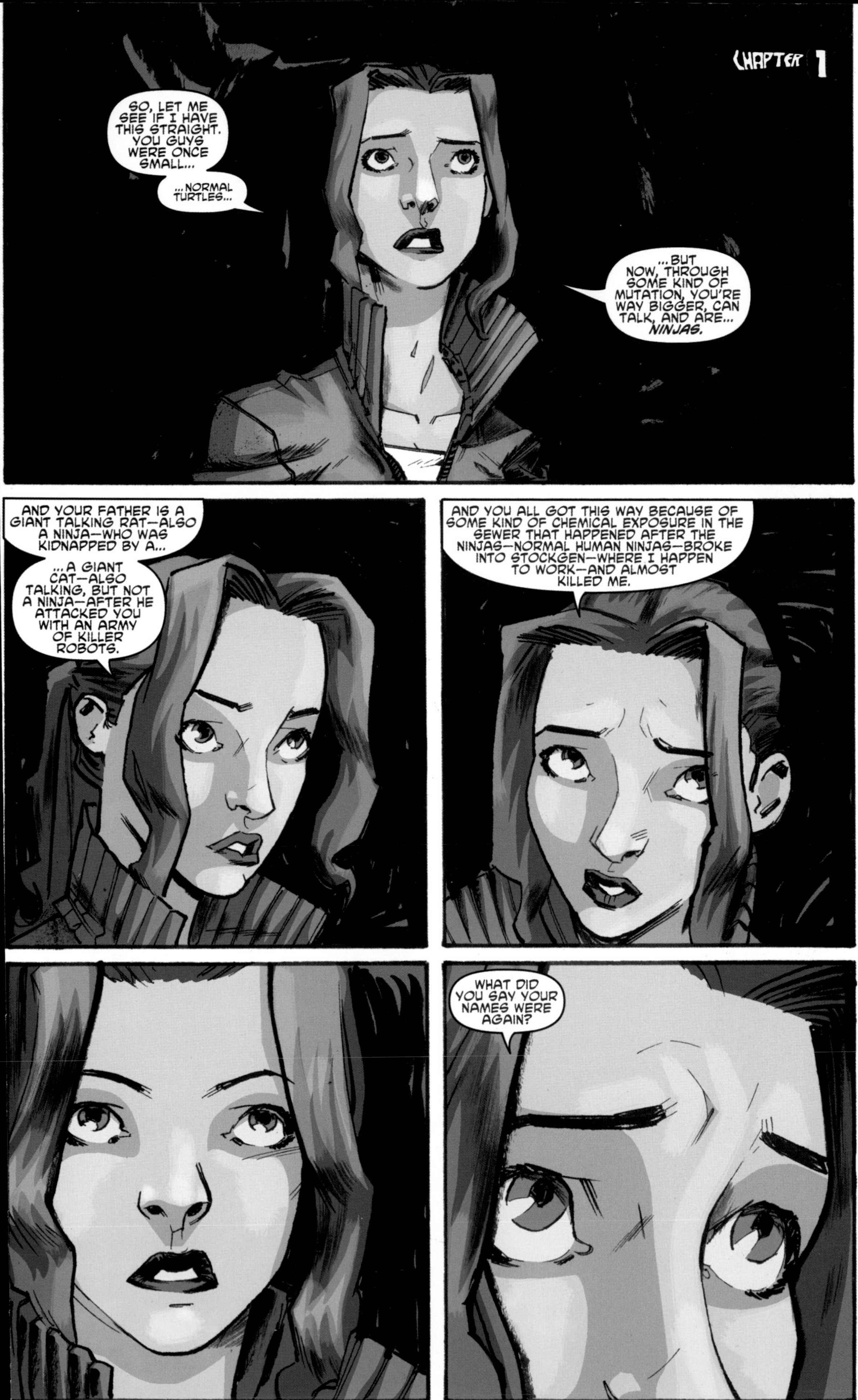
CHAPTER 1
SO, LET ME SEE IF I HAVE THIS STRAIGHT. YOU GUYS WERE ONCE SMALL...
...NORMAL TURTLES...
...BUT NOW, THROUGH SOME KIND OF MUTATION, YOU'RE WAY BIGGER, CAN TALK, AND ARE... NINJAS.
AND YOUR FATHER IS A GIANT TALKING RAT—ALSO A NINJA—WHO WAS KIDNAPPED BY A...
...A GIANT CAT—ALSO TALKING, BUT NOT A NINJA—AFTER HE ATTACKED YOU WITH AN ARMY OF KILLER ROBOTS.
AND YOU ALL GOT THIS WAY BECAUSE OF SOME KIND OF CHEMICAL EXPOSURE IN THE SEWER THAT HAPPENED AFTER THE NINJAS—NORMAL HUMAN NINJAS—BROKE INTO STOCKGEN—WHERE I HAPPEN TO WORK—AND ALMOST KILLED ME.
WHAT DID YOU SAY YOUR NAMES WERE AGAIN?

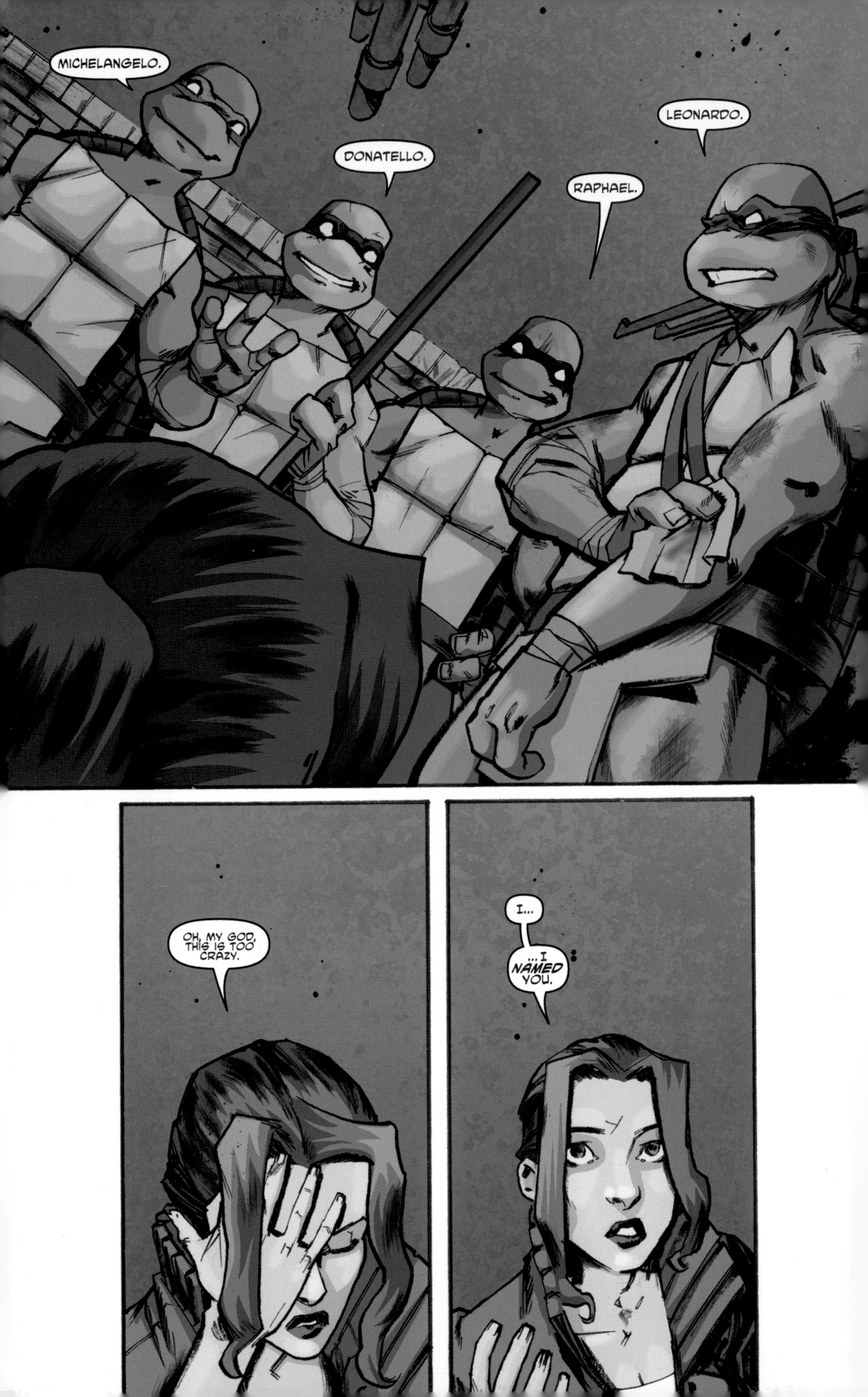
MICHELANGELO.
DONATELLO.
RAPHAEL.
LEONARDO.
OH, MY GOD, THIS IS TOO CRAZY.
I...
...I *NAMED* YOU.

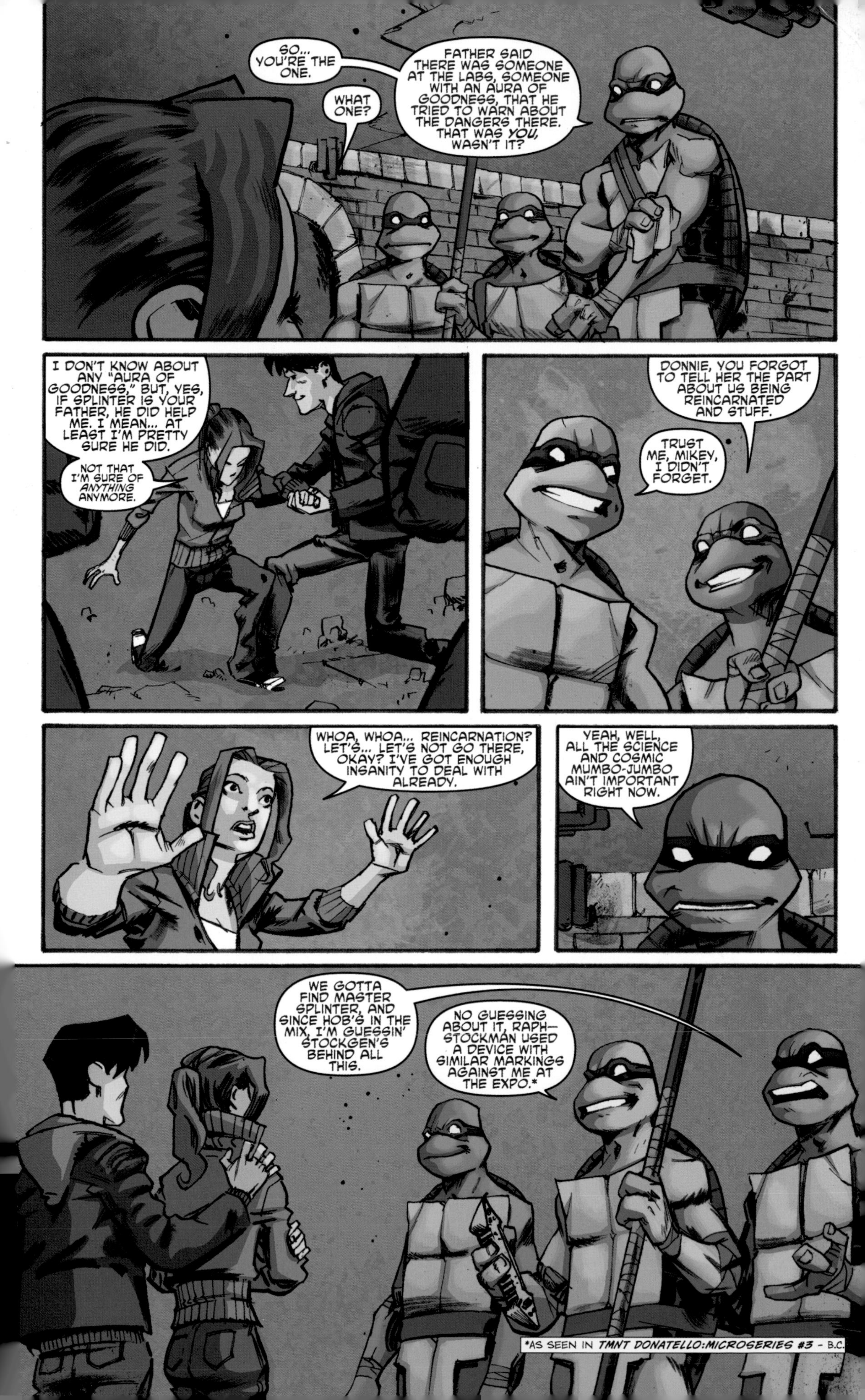
SO... YOU'RE THE ONE.
WHAT ONE?
FATHER SAID THERE WAS SOMEONE AT THE LABS, SOMEONE WITH AN AURA OF GOODNESS, THAT HE TRIED TO WARN ABOUT THE DANGERS THERE. THAT WAS YOU, WASN'T IT?
I DON'T KNOW ABOUT ANY "AURA OF GOODNESS," BUT, YES, IF SPLINTER IS YOUR FATHER, HE DID HELP ME. I MEAN... AT LEAST I'M PRETTY SURE HE DID.
NOT THAT I'M SURE OF ANYTHING ANYMORE.
DONNIE, YOU FORGOT TO TELL HER THE PART ABOUT US BEING REINCARNATED AND STUFF.
TRUST ME, MIKEY, I DIDN'T FORGET.
WHOA, WHOA... REINCARNATION? LET'S... LET'S NOT GO THERE, OKAY? I'VE GOT ENOUGH INSANITY TO DEAL WITH ALREADY.
YEAH, WELL, ALL THE SCIENCE AND COSMIC MUMBO-JUMBO AIN'T IMPORTANT RIGHT NOW.
WE GOTTA FIND MASTER SPLINTER, AND SINCE HOB'S IN THE MIX, I'M GUESSIN' STOCKGEN'S BEHIND ALL THIS.
NO GUESSING ABOUT IT, RAPH—STOCKMAN USED A DEVICE WITH SIMILAR MARKINGS AGAINST ME AT THE EXPO.*
*AS SEEN IN TMNT DONATELLO: MICROSERIES #3 - B.C.

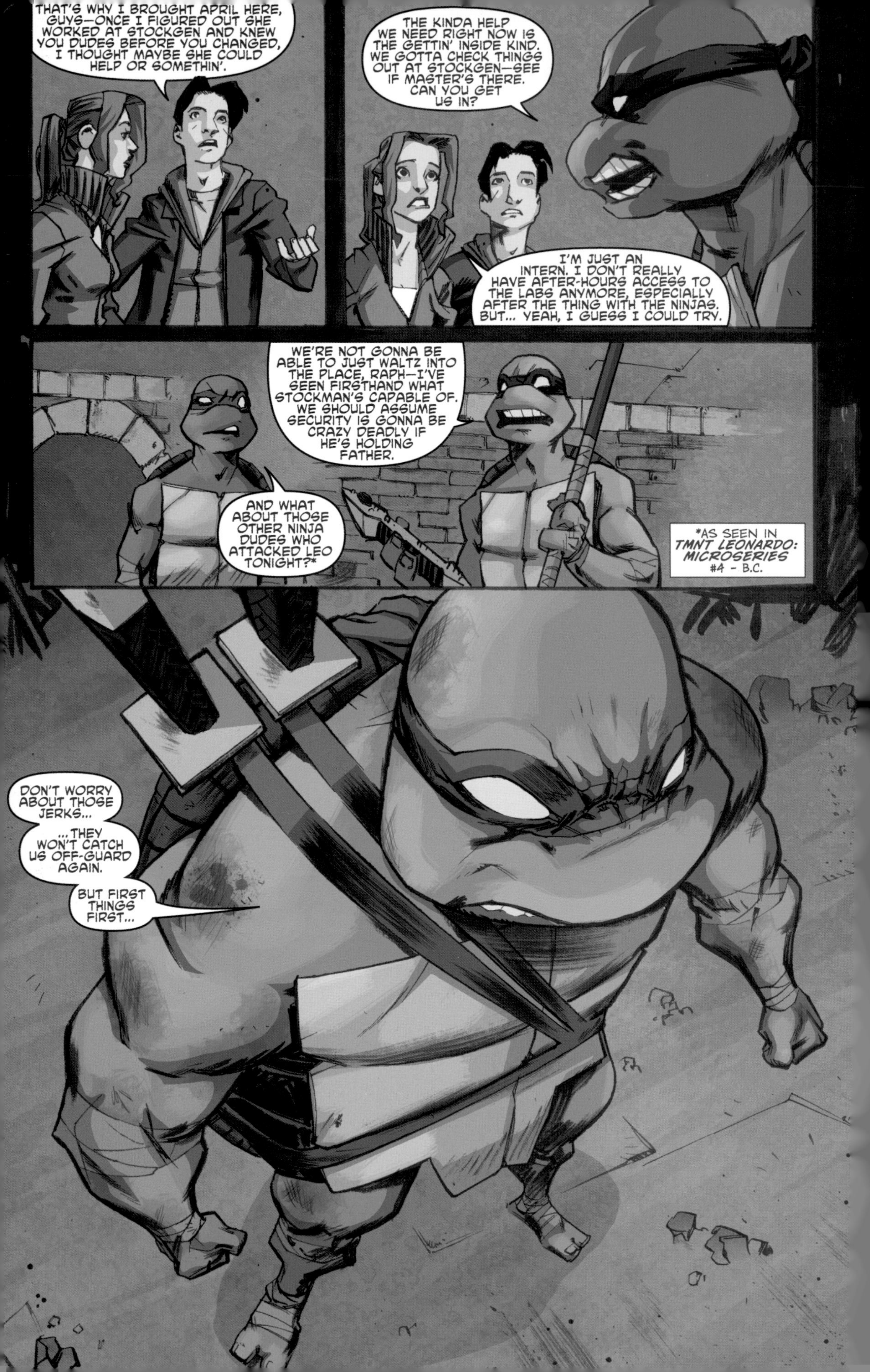
THAT'S WHY I BROUGHT APRIL HERE, GUYS—ONCE I FIGURED OUT SHE WORKED AT STOCKGEN AND KNEW YOU DUDES BEFORE YOU CHANGED, I THOUGHT MAYBE SHE COULD HELP OR SOMETHIN'.
THE KINDA HELP WE NEED RIGHT NOW IS THE GETTIN' INSIDE KIND. WE GOTTA CHECK THINGS OUT AT STOCKGEN—SEE IF MASTER'S THERE. CAN YOU GET US IN?
I'M JUST AN INTERN. I DON'T REALLY HAVE AFTER-HOURS ACCESS TO THE LABS ANYMORE, ESPECIALLY AFTER THE THING WITH THE NINJAS. BUT... YEAH, I GUESS I COULD TRY.
WE'RE NOT GONNA BE ABLE TO JUST WALTZ INTO THE PLACE, RAPH—I'VE SEEN FIRSTHAND WHAT STOCKMAN'S CAPABLE OF. WE SHOULD ASSUME SECURITY IS GONNA BE CRAZY DEADLY IF HE'S HOLDING FATHER.
AND WHAT ABOUT THOSE OTHER NINJA DUDES WHO ATTACKED LEO TONIGHT?*
*AS SEEN IN TMNT LEONARDO: MICROSERIES #4 - B.C.
DON'T WORRY ABOUT THOSE JERKS...
...THEY WON'T CATCH US OFF-GUARD AGAIN.
BUT FIRST THINGS FIRST...

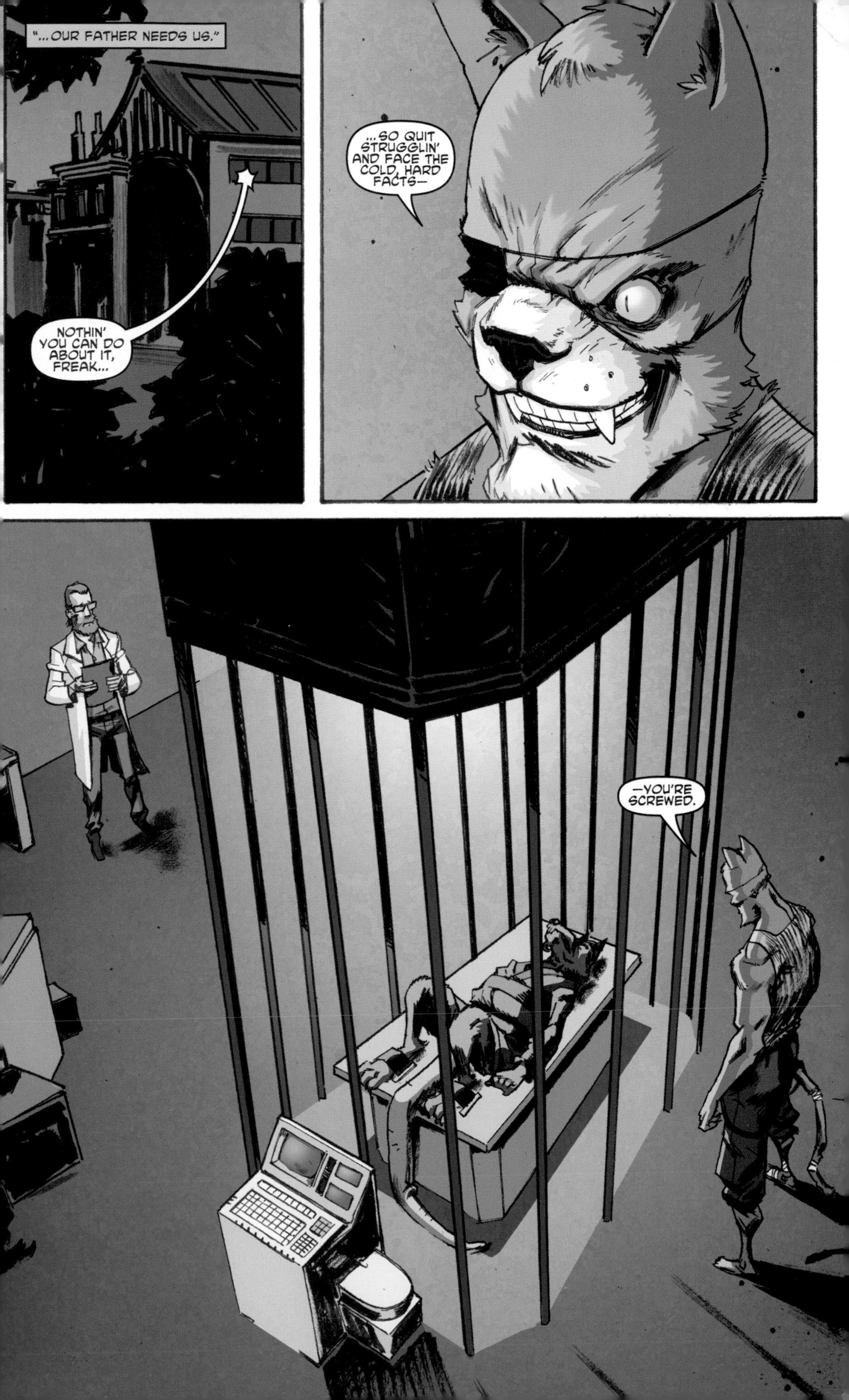
"...OUR FATHER NEEDS US."
NOTHIN' YOU CAN DO ABOUT IT, FREAK...
...SO QUIT STRUGGLIN' AND FACE THE COLD, HARD FACTS—
—YOU'RE SCREWED.

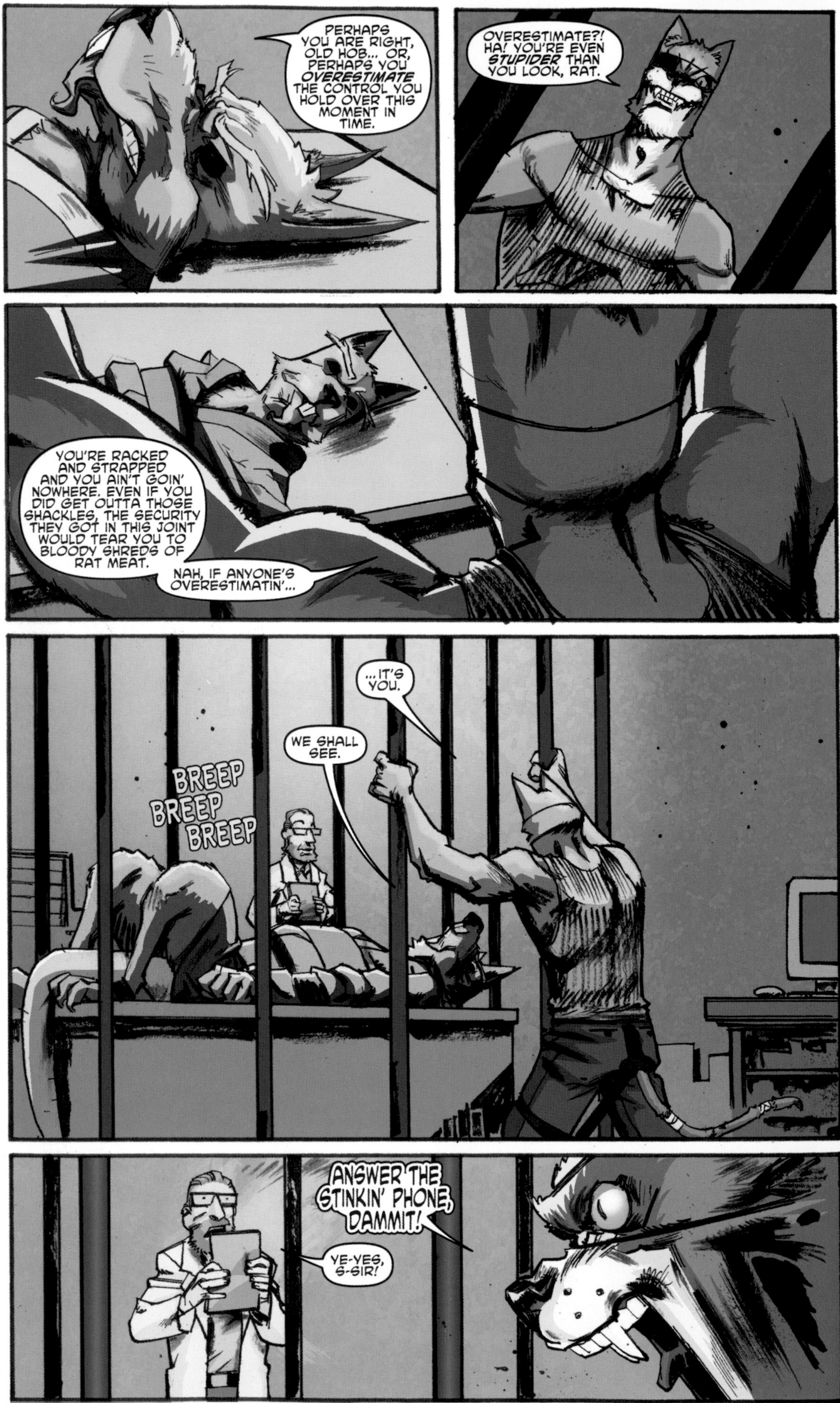
PERHAPS YOU ARE RIGHT, OLD HOB... OR, PERHAPS YOU *OVERESTIMATE* THE CONTROL YOU HOLD OVER THIS MOMENT IN TIME.
OVERESTIMATE?! HA! YOU'RE EVEN *STUPIDER* THAN YOU LOOK, RAT.
YOU'RE RACKED AND STRAPPED AND YOU AIN'T GOIN' NOWHERE. EVEN IF YOU DID GET OUTTA THOSE SHACKLES, THE SECURITY THEY GOT IN THIS JOINT WOULD TEAR YOU TO BLOODY SHREDS OF RAT MEAT.
NAH, IF ANYONE'S OVERESTIMATIN'...
...IT'S YOU.
WE SHALL SEE.
BREEP BREEP BREEP
ANSWER THE STINKIN' PHONE, DAMMIT!
YE-YES, S-SIR!

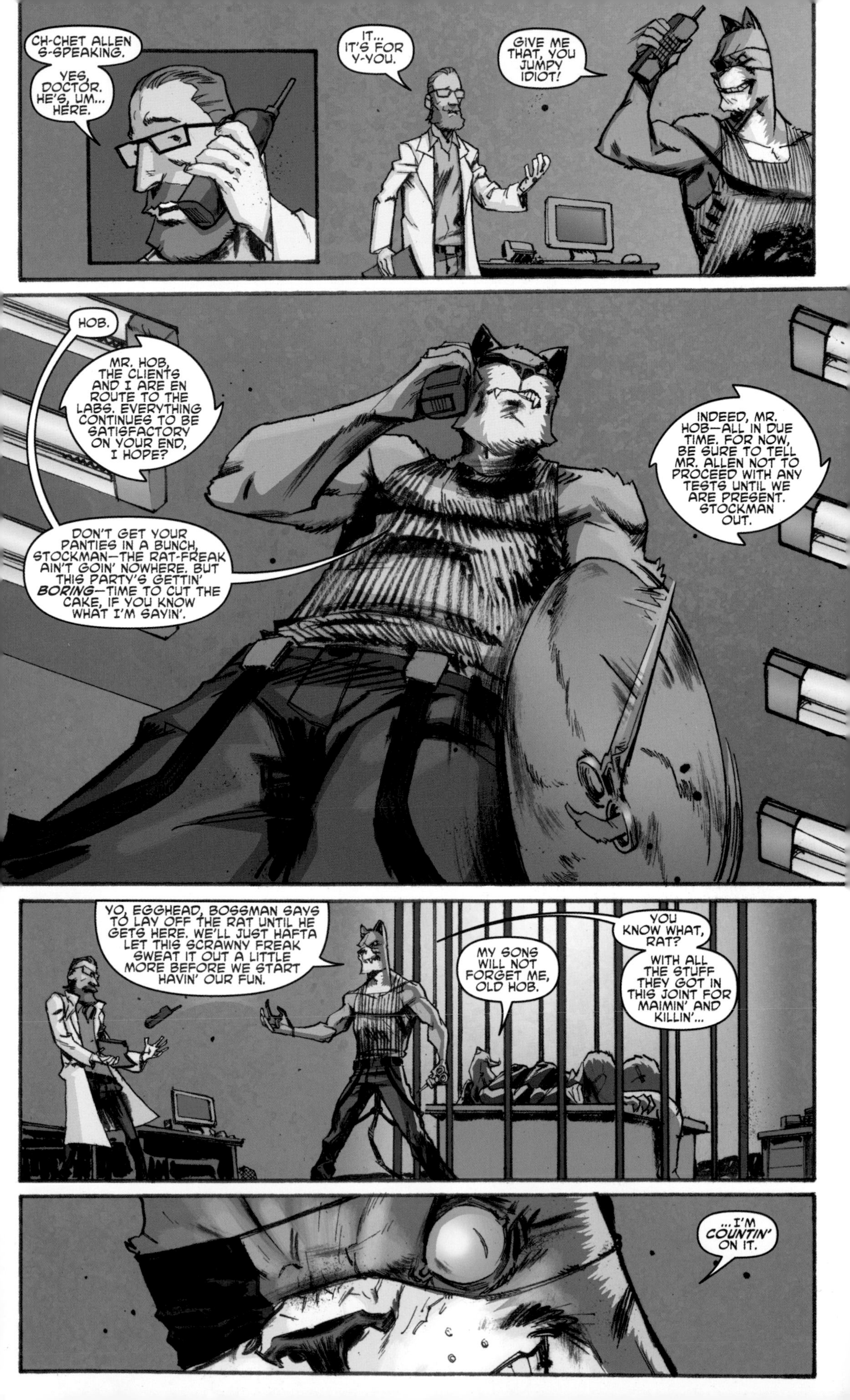
CH-CHET ALLEN S-SPEAKING.
YES, DOCTOR. HE'S, UM... HERE.
IT... IT'S FOR Y-YOU.
GIVE ME THAT, YOU JUMPY IDIOT!
HOB.
MR. HOB, THE CLIENTS AND I ARE EN ROUTE TO THE LABS. EVERYTHING CONTINUES TO BE SATISFACTORY ON YOUR END, I HOPE?
DON'T GET YOUR PANTIES IN A BUNCH, STOCKMAN—THE RAT-FREAK AIN'T GOIN' NOWHERE. BUT THIS PARTY'S GETTIN' *BORING*—TIME TO CUT THE CAKE, IF YOU KNOW WHAT I'M SAYIN'.
INDEED, MR. HOB—ALL IN DUE TIME. FOR NOW, BE SURE TO TELL MR. ALLEN NOT TO PROCEED WITH ANY TESTS UNTIL WE ARE PRESENT. STOCKMAN OUT.
YO, EGGHEAD, BOSSMAN SAYS TO LAY OFF THE RAT UNTIL HE GETS HERE. WE'LL JUST HAFTA LET THIS SCRAWNY FREAK SWEAT IT OUT A LITTLE MORE BEFORE WE START HAVIN' OUR FUN.
MY SONS WILL NOT FORGET ME, OLD HOB.
YOU KNOW WHAT, RAT?
WITH ALL THE STUFF THEY GOT IN THIS JOINT FOR MAIMIN' AND KILLIN'...
...I'M *COUNTIN'* ON IT.

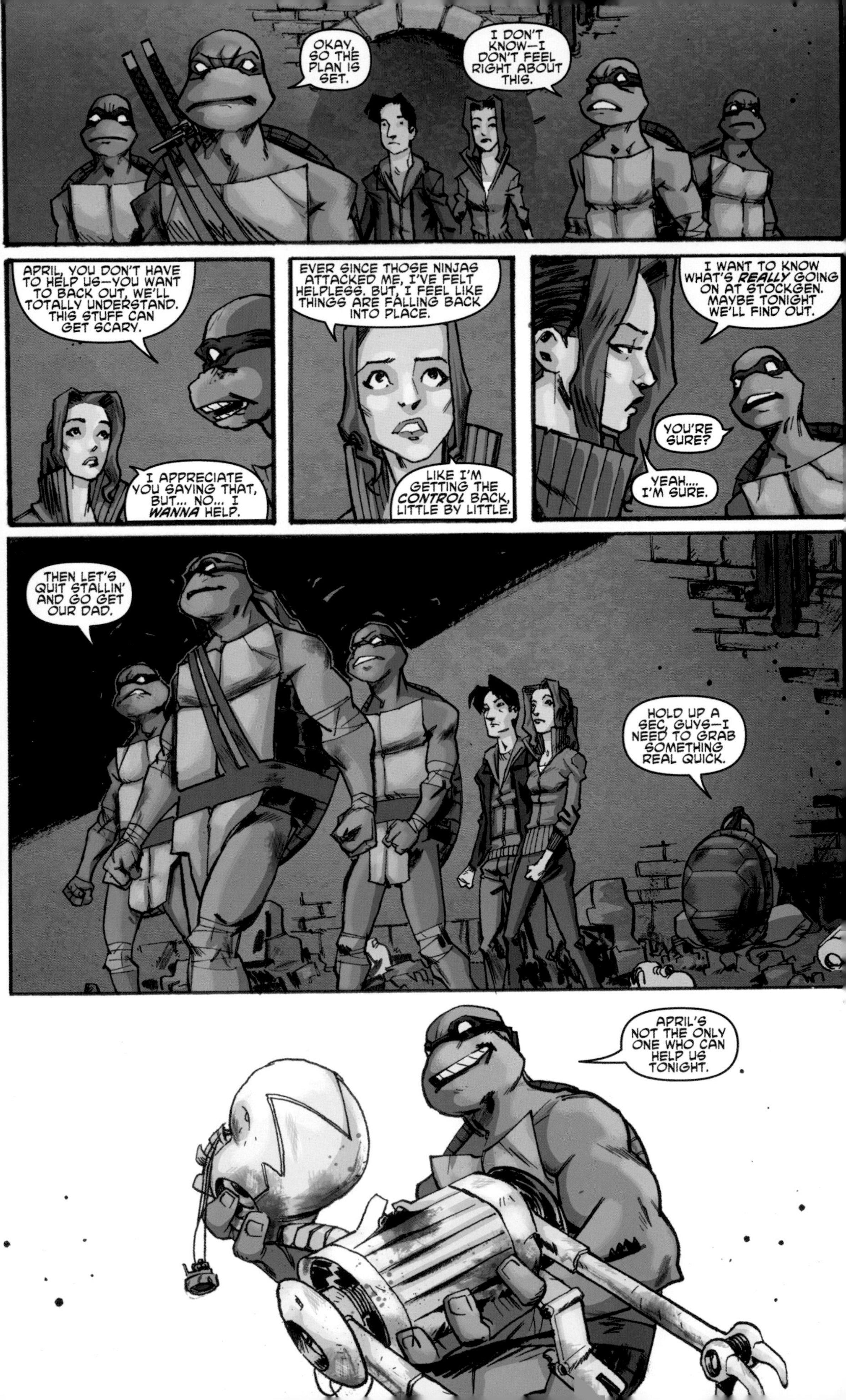
OKAY, SO THE PLAN IS SET.
I DON'T KNOW—I DON'T FEEL RIGHT ABOUT THIS.
APRIL, YOU DON'T HAVE TO HELP US—YOU WANT TO BACK OUT, WE'LL TOTALLY UNDERSTAND. THIS STUFF CAN GET SCARY.
I APPRECIATE YOU SAYING THAT, BUT... NO... I WANNA HELP.
EVER SINCE THOSE NINJAS ATTACKED ME, I'VE FELT HELPLESS. BUT, I FEEL LIKE THINGS ARE FALLING BACK INTO PLACE.
LIKE I'M GETTING THE CONTROL BACK, LITTLE BY LITTLE.
I WANT TO KNOW WHAT'S REALLY GOING ON AT STOCKGEN. MAYBE TONIGHT WE'LL FIND OUT.
YOU'RE SURE?
YEAH.... I'M SURE.
THEN LET'S QUIT STALLIN' AND GO GET OUR DAD.
HOLD UP A SEC, GUYS—I NEED TO GRAB SOMETHING REAL QUICK.
APRIL'S NOT THE ONLY ONE WHO CAN HELP US TONIGHT.

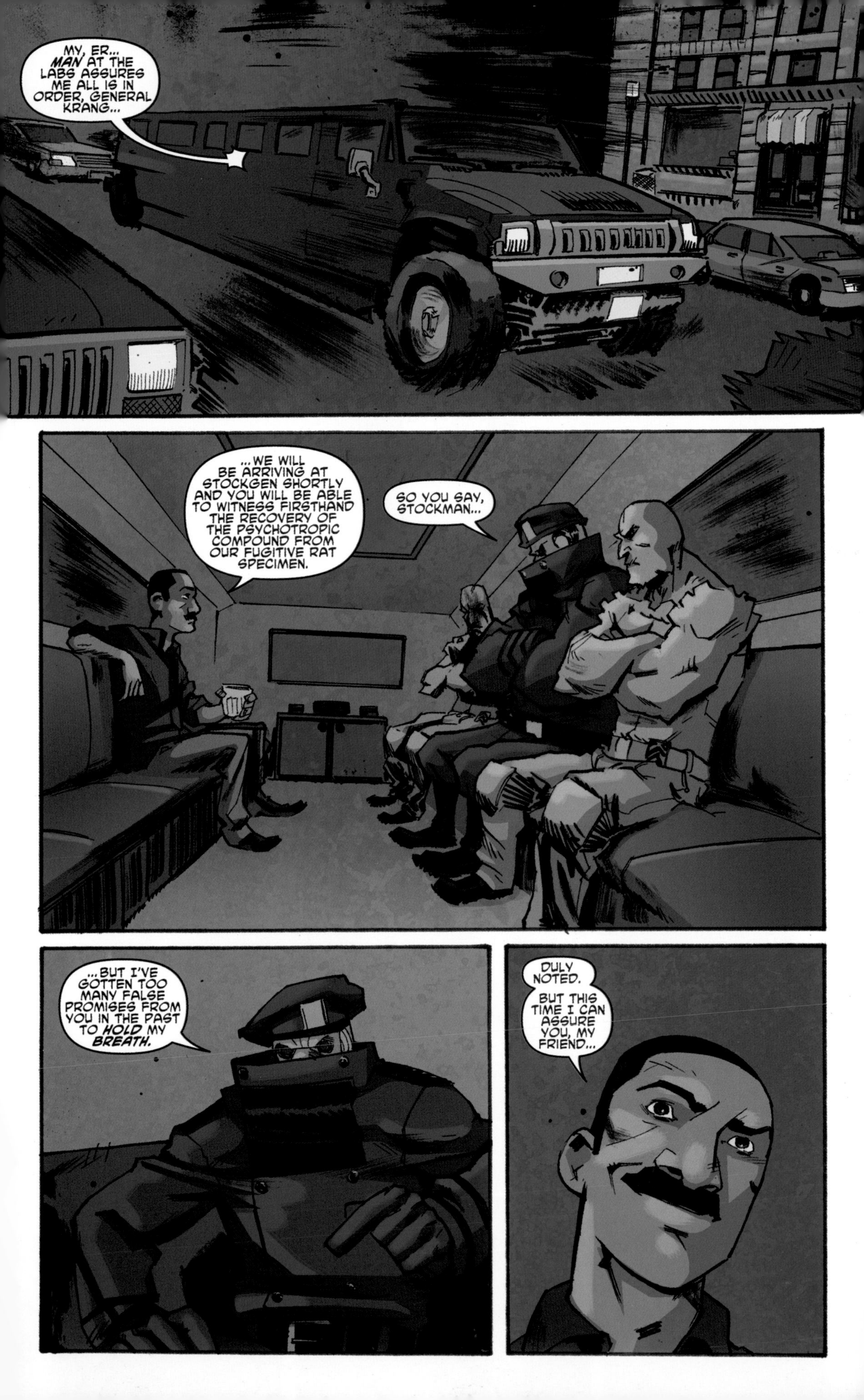
MY, ER... MAN AT THE LABS ASSURES ME ALL IS IN ORDER, GENERAL KRANG...
...WE WILL BE ARRIVING AT STOCKGEN SHORTLY AND YOU WILL BE ABLE TO WITNESS FIRSTHAND THE RECOVERY OF THE PSYCHOTROPIC COMPOUND FROM OUR FUGITIVE RAT SPECIMEN.
SO YOU SAY, STOCKMAN...
...BUT I'VE GOTTEN TOO MANY FALSE PROMISES FROM YOU IN THE PAST TO HOLD MY BREATH.
DULY NOTED.
BUT THIS TIME I CAN ASSURE YOU, MY FRIEND...

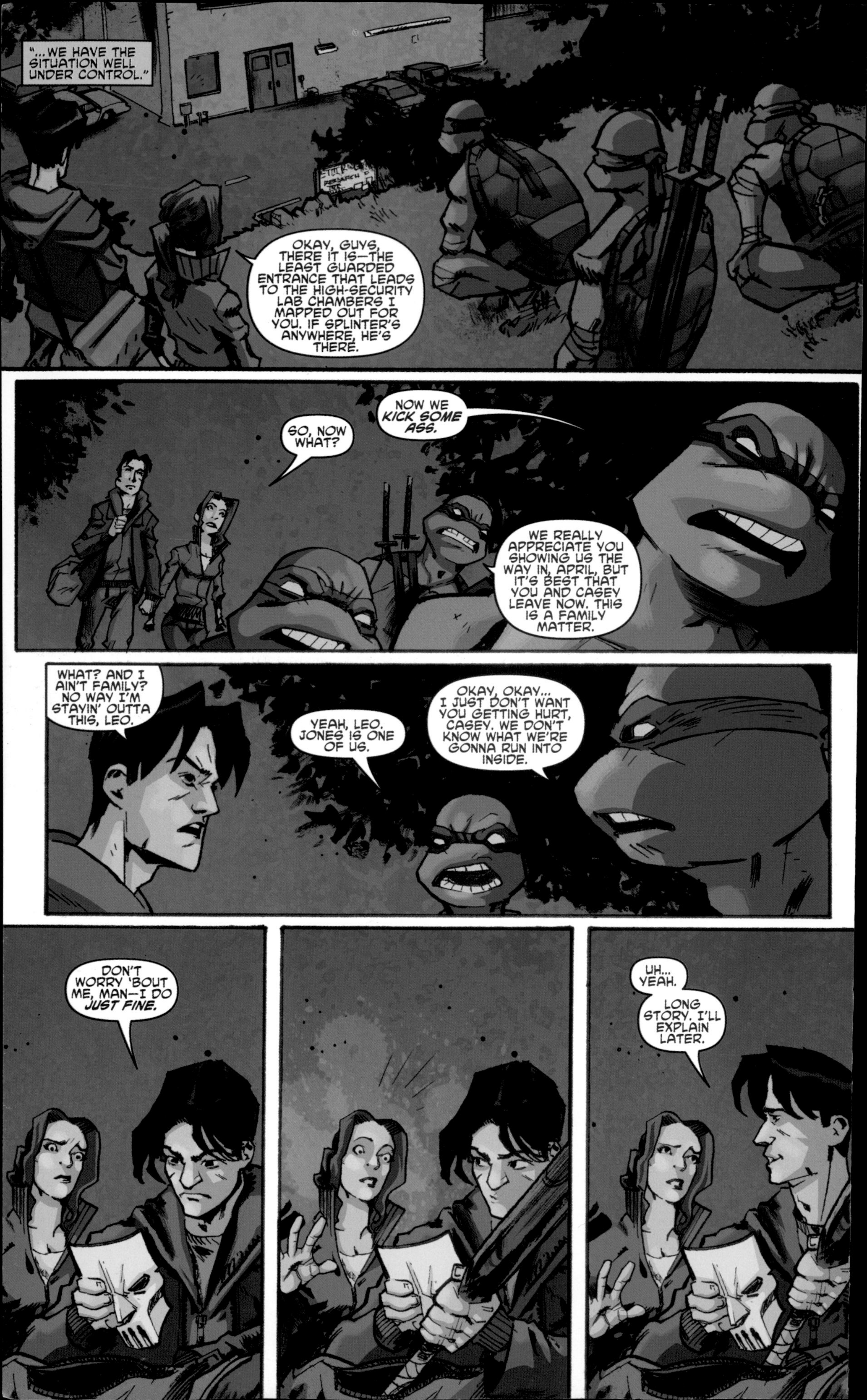
"...WE HAVE THE SITUATION WELL UNDER CONTROL."
OKAY, GUYS, THERE IT IS—THE LEAST GUARDED ENTRANCE THAT LEADS TO THE HIGH-SECURITY LAB CHAMBERS I MAPPED OUT FOR YOU. IF SPLINTER'S ANYWHERE, HE'S THERE.
SO, NOW WHAT?
NOW WE *KICK SOME ASS.*
WE REALLY APPRECIATE YOU SHOWING US THE WAY IN, APRIL, BUT IT'S BEST THAT YOU AND CASEY LEAVE NOW. THIS IS A FAMILY MATTER.
WHAT? AND I AIN'T FAMILY? NO WAY I'M STAYIN' OUTTA THIS, LEO.
YEAH, LEO. JONES IS ONE OF US.
OKAY, OKAY... I JUST DON'T WANT YOU GETTING HURT, CASEY. WE DON'T KNOW WHAT WE'RE GONNA RUN INTO INSIDE.
DON'T WORRY 'BOUT ME, MAN—I DO *JUST FINE.*
UH... YEAH.
LONG STORY. I'LL EXPLAIN LATER.

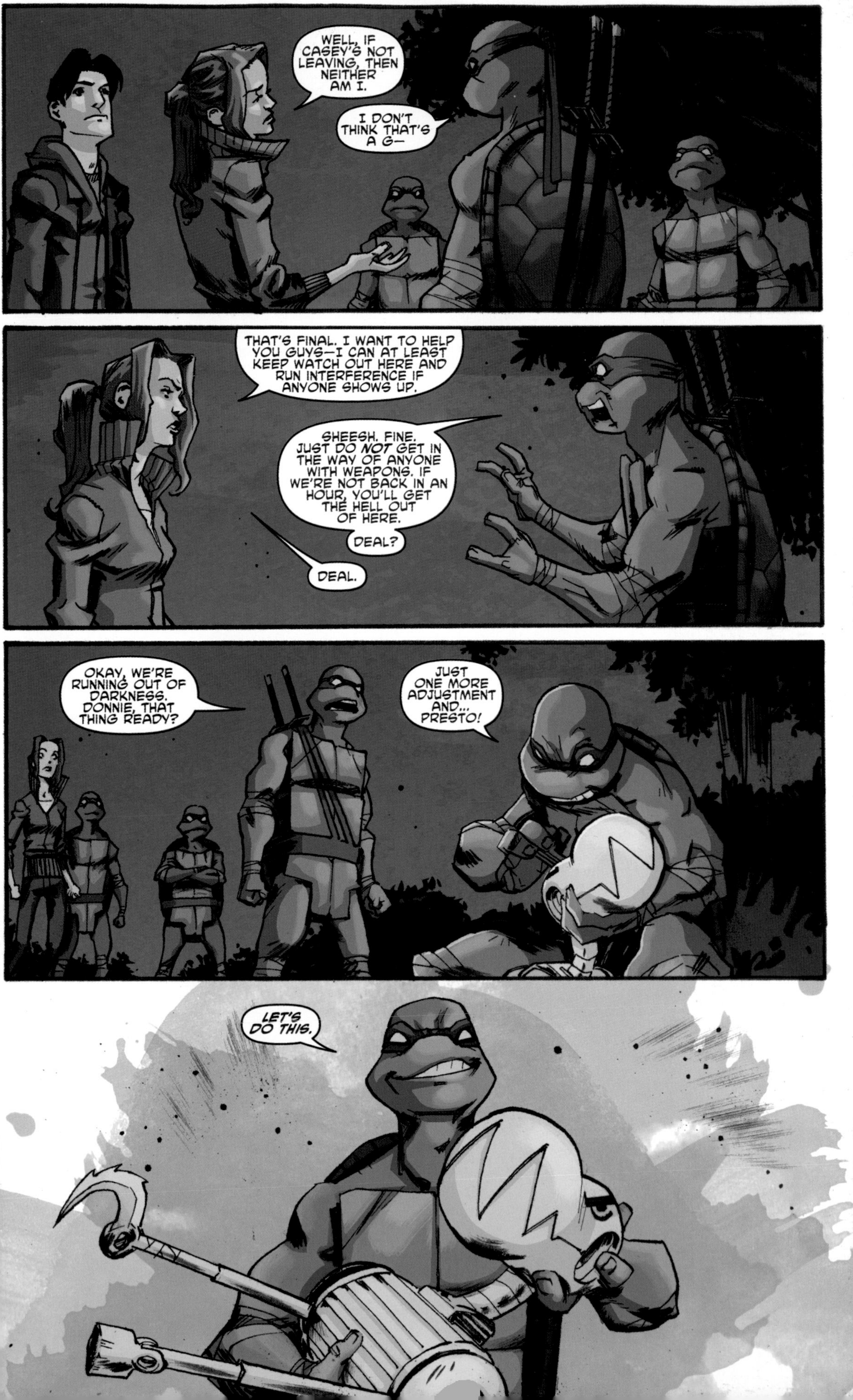
WELL, IF CASEY'S NOT LEAVING, THEN NEITHER AM I.
I DON'T THINK THAT'S A G—
THAT'S FINAL. I WANT TO HELP YOU GUYS—I CAN AT LEAST KEEP WATCH OUT HERE AND RUN INTERFERENCE IF ANYONE SHOWS UP.
SHEESH. FINE. JUST DO *NOT* GET IN THE WAY OF ANYONE WITH WEAPONS. IF WE'RE NOT BACK IN AN HOUR, YOU'LL GET THE HELL OUT OF HERE.
DEAL?
DEAL.
OKAY, WE'RE RUNNING OUT OF DARKNESS. DONNIE, THAT THING READY?
JUST ONE MORE ADJUSTMENT AND... PRESTO!
LET'S DO THIS.

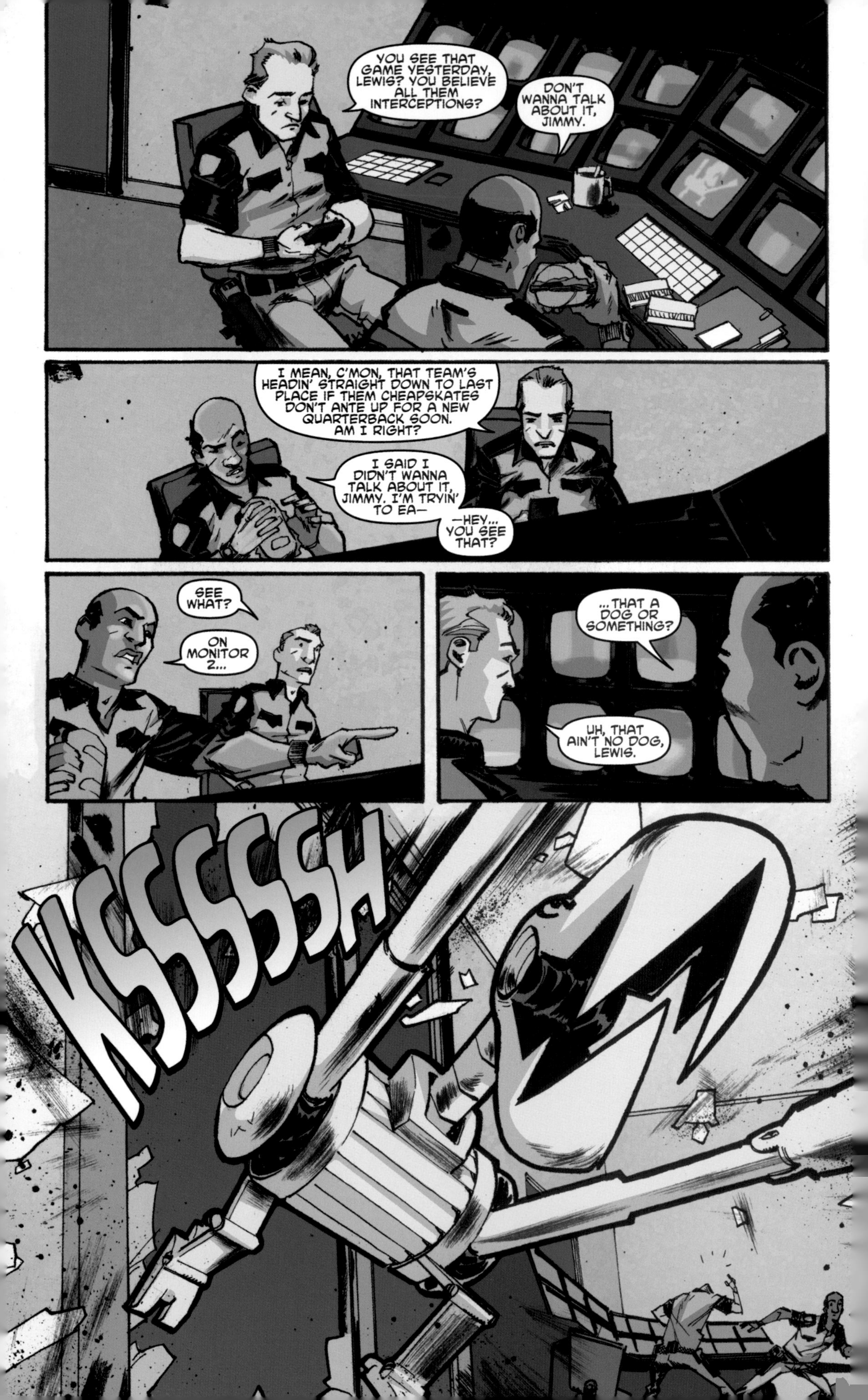
YOU SEE THAT GAME YESTERDAY, LEWIS? YOU BELIEVE ALL THEM INTERCEPTIONS?
DON'T WANNA TALK ABOUT IT, JIMMY.
I MEAN, C'MON, THAT TEAM'S HEADIN' STRAIGHT DOWN TO LAST PLACE IF THEM CHEAPSKATES DON'T ANTE UP FOR A NEW QUARTERBACK SOON. AM I RIGHT?
I SAID I DIDN'T WANNA TALK ABOUT IT, JIMMY. I'M TRYIN' TO EA—
—HEY... YOU SEE THAT?
SEE WHAT?
ON MONITOR 2...
...THAT A DOG OR SOMETHING?
UH, THAT AIN'T NO DOG, LEWIS.
KSSSSSH

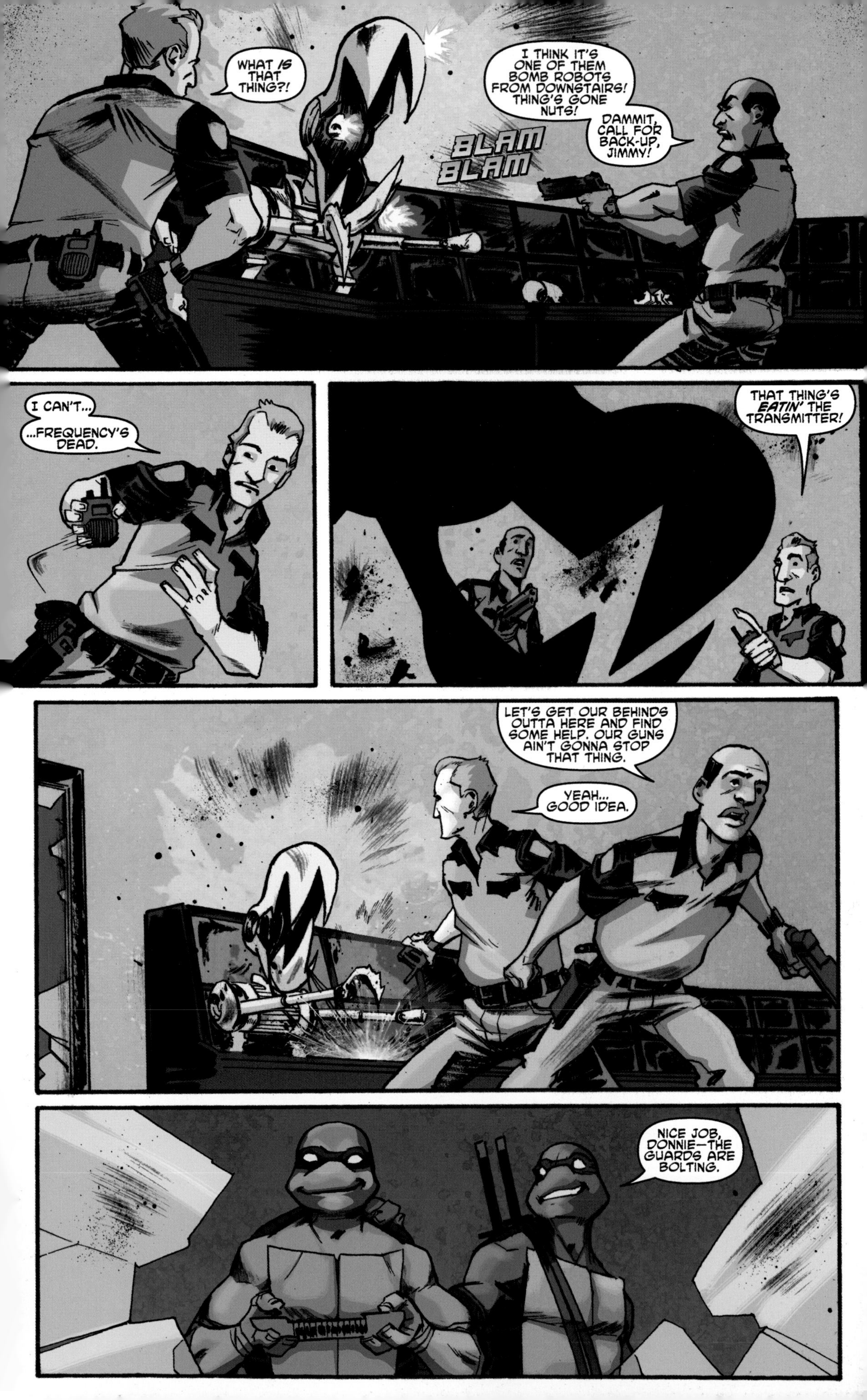
WHAT IS THAT THING?!
I THINK IT'S ONE OF THEM BOMB ROBOTS FROM DOWNSTAIRS! THING'S GONE NUTS!
BLAM BLAM
DAMMIT, CALL FOR BACK-UP, JIMMY!
I CAN'T...
...FREQUENCY'S DEAD.
THAT THING'S EATIN' THE TRANSMITTER!
LET'S GET OUR BEHINDS OUTTA HERE AND FIND SOME HELP. OUR GUNS AIN'T GONNA STOP THAT THING.
YEAH... GOOD IDEA.
NICE JOB, DONNIE—THE GUARDS ARE BOLTING.

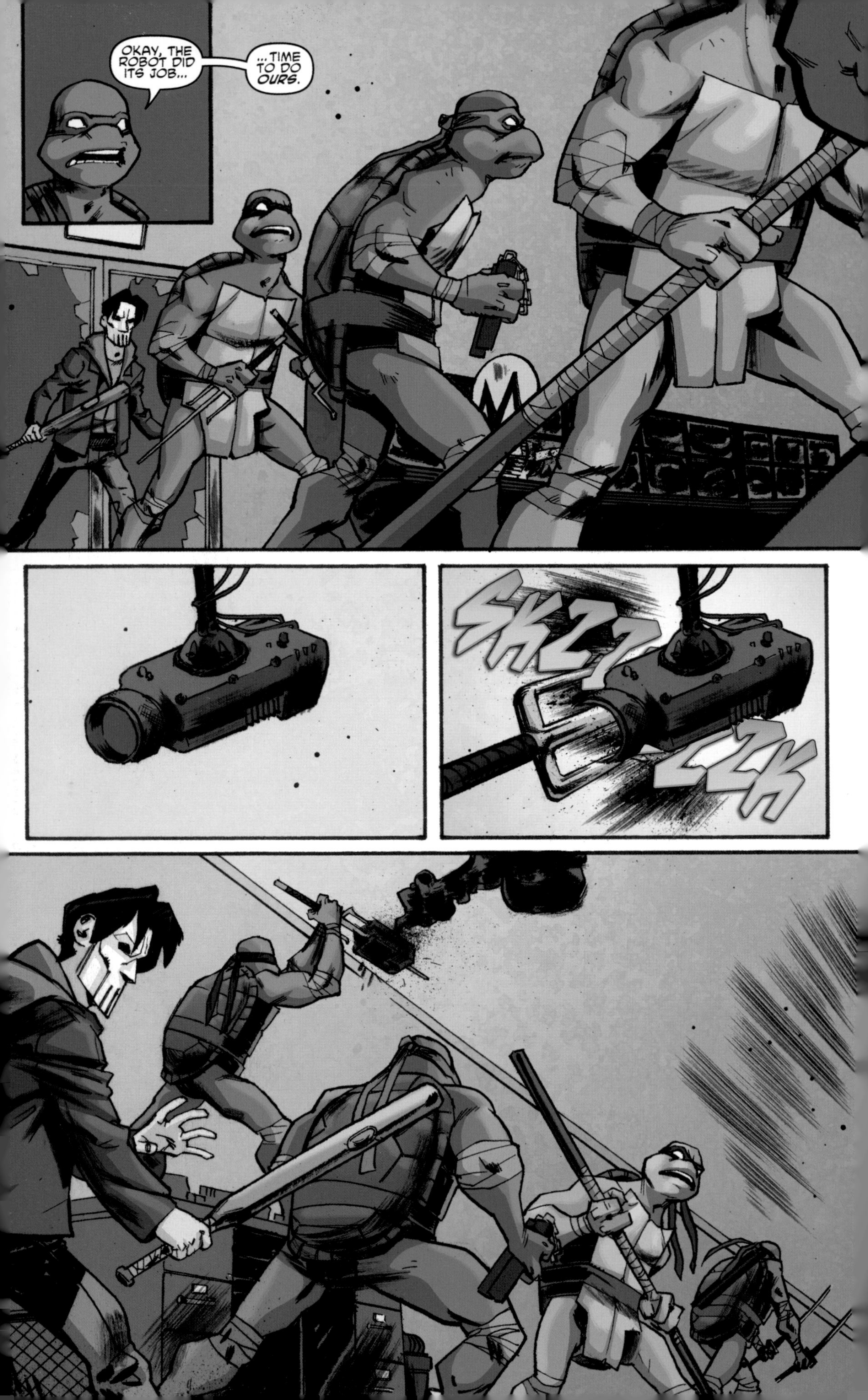
OKAY, THE ROBOT DID ITS JOB...
...TIME TO DO OURS.
SKZZ
ZZK

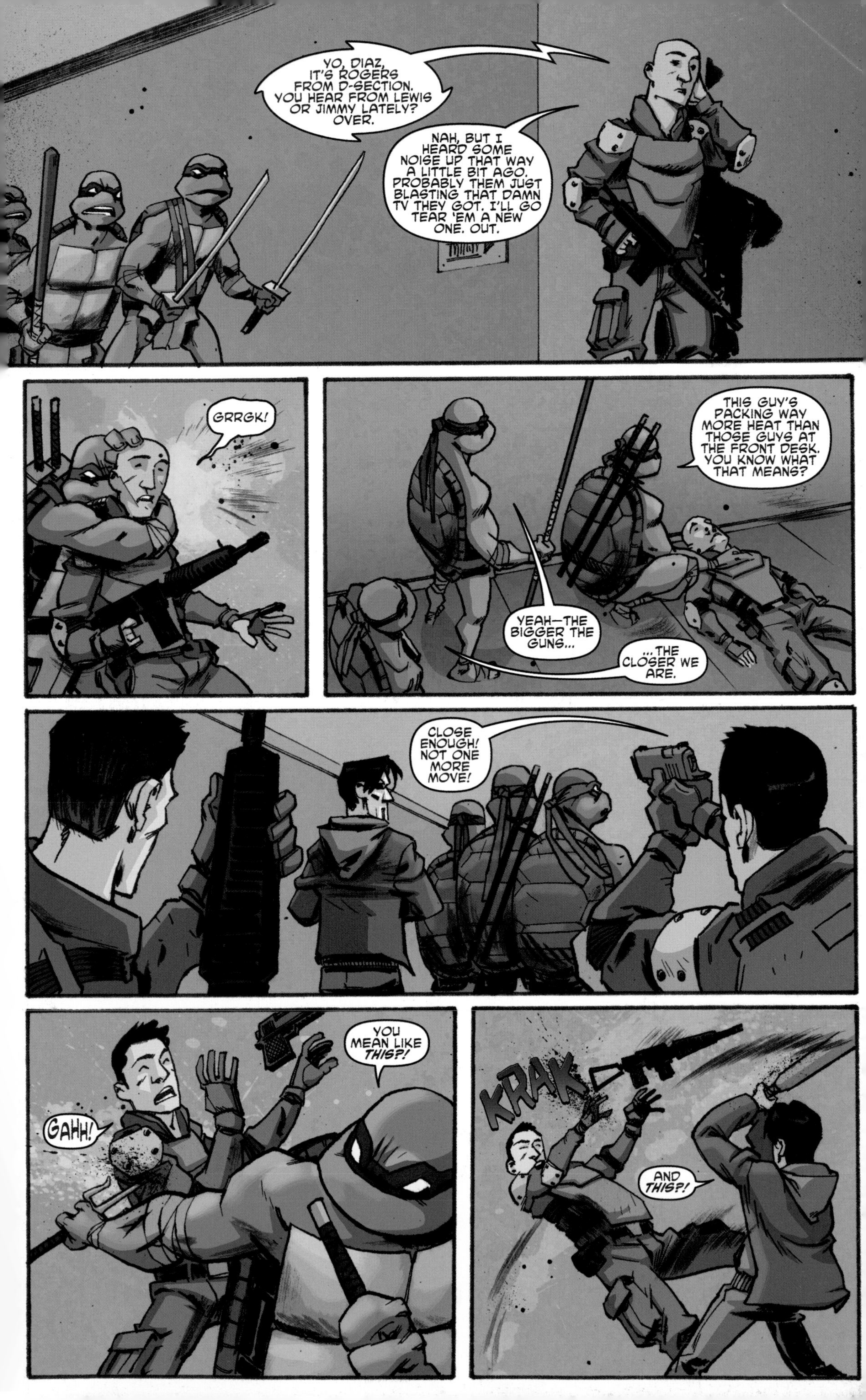
YO, DIAZ, IT'S ROGERS FROM D-SECTION. YOU HEAR FROM LEWIS OR JIMMY LATELY? OVER.
NAH, BUT I HEARD SOME NOISE UP THAT WAY A LITTLE BIT AGO. PROBABLY THEM JUST BLASTING THAT DAMN TV THEY GOT. I'LL GO TEAR 'EM A NEW ONE. OUT.
GRRGK!
THIS GUY'S PACKING WAY MORE HEAT THAN THOSE GUYS AT THE FRONT DESK. YOU KNOW WHAT THAT MEANS?
YEAH—THE BIGGER THE GUNS...
...THE CLOSER WE ARE.
CLOSE ENOUGH! NOT ONE MORE MOVE!
YOU MEAN LIKE *THIS?!*
GAHH!
KRAK
AND *THIS?!*

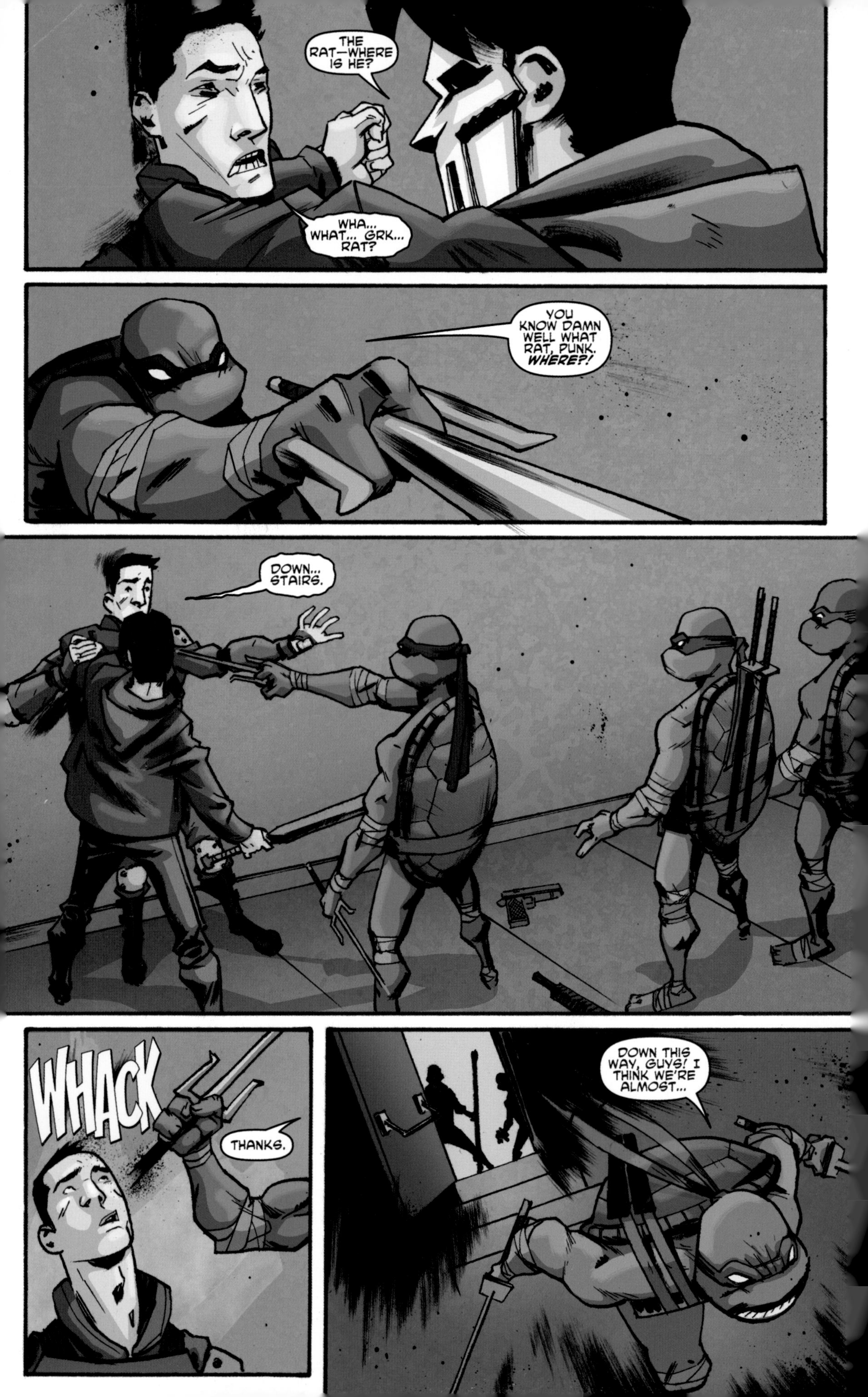
THE RAT—WHERE IS HE?
WHA... WHAT... GRK... RAT?
YOU KNOW DAMN WELL WHAT RAT, PUNK. *WHERE?!*
DOWN... STAIRS.
WHACK
THANKS.
DOWN THIS WAY, GUYS! I THINK WE'RE ALMOST...

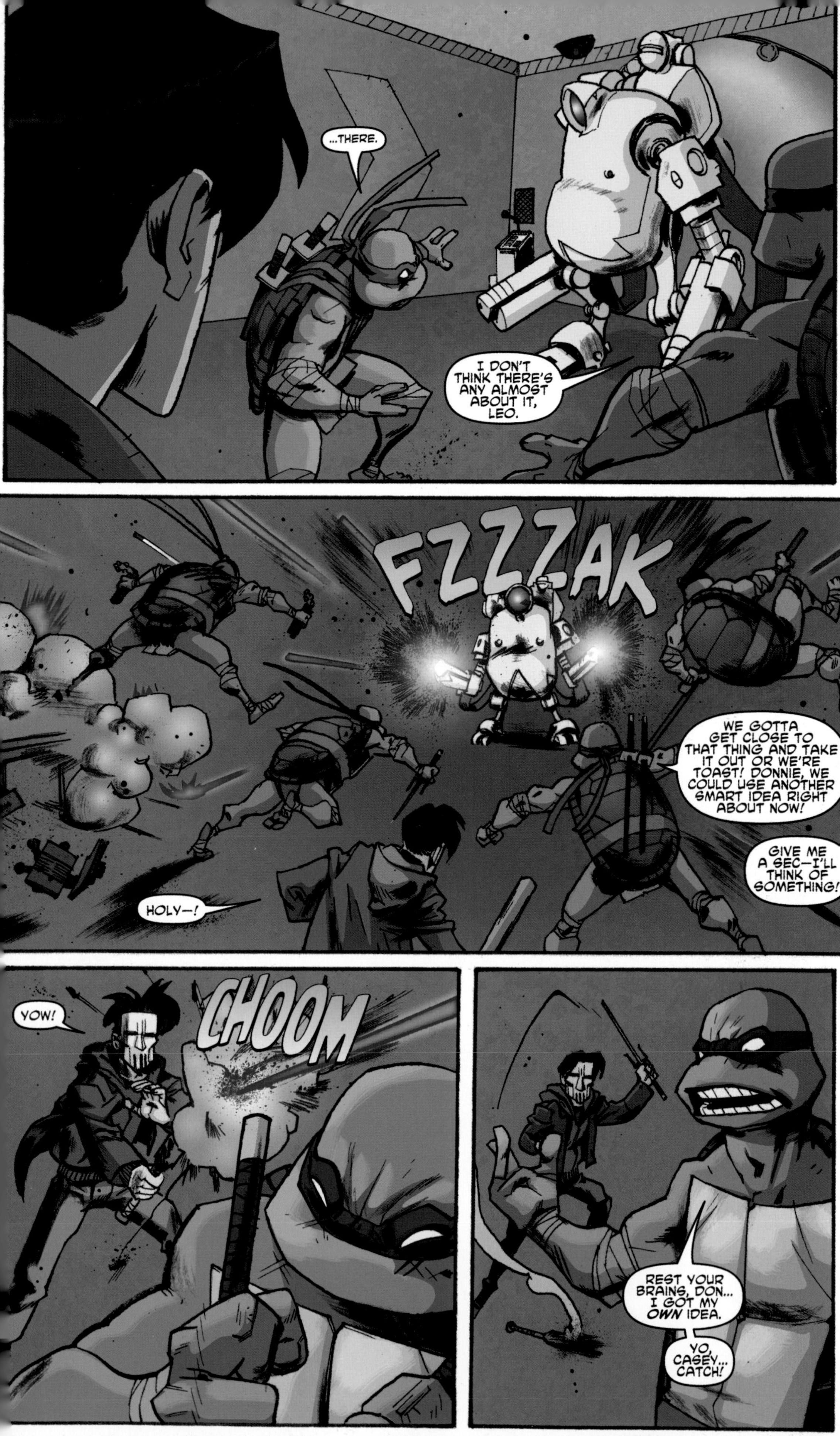
...THERE.
I DON'T THINK THERE'S ANY ALMOST ABOUT IT, LEO.
FZZZAK
WE GOTTA GET CLOSE TO THAT THING AND TAKE IT OUT OR WE'RE TOAST! DONNIE, WE COULD USE ANOTHER SMART IDEA RIGHT ABOUT NOW!
GIVE ME A SEC—I'LL THINK OF SOMETHING!
HOLY—!
YOW!
CHOOM
REST YOUR BRAINS, DON... I GOT MY *OWN* IDEA.
YO, CASEY... CATCH!

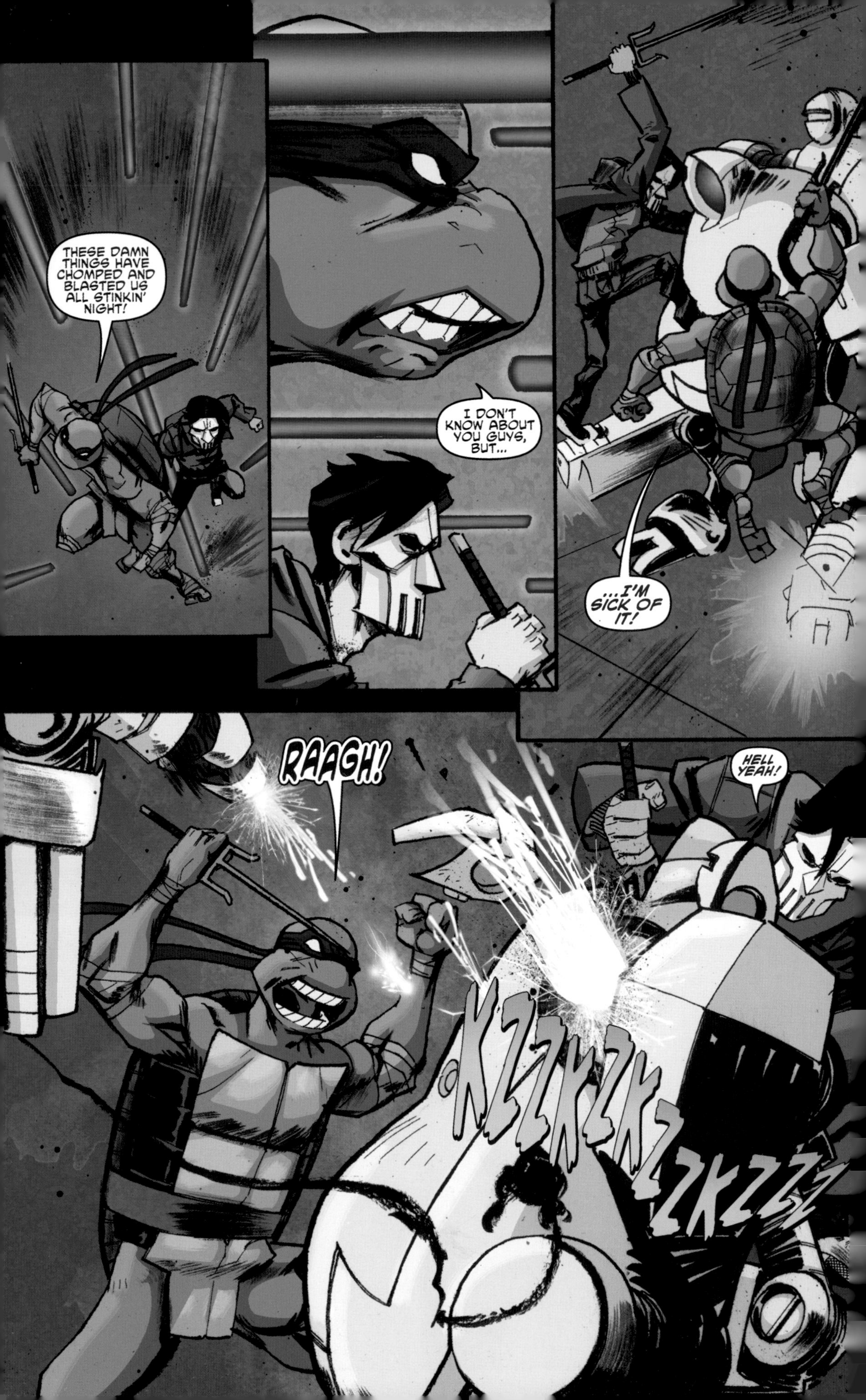

THESE DAMN THINGS HAVE CHOMPED AND BLASTED US ALL STINKIN' NIGHT!
I DON'T KNOW ABOUT YOU GUYS, BUT...
...I'M SICK OF IT!
RAAGH!
HELL YEAH!
KZZKZKZZKZZZ

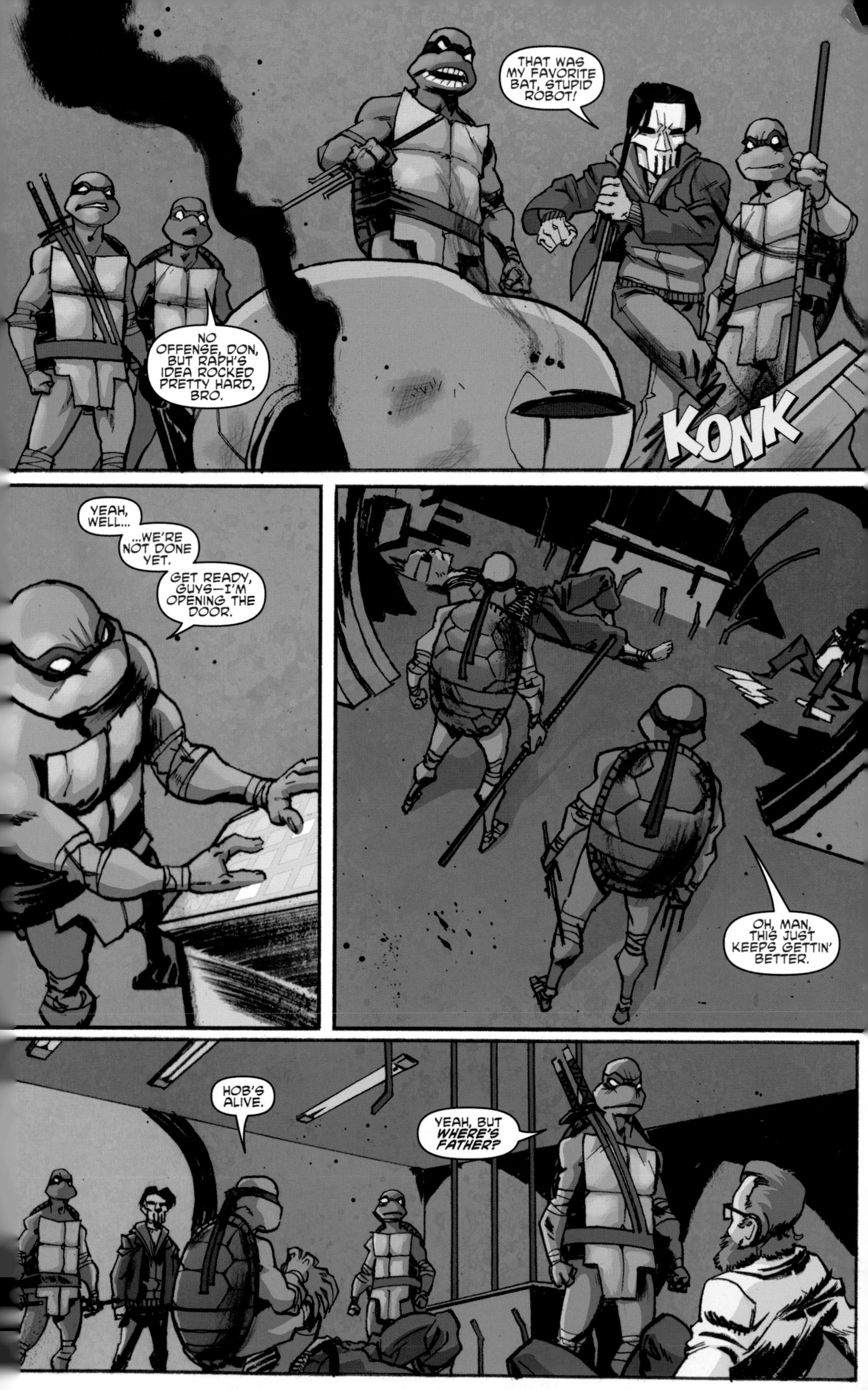
THAT WAS MY FAVORITE BAT, STUPID ROBOT!
NO OFFENSE, DON, BUT RAPH'S IDEA ROCKED PRETTY HARD, BRO.
KONK
YEAH, WELL...
...WE'RE NOT DONE YET.
GET READY, GUYS—I'M OPENING THE DOOR.
OH, MAN, THIS JUST KEEPS GETTIN' BETTER.
HOB'S ALIVE.
YEAH, BUT WHERE'S FATHER?

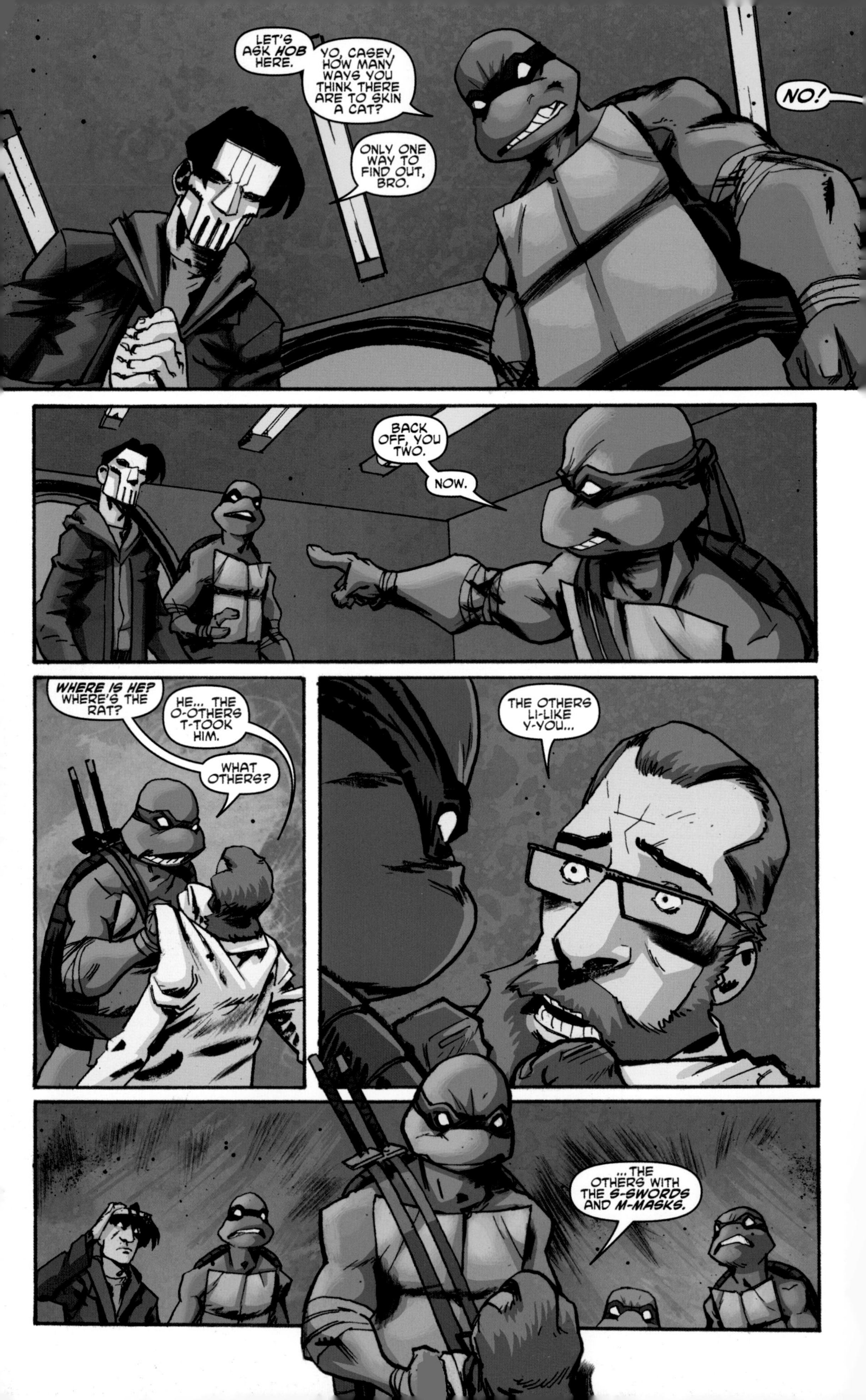
LET'S ASK HOB HERE.
YO, CASEY, HOW MANY WAYS YOU THINK THERE ARE TO SKIN A CAT?
ONLY ONE WAY TO FIND OUT, BRO.
NO!
BACK OFF, YOU TWO.
NOW.
WHERE IS HE? WHERE'S THE RAT?
HE... THE O-OTHERS T-TOOK HIM.
WHAT OTHERS?
THE OTHERS LI-LIKE Y-YOU...
...THE OTHERS WITH THE S-SWORDS AND M-MASKS.

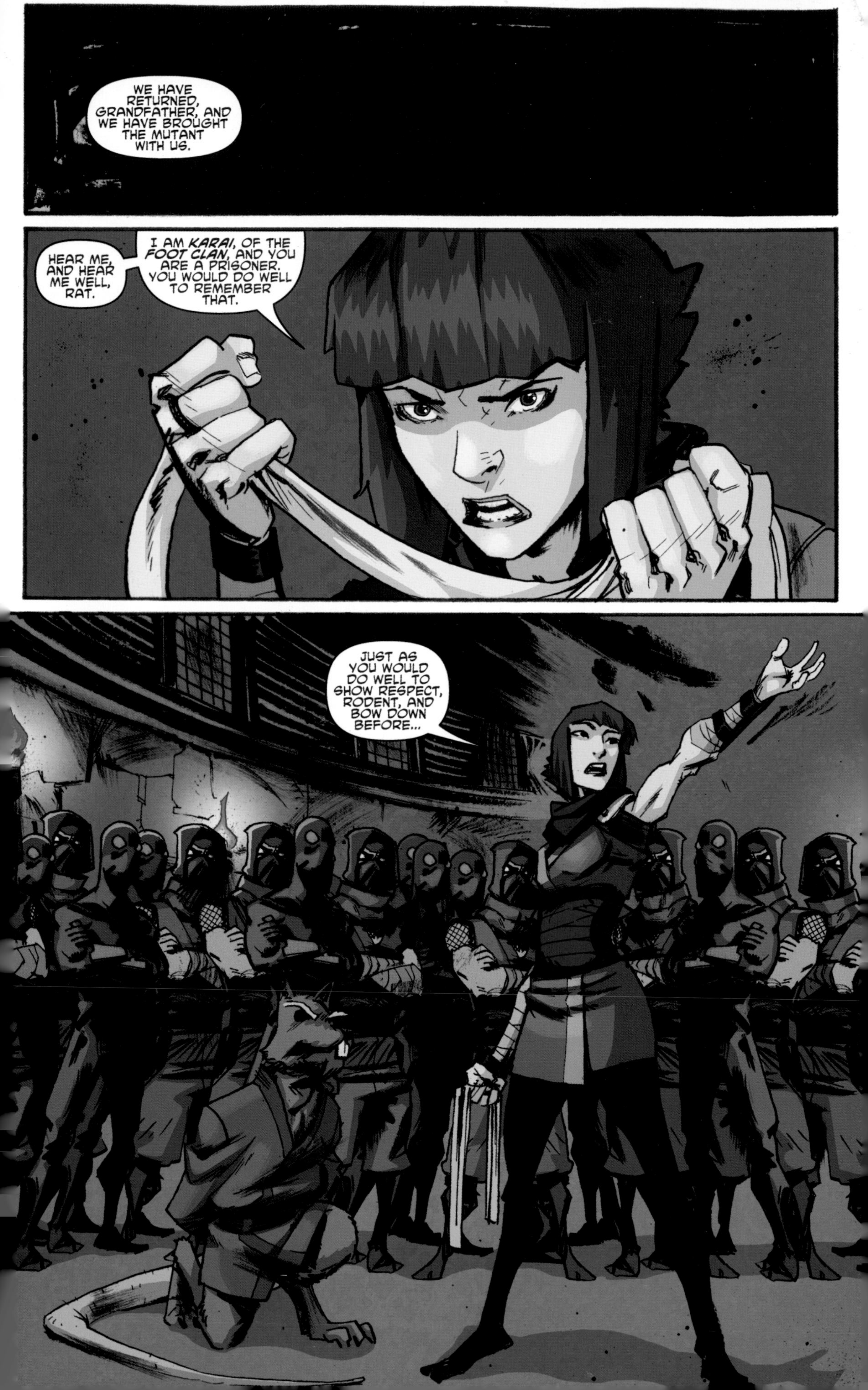
WE HAVE RETURNED, GRANDFATHER, AND WE HAVE BROUGHT THE MUTANT WITH US.
HEAR ME, AND HEAR ME WELL, RAT.
I AM KARAI, OF THE FOOT CLAN, AND YOU ARE A PRISONER. YOU WOULD DO WELL TO REMEMBER THAT.
JUST AS YOU WOULD DO WELL TO SHOW RESPECT, RODENT, AND BOW DOWN BEFORE...

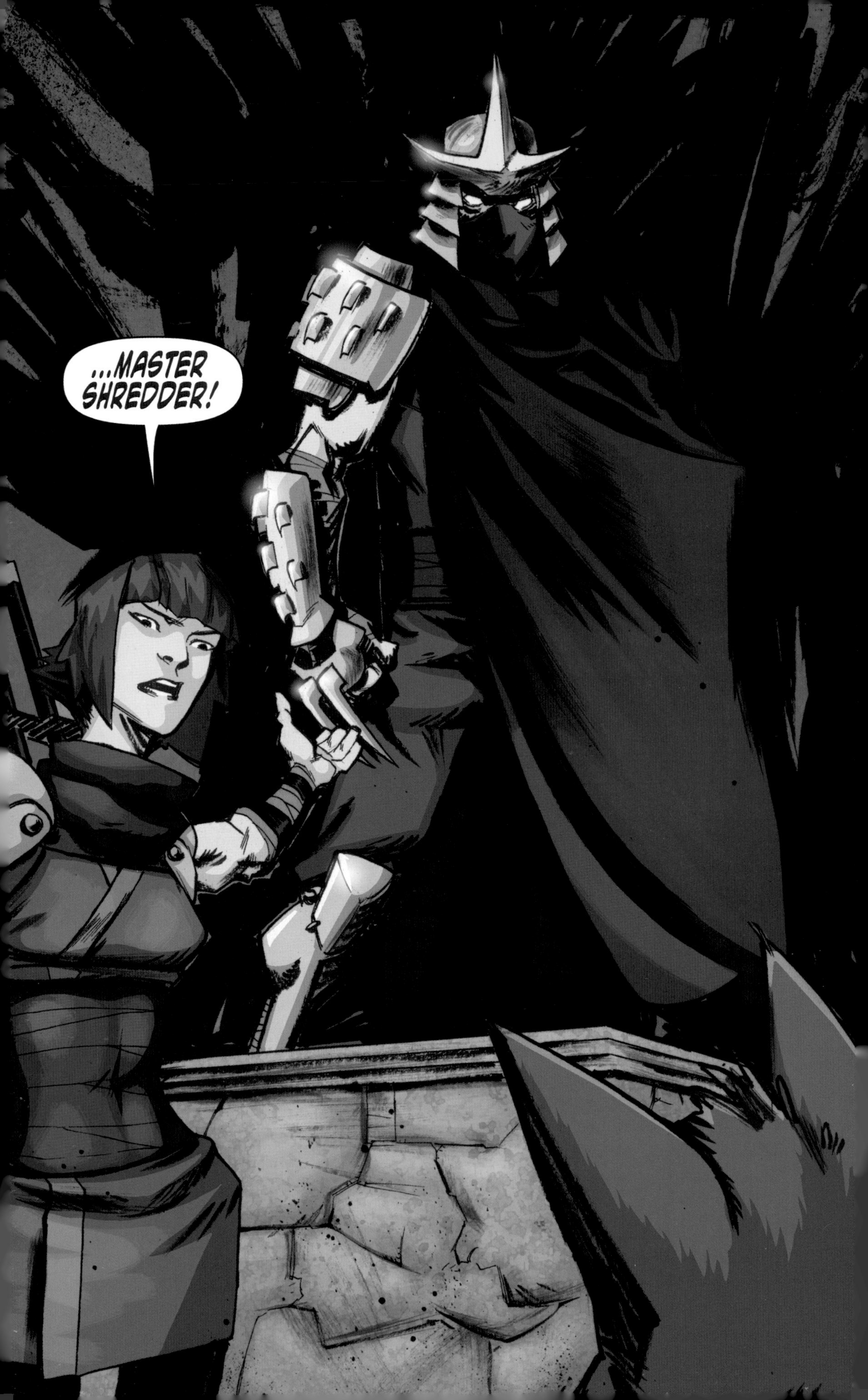
...MASTER SHREDDER!

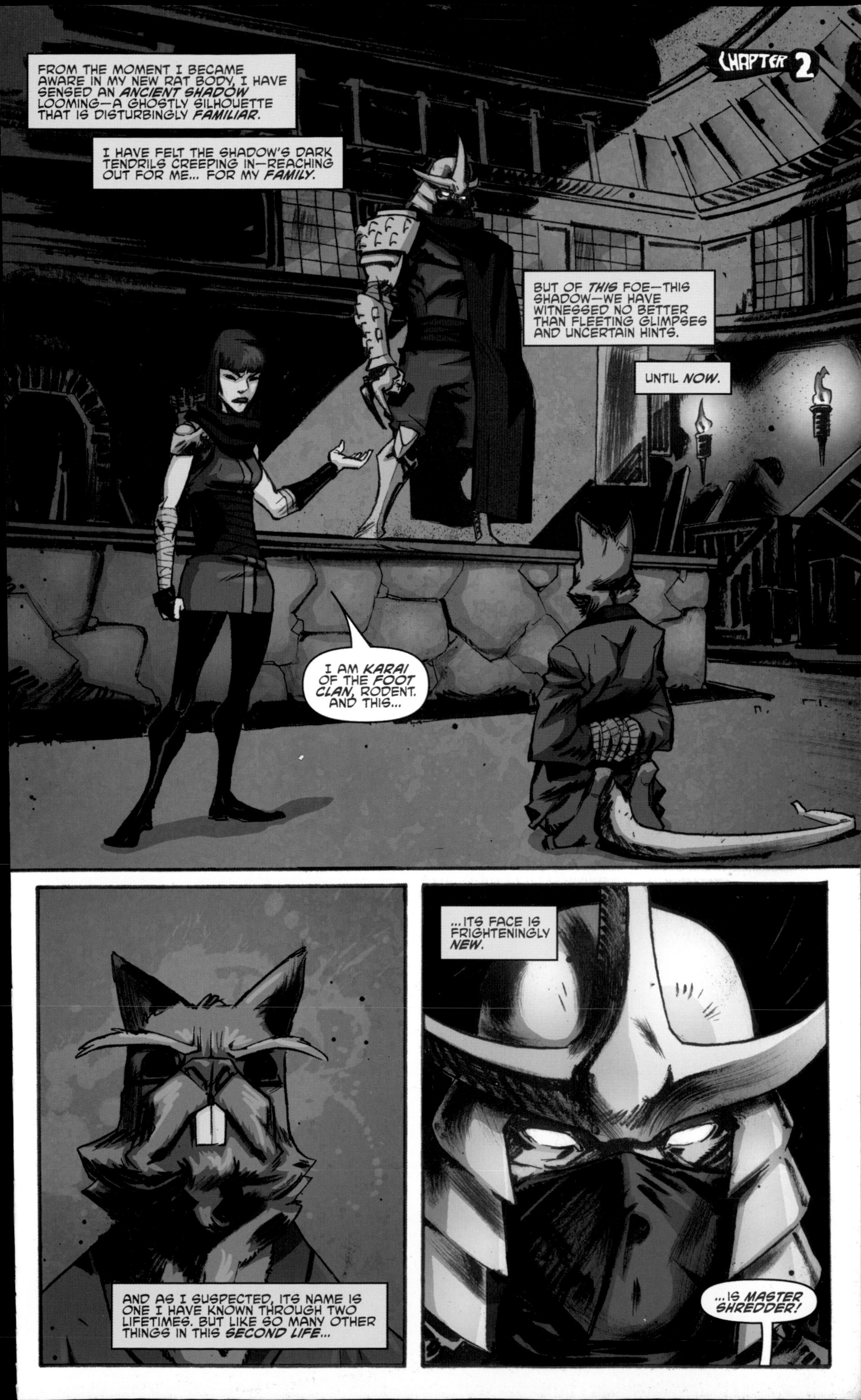
CHAPTER 2
FROM THE MOMENT I BECAME AWARE IN MY NEW RAT BODY, I HAVE SENSED AN ANCIENT SHADOW LOOMING—A GHOSTLY SILHOUETTE THAT IS DISTURBINGLY FAMILIAR.
I HAVE FELT THE SHADOW'S DARK TENDRILS CREEPING IN—REACHING OUT FOR ME... FOR MY FAMILY.
BUT OF THIS FOE—THIS SHADOW—WE HAVE WITNESSED NO BETTER THAN FLEETING GLIMPSES AND UNCERTAIN HINTS.
UNTIL NOW.
I AM KARAI OF THE FOOT CLAN, RODENT. AND THIS...
AND AS I SUSPECTED, ITS NAME IS ONE I HAVE KNOWN THROUGH TWO LIFETIMES. BUT LIKE SO MANY OTHER THINGS IN THIS SECOND LIFE...
...ITS FACE IS FRIGHTENINGLY NEW.
...IS MASTER SHREDDER!

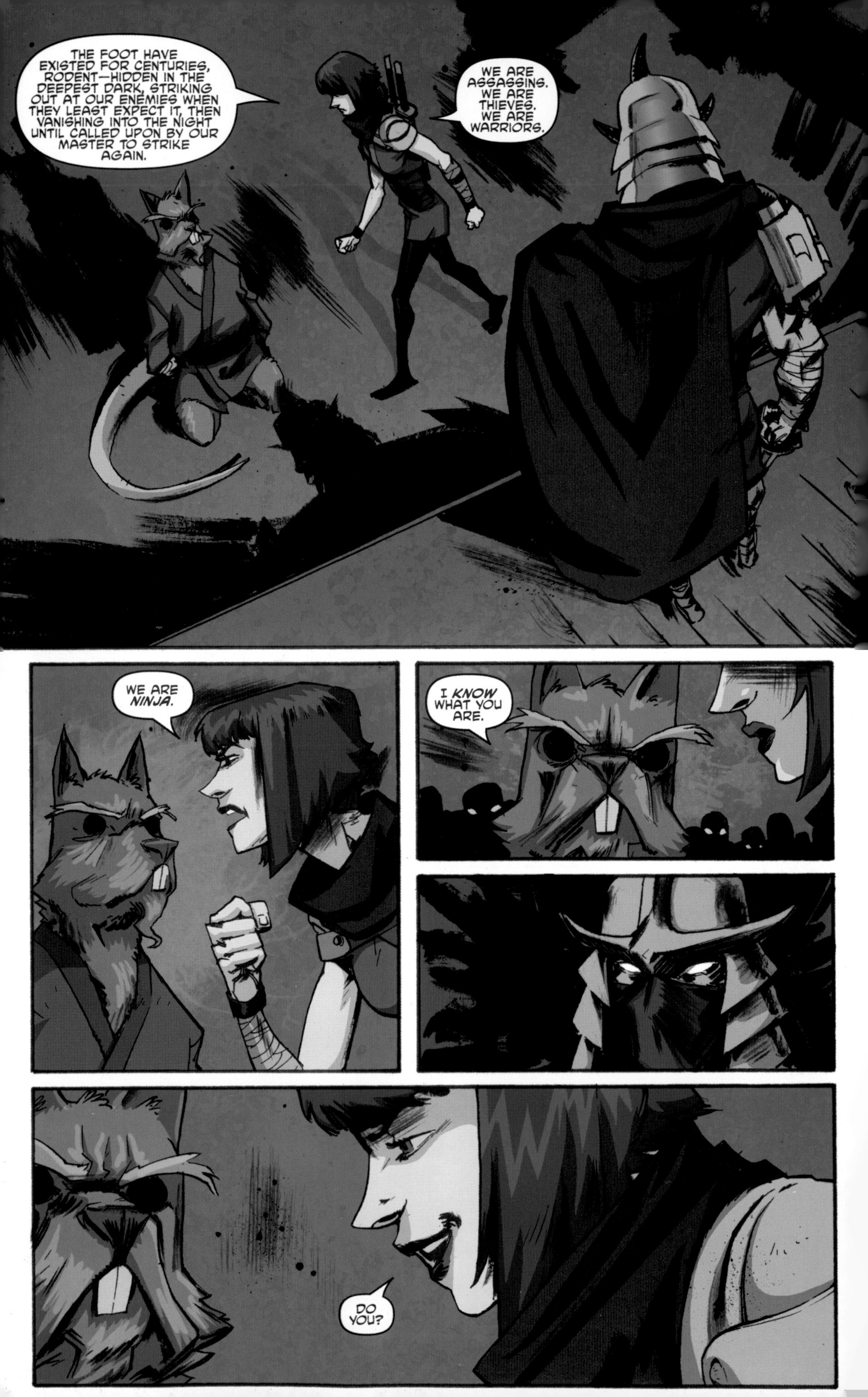
THE FOOT HAVE EXISTED FOR CENTURIES, RODENT—HIDDEN IN THE DEEPEST DARK, STRIKING OUT AT OUR ENEMIES WHEN THEY LEAST EXPECT IT, THEN VANISHING INTO THE NIGHT UNTIL CALLED UPON BY OUR MASTER TO STRIKE AGAIN.
WE ARE ASSASSINS. WE ARE THIEVES. WE ARE WARRIORS.
WE ARE *NINJA*.
I *KNOW* WHAT YOU ARE.
DO YOU?

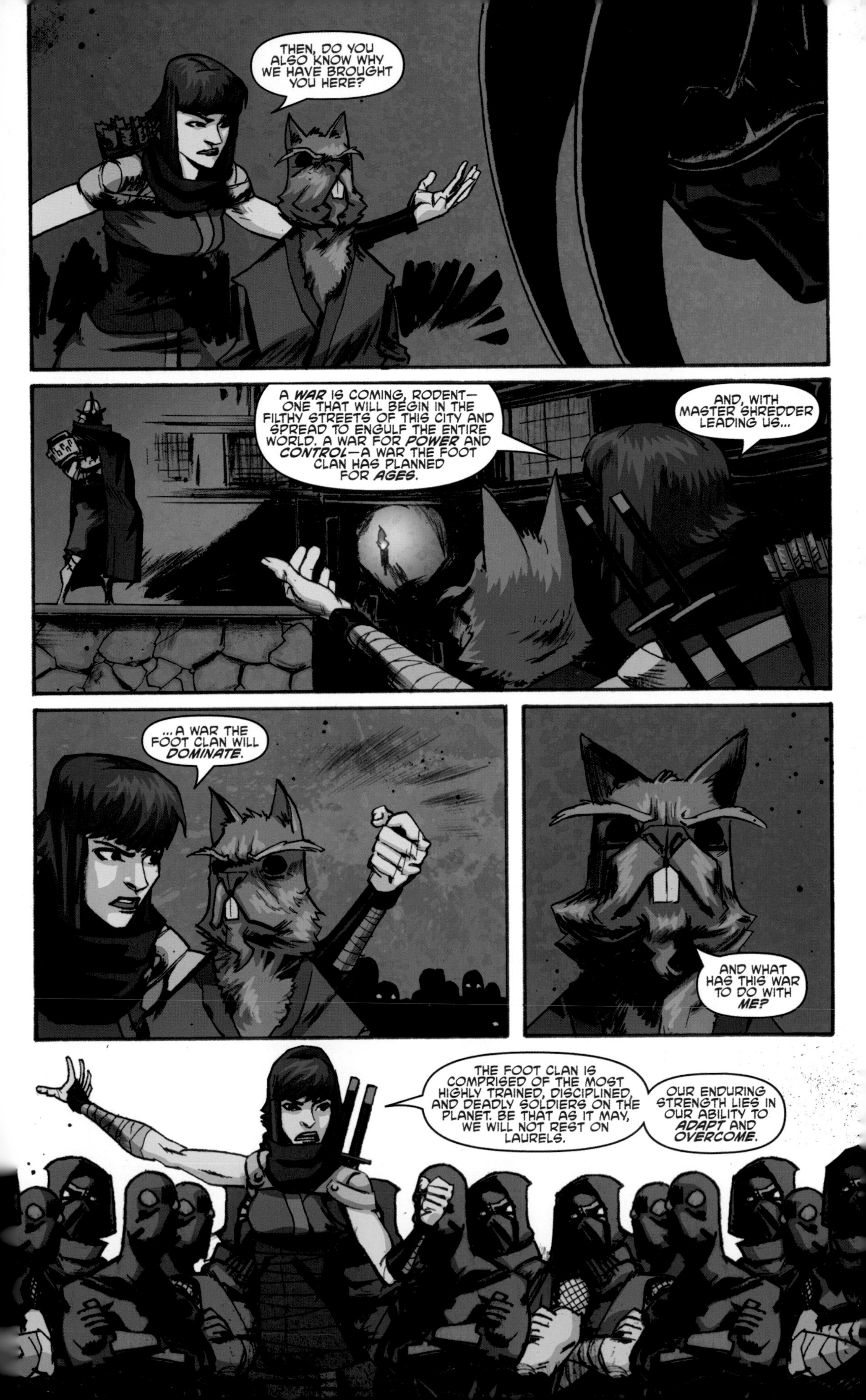
THEN, DO YOU ALSO KNOW WHY WE HAVE BROUGHT YOU HERE?
A WAR IS COMING, RODENT—ONE THAT WILL BEGIN IN THE FILTHY STREETS OF THIS CITY AND SPREAD TO ENGULF THE ENTIRE WORLD. A WAR FOR POWER AND CONTROL—A WAR THE FOOT CLAN HAS PLANNED FOR AGES.
AND, WITH MASTER SHREDDER LEADING US...
...A WAR THE FOOT CLAN WILL DOMINATE.
AND WHAT HAS THIS WAR TO DO WITH ME?
THE FOOT CLAN IS COMPRISED OF THE MOST HIGHLY TRAINED, DISCIPLINED, AND DEADLY SOLDIERS ON THE PLANET. BE THAT AS IT MAY, WE WILL NOT REST ON LAURELS.
OUR ENDURING STRENGTH LIES IN OUR ABILITY TO ADAPT AND OVERCOME.

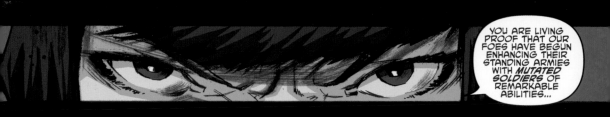

YOU ARE LIVING PROOF THAT OUR FOES HAVE BEGUN ENHANCING THEIR STANDING ARMIES WITH *MUTATED SOLDIERS* OF REMARKABLE ABILITIES...

...AS HAVE *WE*.

YOU HAVE NOT ANSWERED MY QUESTION—WHAT DOES THIS HAVE TO DO WITH ME?

YOU HAVE THE OPPORTUNITY TO JOIN US TODAY, MUTANT. TO BECOME A SOLDIER FOR THE FOOT CLAN.

BUT FIRST...

...A *TEST!*

SB

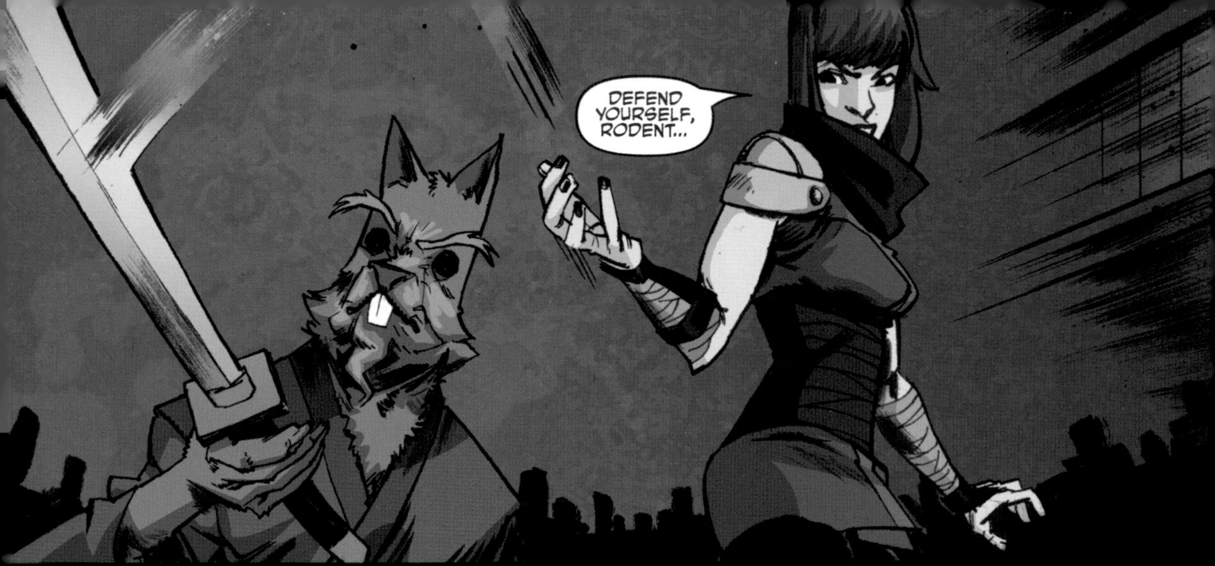
DEFEND YOURSELF, RODENT...

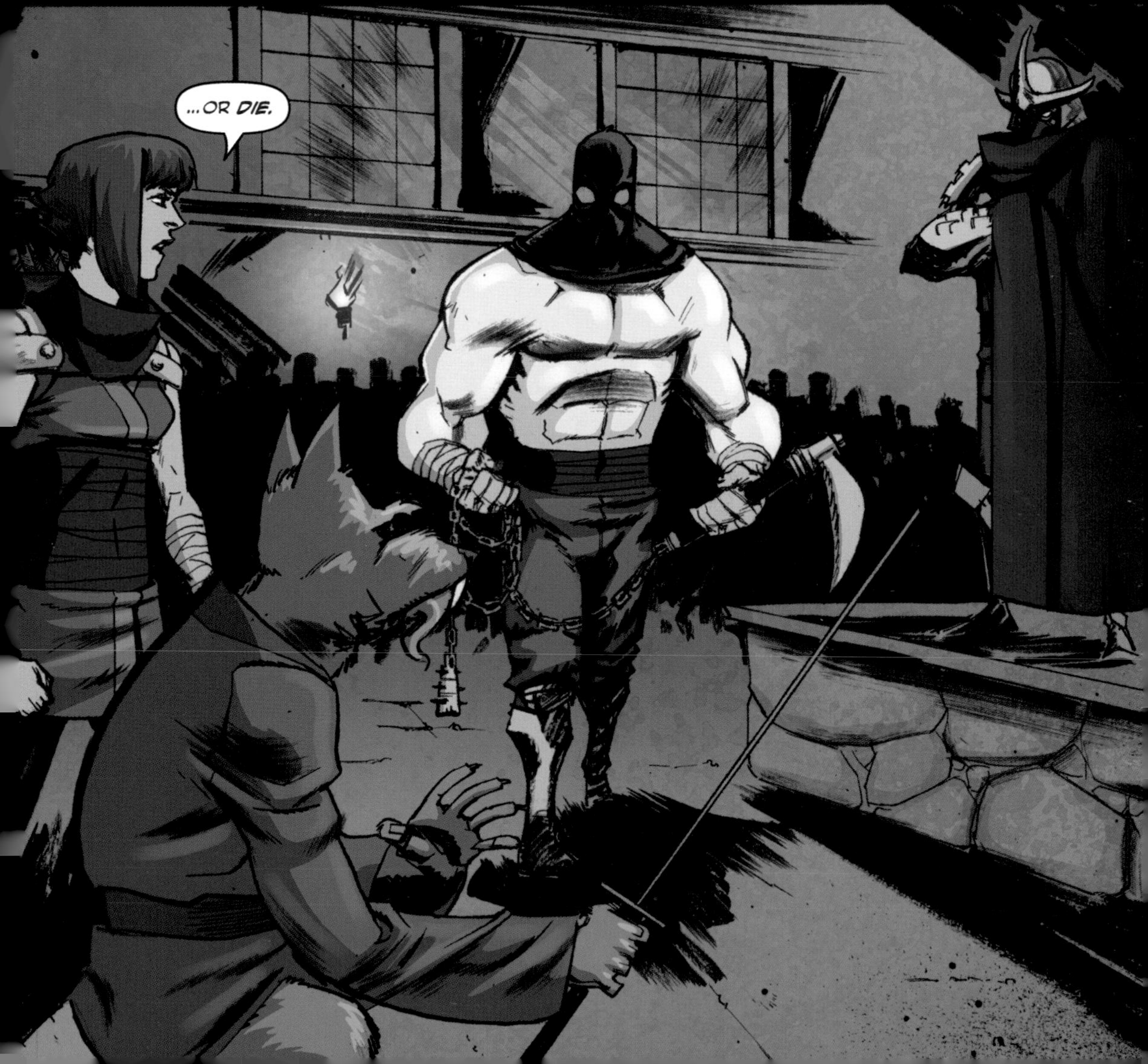
...OR DIE.

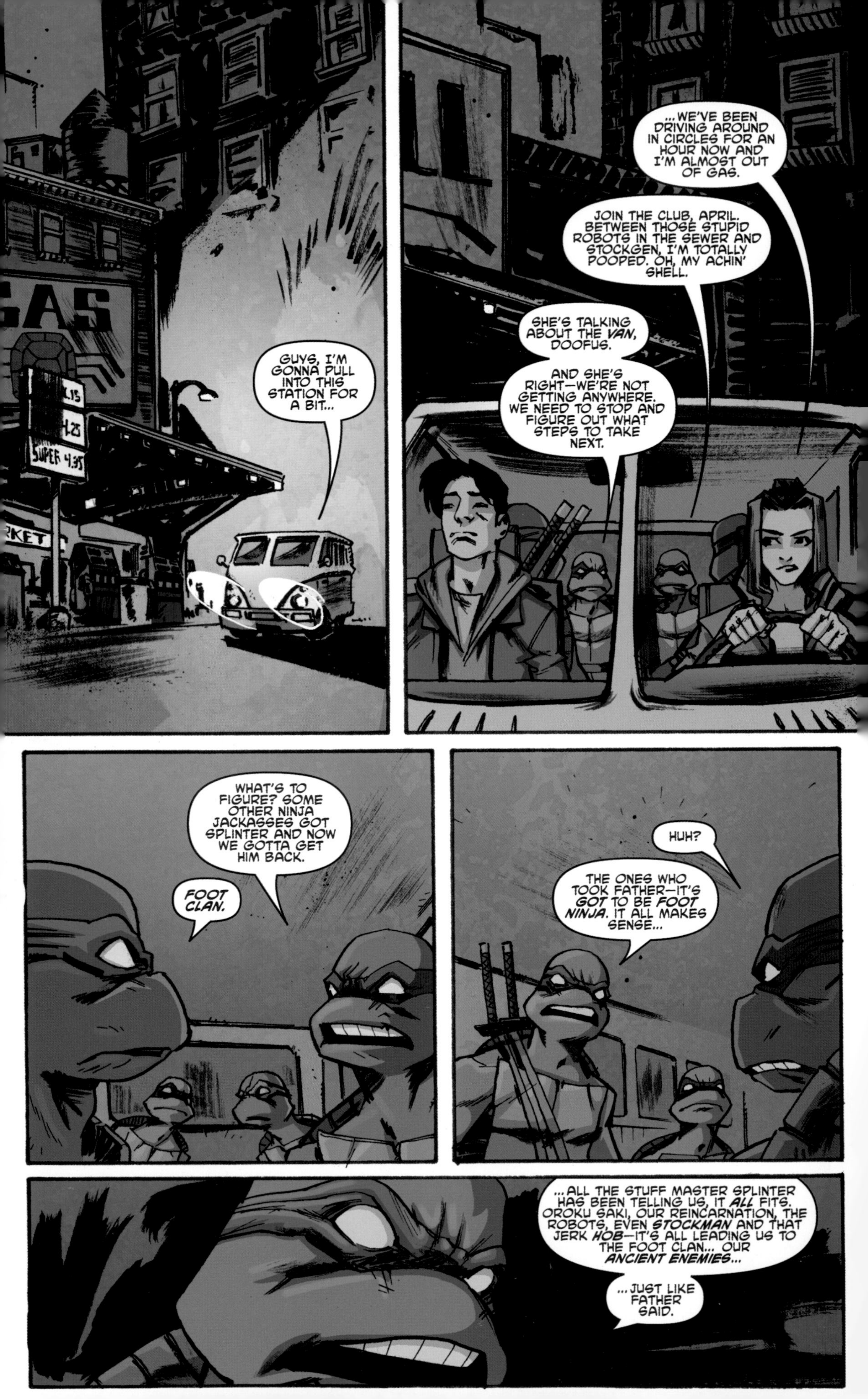
GAS
SUPER 4.35
RKET
GUYS, I'M GONNA PULL INTO THIS STATION FOR A BIT...
...WE'VE BEEN DRIVING AROUND IN CIRCLES FOR AN HOUR NOW AND I'M ALMOST OUT OF GAS.
JOIN THE CLUB, APRIL. BETWEEN THOSE STUPID ROBOTS IN THE SEWER AND STOCKGEN, I'M TOTALLY POOPED. OH, MY ACHIN' SHELL.
SHE'S TALKING ABOUT THE *VAN*, DOOFUS.
AND SHE'S RIGHT—WE'RE NOT GETTING ANYWHERE. WE NEED TO STOP AND FIGURE OUT WHAT STEPS TO TAKE NEXT.
WHAT'S TO FIGURE? SOME OTHER NINJA JACKASSES GOT SPLINTER AND NOW WE GOTTA GET HIM BACK.
FOOT CLAN.
HUH?
THE ONES WHO TOOK FATHER—IT'S *GOT* TO BE *FOOT NINJA*. IT ALL MAKES SENSE...
...ALL THE STUFF MASTER SPLINTER HAS BEEN TELLING US, IT *ALL* FITS. OROKU SAKI, OUR REINCARNATION, THE ROBOTS, EVEN *STOCKMAN* AND THAT JERK *HOB*—IT'S ALL LEADING US TO THE FOOT CLAN... OUR *ANCIENT ENEMIES*...
...JUST LIKE FATHER SAID.

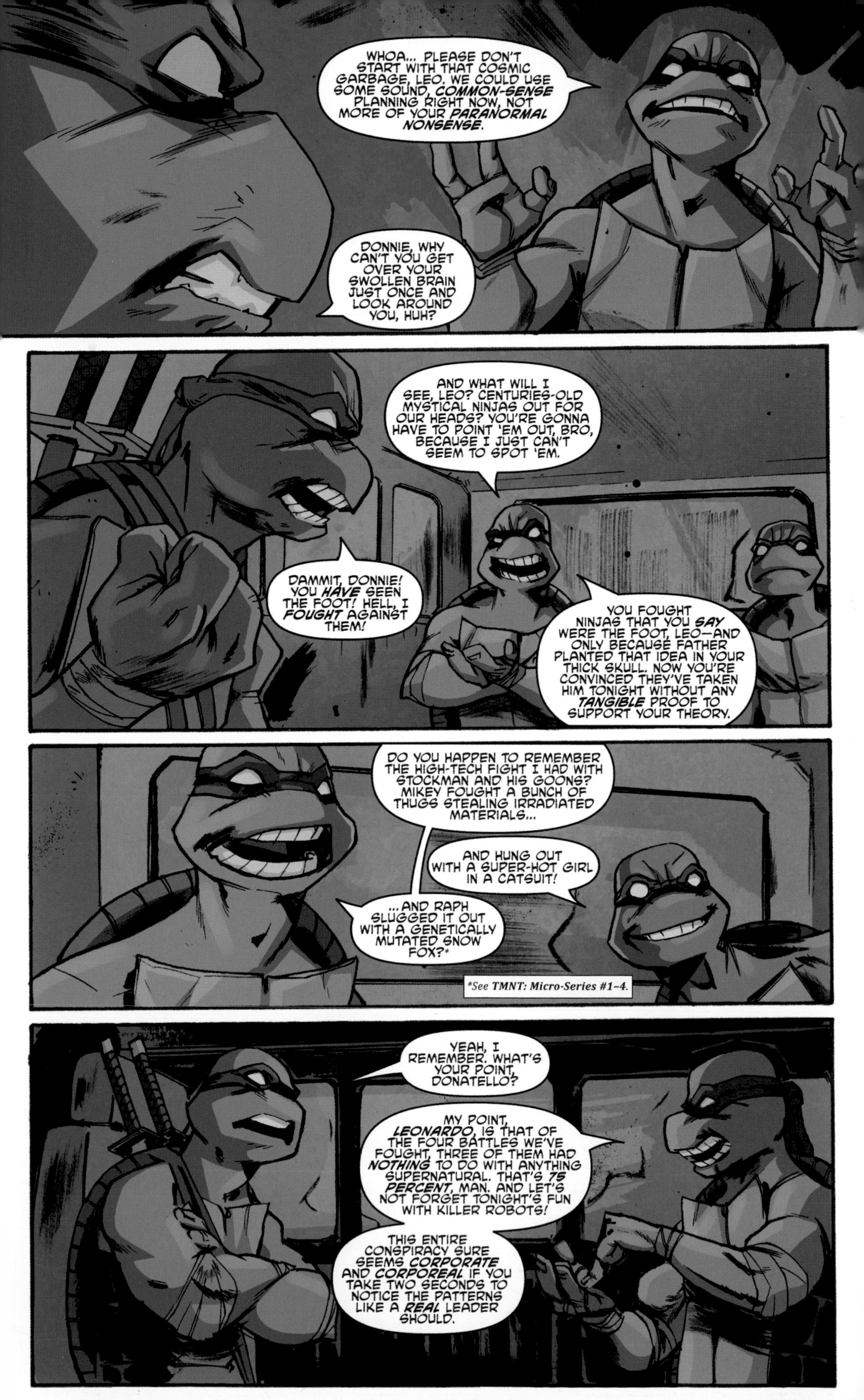
WHOA... PLEASE DON'T START WITH THAT COSMIC GARBAGE, LEO. WE COULD USE SOME SOUND, COMMON-SENSE PLANNING RIGHT NOW, NOT MORE OF YOUR PARANORMAL NONSENSE.
DONNIE, WHY CAN'T YOU GET OVER YOUR SWOLLEN BRAIN JUST ONCE AND LOOK AROUND YOU, HUH?
AND WHAT WILL I SEE, LEO? CENTURIES-OLD MYSTICAL NINJAS OUT FOR OUR HEADS? YOU'RE GONNA HAVE TO POINT 'EM OUT, BRO, BECAUSE I JUST CAN'T SEEM TO SPOT 'EM.
DAMMIT, DONNIE! YOU HAVE SEEN THE FOOT! HELL, I FOUGHT AGAINST THEM!
YOU FOUGHT NINJAS THAT YOU SAY WERE THE FOOT, LEO—AND ONLY BECAUSE FATHER PLANTED THAT IDEA IN YOUR THICK SKULL. NOW YOU'RE CONVINCED THEY'VE TAKEN HIM TONIGHT WITHOUT ANY TANGIBLE PROOF TO SUPPORT YOUR THEORY.
DO YOU HAPPEN TO REMEMBER THE HIGH-TECH FIGHT I HAD WITH STOCKMAN AND HIS GOONS? MIKEY FOUGHT A BUNCH OF THUGS STEALING IRRADIATED MATERIALS...
AND HUNG OUT WITH A SUPER-HOT GIRL IN A CATSUIT!
...AND RAPH SLUGGED IT OUT WITH A GENETICALLY MUTATED SNOW FOX?*
*See TMNT: Micro-Series #1–4.
YEAH, I REMEMBER. WHAT'S YOUR POINT, DONATELLO?
MY POINT, LEONARDO, IS THAT OF THE FOUR BATTLES WE'VE FOUGHT, THREE OF THEM HAD NOTHING TO DO WITH ANYTHING SUPERNATURAL. THAT'S 75 PERCENT, MAN. AND LET'S NOT FORGET TONIGHT'S FUN WITH KILLER ROBOTS!
THIS ENTIRE CONSPIRACY SURE SEEMS CORPORATE AND CORPOREAL IF YOU TAKE TWO SECONDS TO NOTICE THE PATTERNS LIKE A REAL LEADER SHOULD.

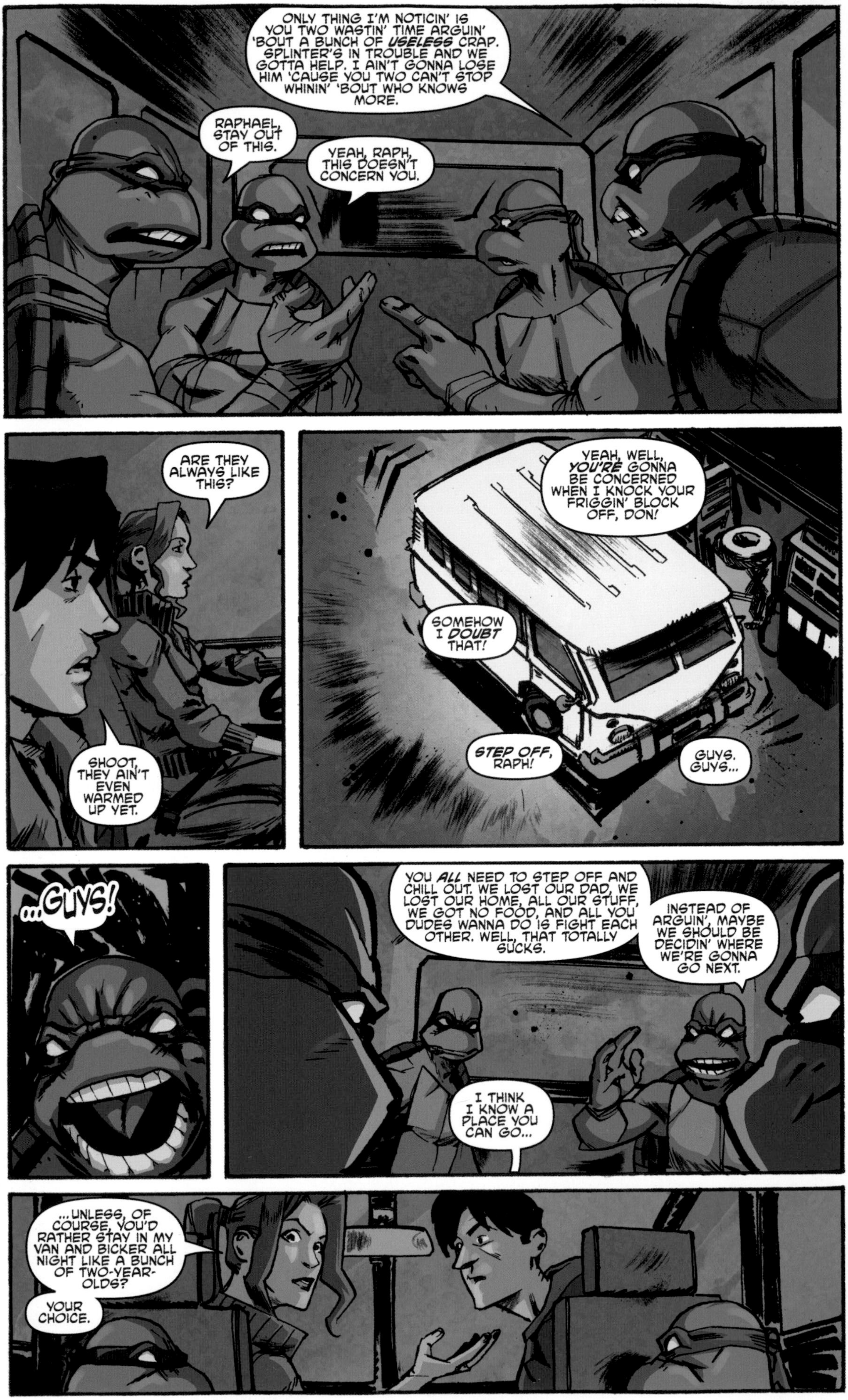
ONLY THING I'M NOTICIN' IS YOU TWO WASTIN' TIME ARGUIN' 'BOUT A BUNCH OF USELESS CRAP. SPLINTER'S IN TROUBLE AND WE GOTTA HELP. I AIN'T GONNA LOSE HIM 'CAUSE YOU TWO CAN'T STOP WHININ' 'BOUT WHO KNOWS MORE.
RAPHAEL, STAY OUT OF THIS.
YEAH, RAPH, THIS DOESN'T CONCERN YOU.
ARE THEY ALWAYS LIKE THIS?
SHOOT, THEY AIN'T EVEN WARMED UP YET.
YEAH, WELL, YOU'RE GONNA BE CONCERNED WHEN I KNOCK YOUR FRIGGIN' BLOCK OFF, DON!
SOMEHOW I DOUBT THAT!
STEP OFF, RAPH!
GUYS. GUYS...
...GUYS!
YOU ALL NEED TO STEP OFF AND CHILL OUT. WE LOST OUR DAD, WE LOST OUR HOME, ALL OUR STUFF, WE GOT NO FOOD, AND ALL YOU DUDES WANNA DO IS FIGHT EACH OTHER. WELL, THAT TOTALLY SUCKS.
INSTEAD OF ARGUIN', MAYBE WE SHOULD BE DECIDIN' WHERE WE'RE GONNA GO NEXT.
I THINK I KNOW A PLACE YOU CAN GO...
...UNLESS, OF COURSE, YOU'D RATHER STAY IN MY VAN AND BICKER ALL NIGHT LIKE A BUNCH OF TWO-YEAR-OLDS?
YOUR CHOICE.

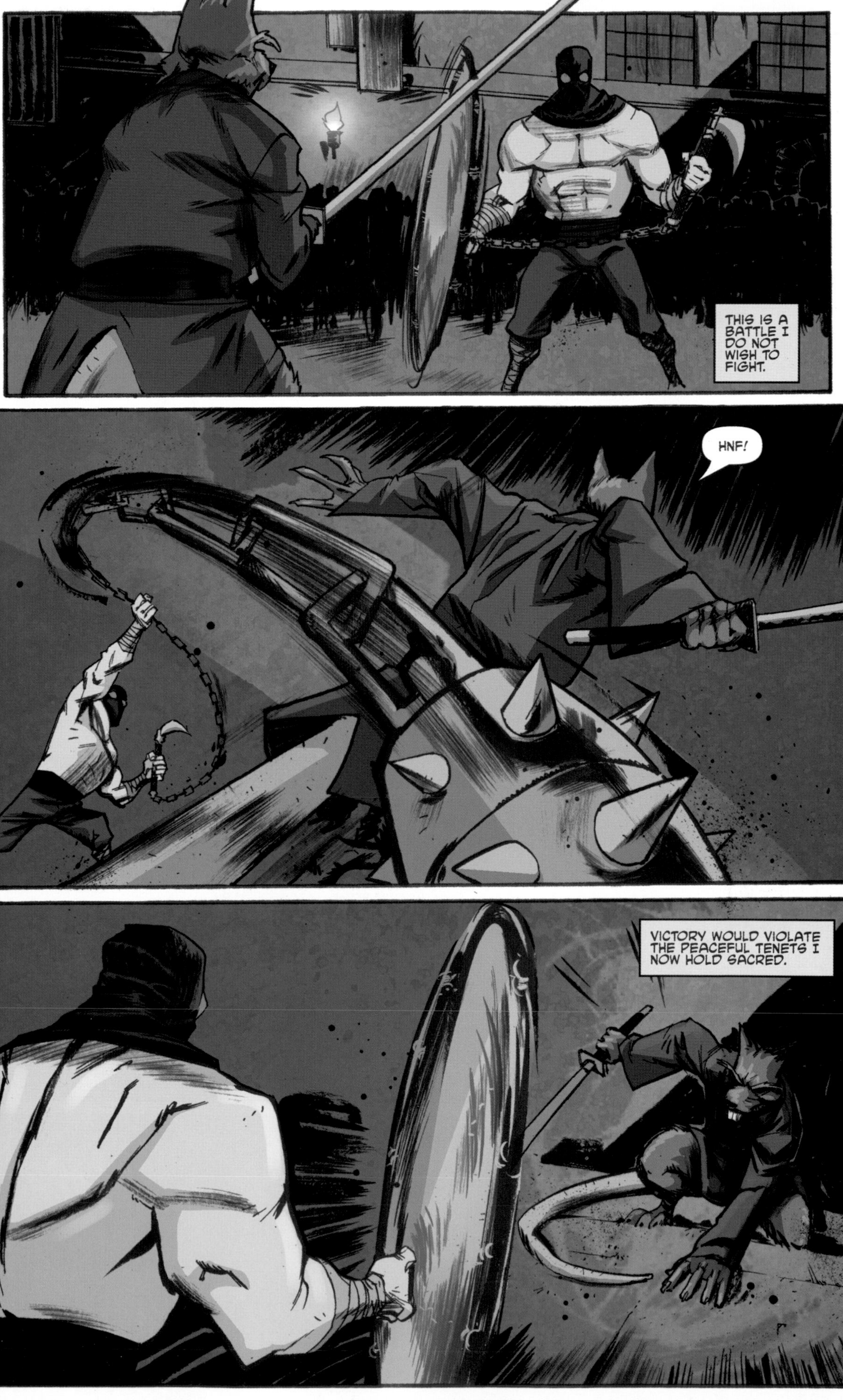
THIS IS A BATTLE I DO NOT WISH TO FIGHT.
HNF!
VICTORY WOULD VIOLATE THE PEACEFUL TENETS I NOW HOLD SACRED.

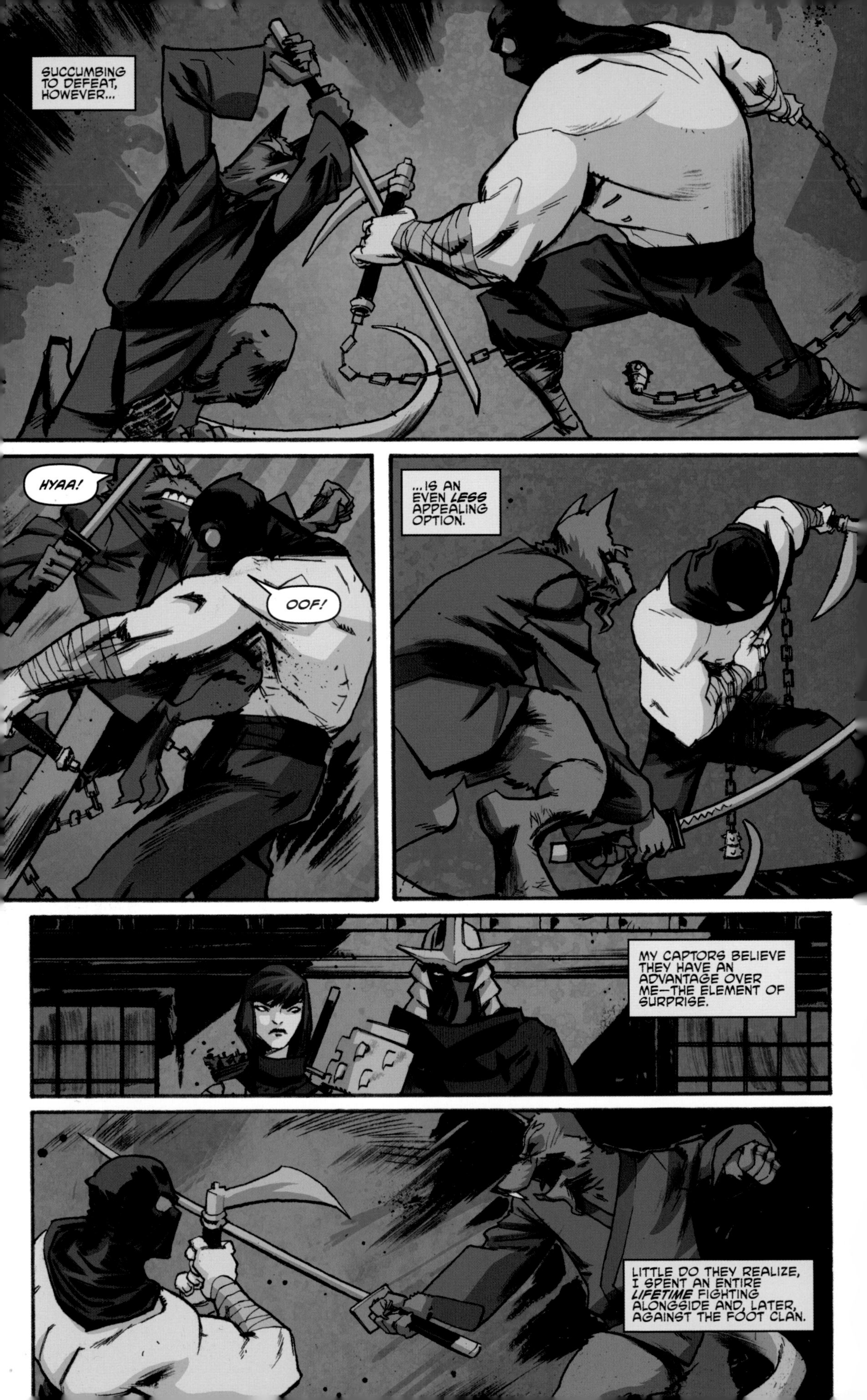
SUCCUMBING TO DEFEAT, HOWEVER...
HYAA!
OOF!
...IS AN EVEN *LESS* APPEALING OPTION.
MY CAPTORS BELIEVE THEY HAVE AN ADVANTAGE OVER ME—THE ELEMENT OF SURPRISE.
LITTLE DO THEY REALIZE, I SPENT AN ENTIRE *LIFETIME* FIGHTING ALONGSIDE AND, LATER, AGAINST THE FOOT CLAN.

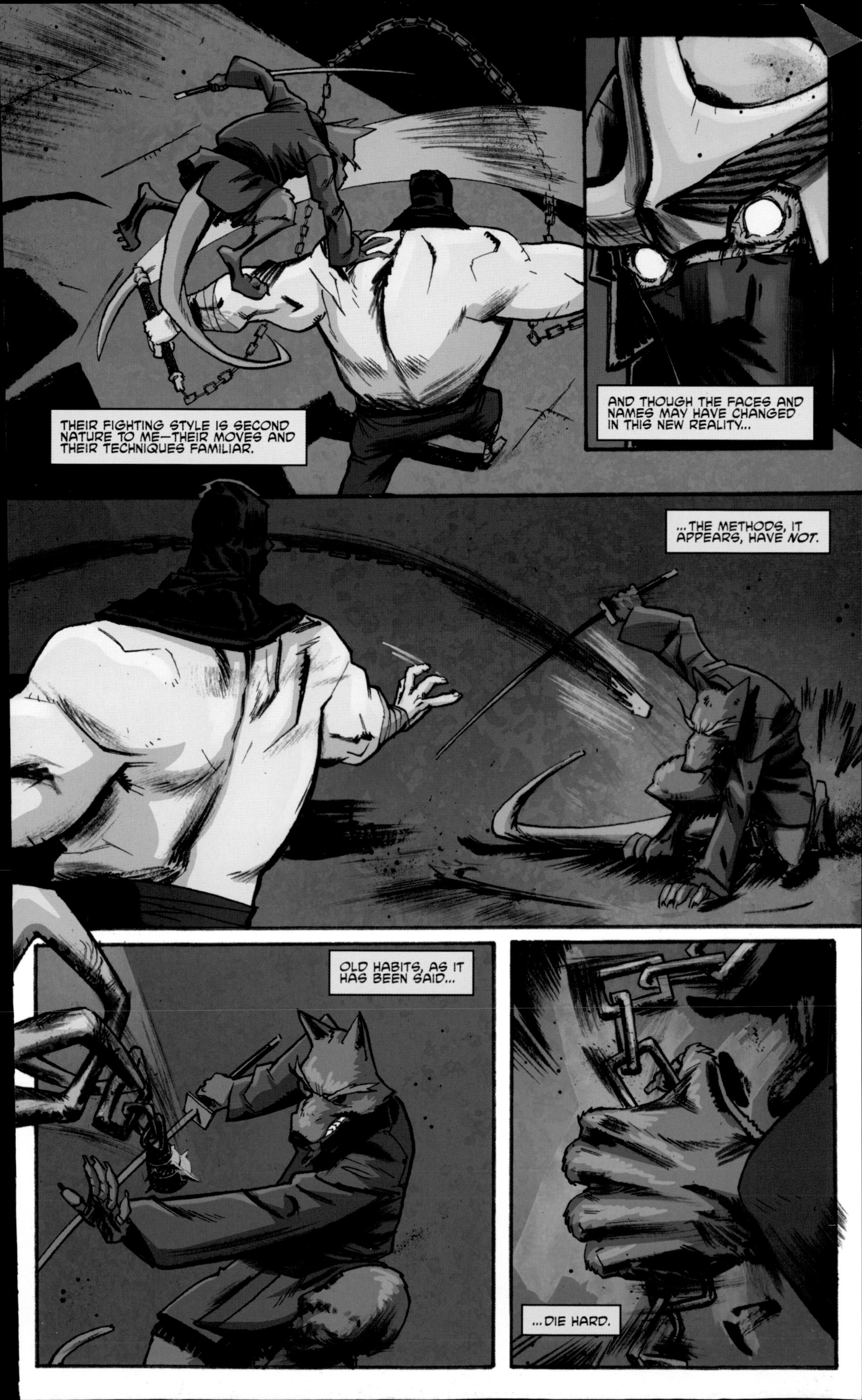
THEIR FIGHTING STYLE IS SECOND NATURE TO ME—THEIR MOVES AND THEIR TECHNIQUES FAMILIAR.
AND THOUGH THE FACES AND NAMES MAY HAVE CHANGED IN THIS NEW REALITY...
...THE METHODS, IT APPEARS, HAVE *NOT*.
OLD HABITS, AS IT HAS BEEN SAID...
...DIE HARD.

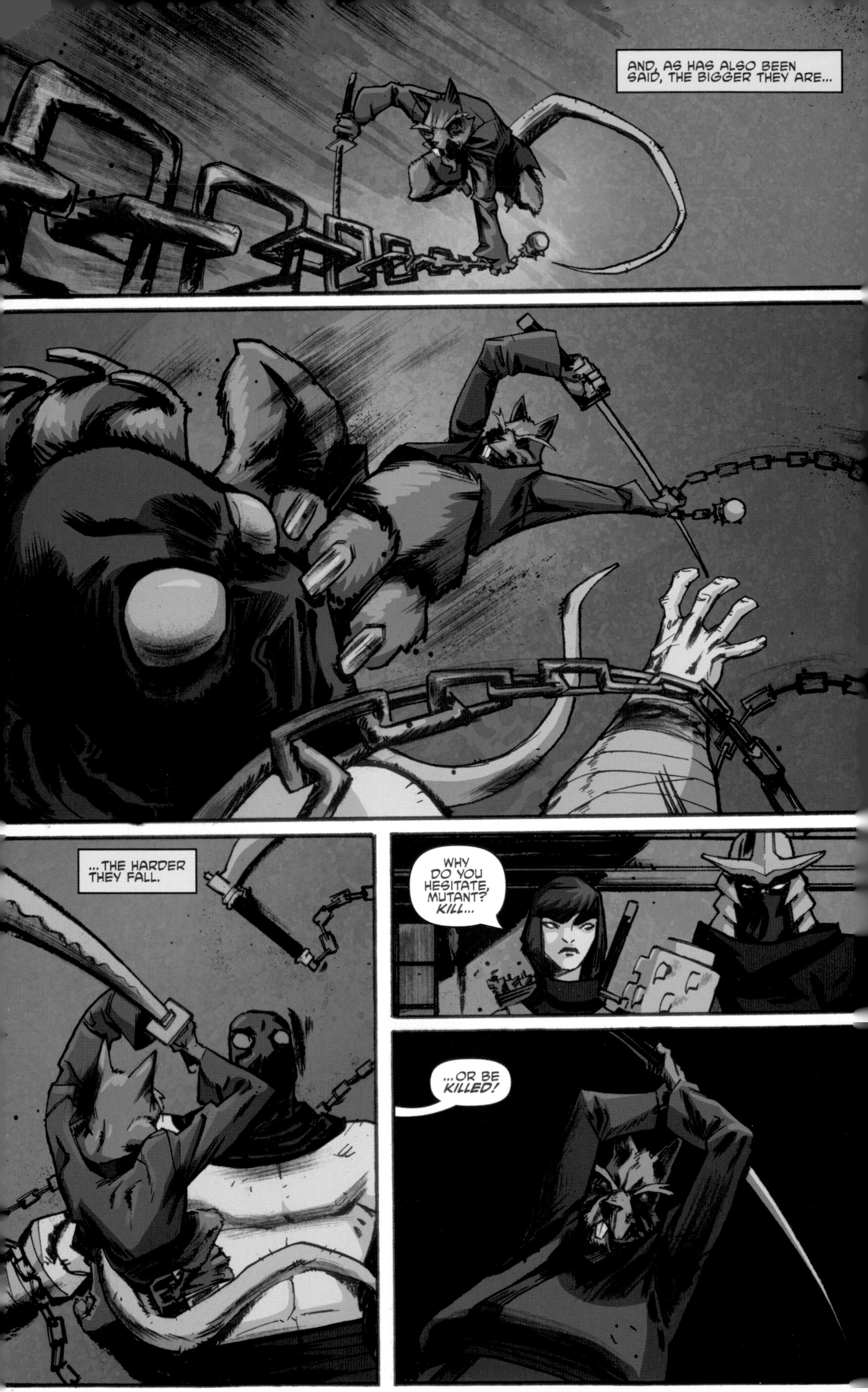
AND, AS HAS ALSO BEEN SAID, THE BIGGER THEY ARE...
...THE HARDER THEY FALL.
WHY DO YOU HESITATE, MUTANT? KILL...
...OR BE KILLED!

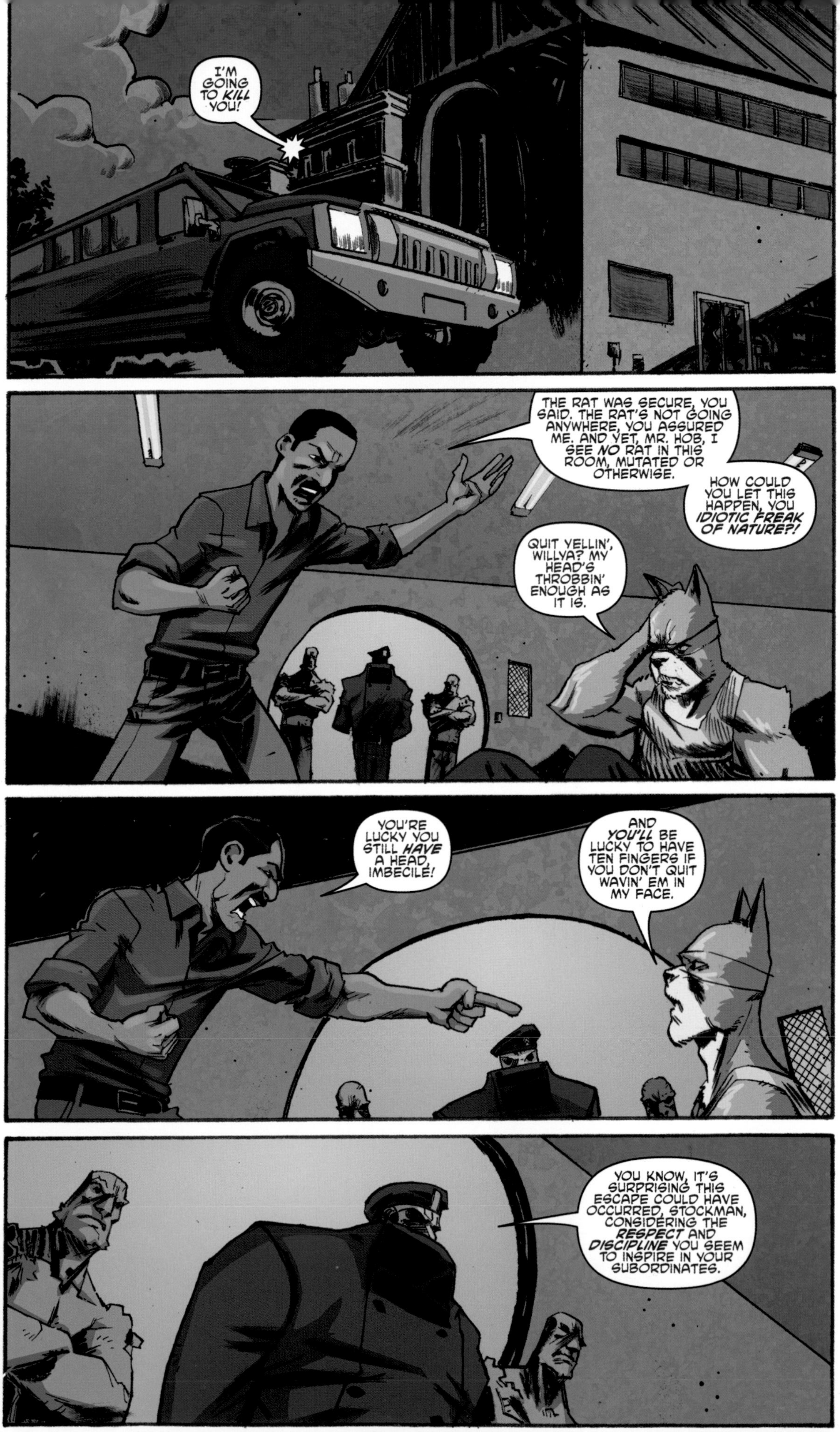

I'M GOING TO KILL YOU!
THE RAT WAS SECURE, YOU SAID. THE RAT'S NOT GOING ANYWHERE, YOU ASSURED ME. AND YET, MR. HOB, I SEE NO RAT IN THIS ROOM, MUTATED OR OTHERWISE.
HOW COULD YOU LET THIS HAPPEN, YOU IDIOTIC FREAK OF NATURE?!
QUIT YELLIN', WILLYA? MY HEAD'S THROBBIN' ENOUGH AS IT IS.
YOU'RE LUCKY YOU STILL HAVE A HEAD, IMBECILE!
AND YOU'LL BE LUCKY TO HAVE TEN FINGERS IF YOU DON'T QUIT WAVIN' EM IN MY FACE.
YOU KNOW, IT'S SURPRISING THIS ESCAPE COULD HAVE OCCURRED, STOCKMAN, CONSIDERING THE RESPECT AND DISCIPLINE YOU SEEM TO INSPIRE IN YOUR SUBORDINATES.

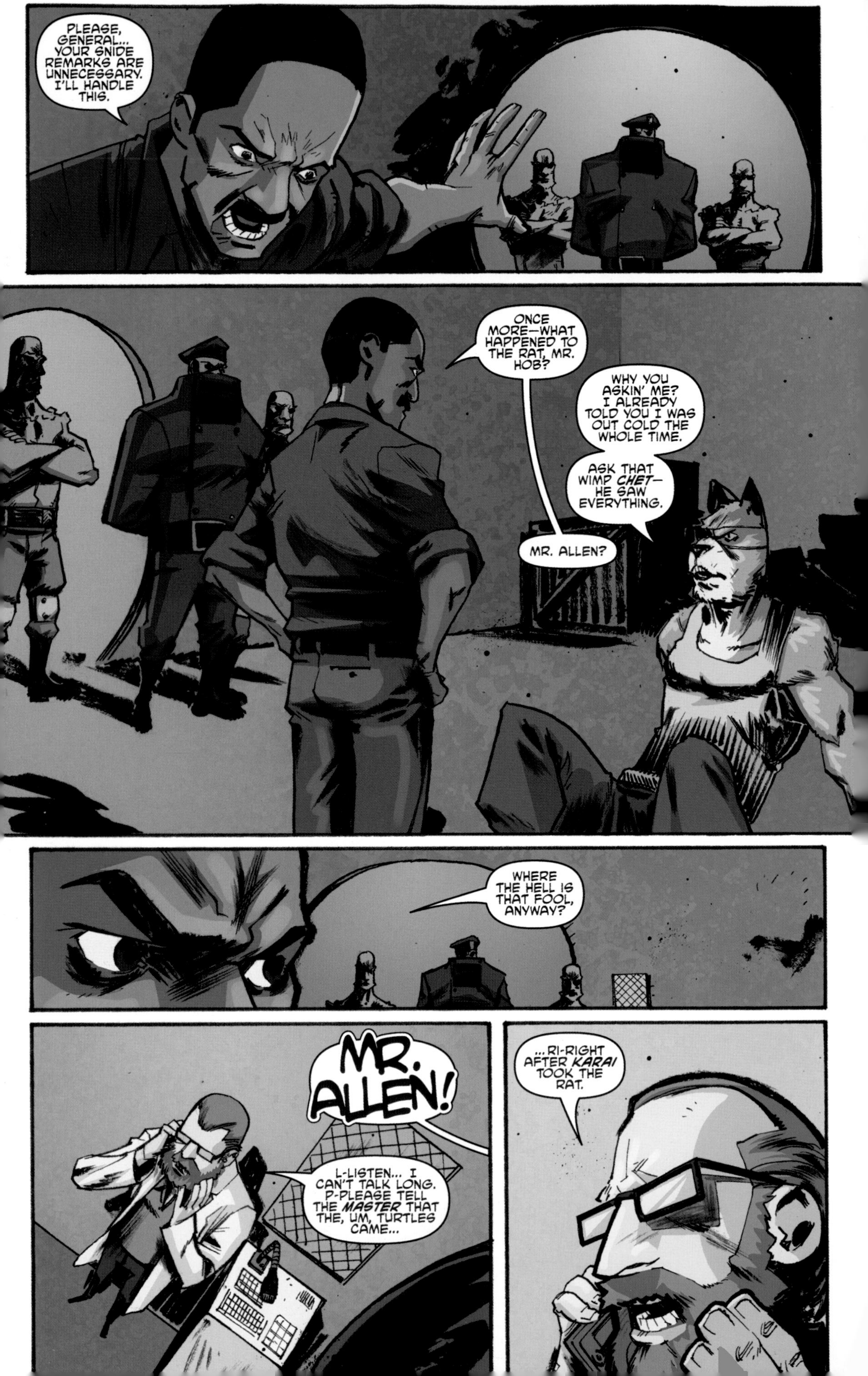
PLEASE, GENERAL... YOUR SNIDE REMARKS ARE UNNECESSARY. I'LL HANDLE THIS.
ONCE MORE—WHAT HAPPENED TO THE RAT, MR. HOB?
WHY YOU ASKIN' ME? I ALREADY TOLD YOU I WAS OUT COLD THE WHOLE TIME.
ASK THAT WIMP CHET—HE SAW EVERYTHING.
MR. ALLEN?
WHERE THE HELL IS THAT FOOL, ANYWAY?
MR. ALLEN!
L-LISTEN... I CAN'T TALK LONG. P-PLEASE TELL THE MASTER THAT THE, UM, TURTLES CAME...
...RI-RIGHT AFTER KARAI TOOK THE RAT.

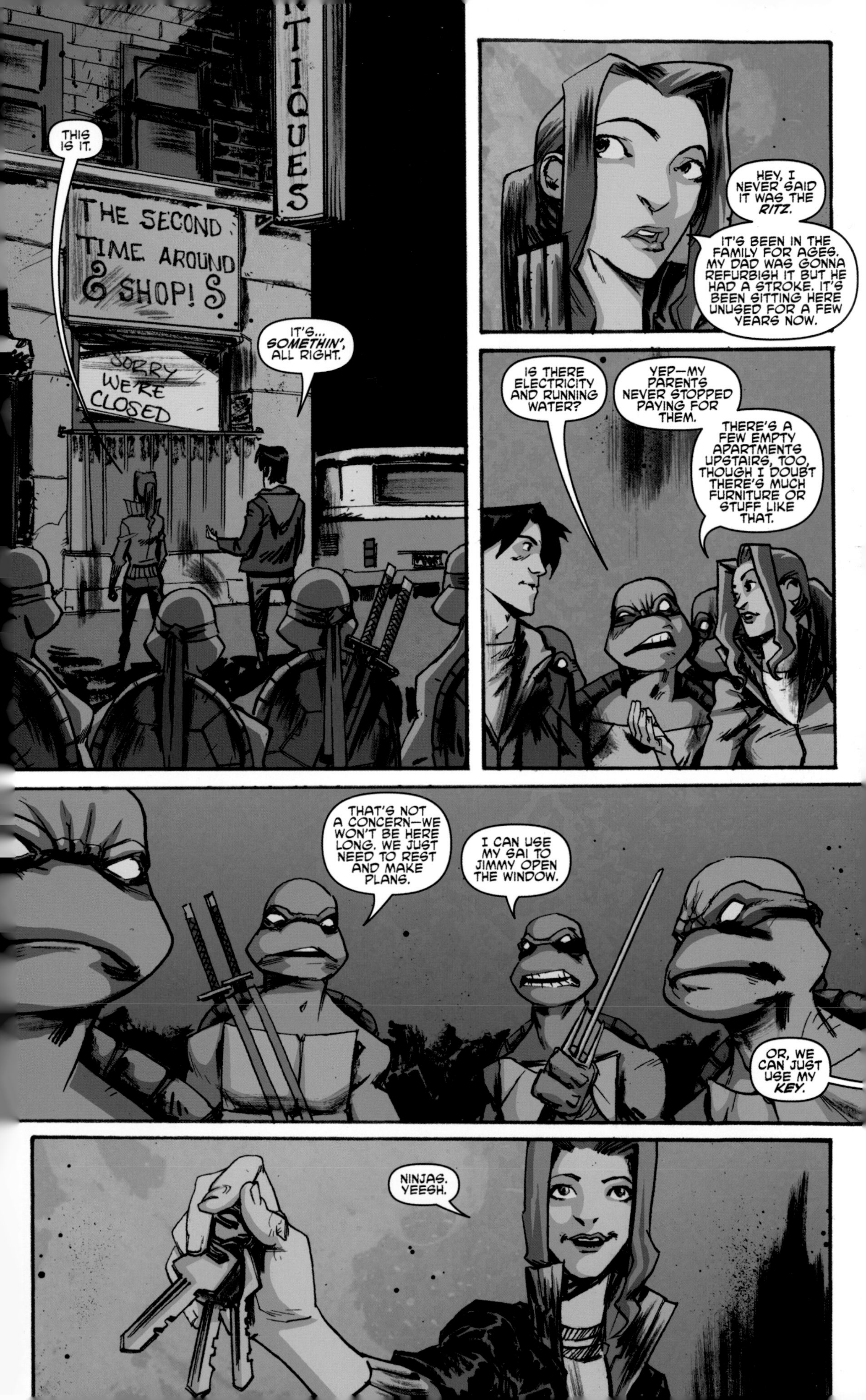

NTIQUES
THE SECOND TIME AROUND & SHOP! S
SORRY WE'RE CLOSED
THIS IS IT.
IT'S... SOMETHIN', ALL RIGHT.
HEY, I NEVER SAID IT WAS THE RITZ.
IT'S BEEN IN THE FAMILY FOR AGES. MY DAD WAS GONNA REFURBISH IT BUT HE HAD A STROKE. IT'S BEEN SITTING HERE UNUSED FOR A FEW YEARS NOW.
IS THERE ELECTRICITY AND RUNNING WATER?
YEP—MY PARENTS NEVER STOPPED PAYING FOR THEM.
THERE'S A FEW EMPTY APARTMENTS UPSTAIRS, TOO, THOUGH I DOUBT THERE'S MUCH FURNITURE OR STUFF LIKE THAT.
THAT'S NOT A CONCERN—WE WON'T BE HERE LONG. WE JUST NEED TO REST AND MAKE PLANS.
I CAN USE MY SAI TO JIMMY OPEN THE WINDOW.
OR, WE CAN JUST USE MY KEY.
NINJAS. YEESH.

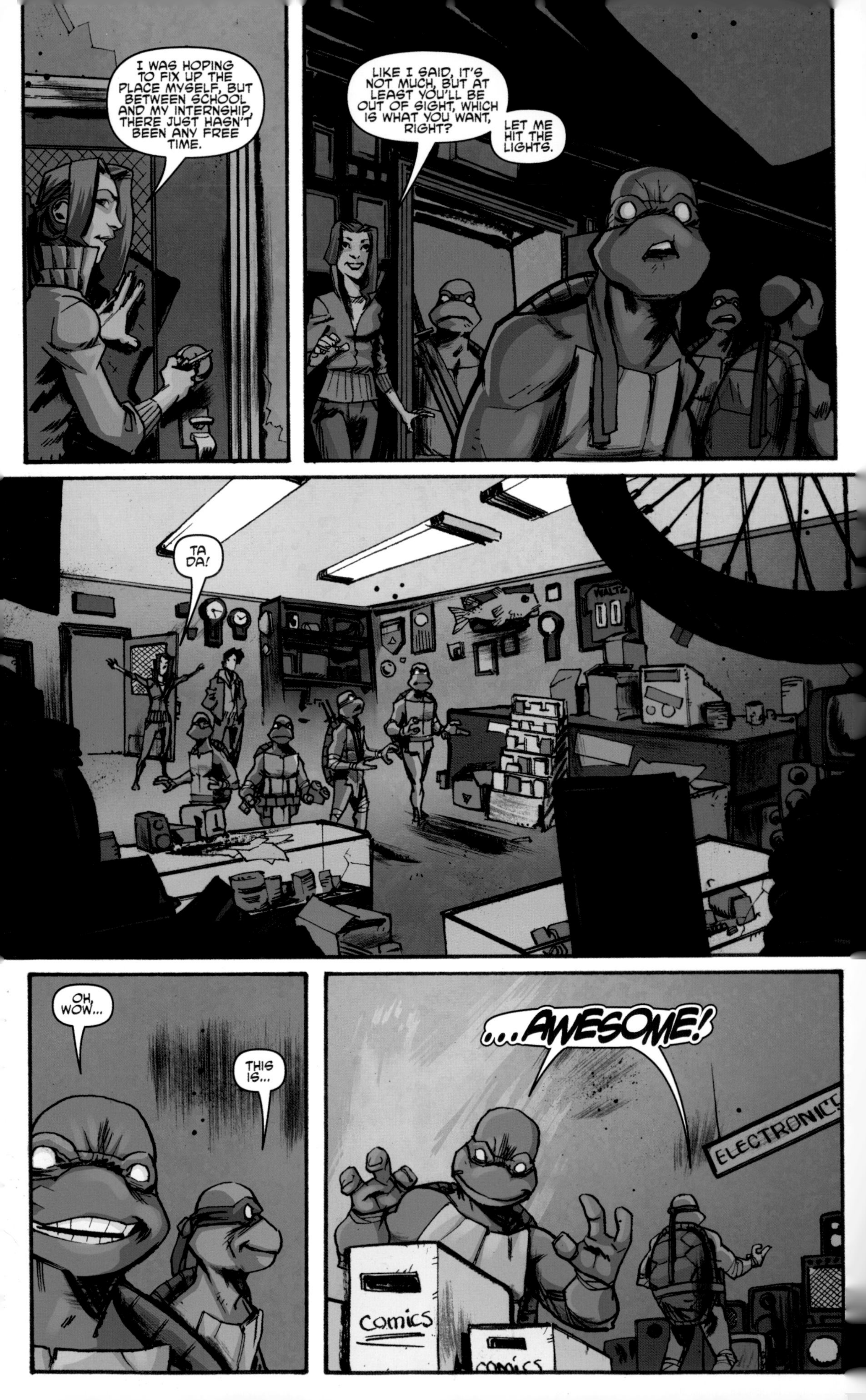
I WAS HOPING TO FIX UP THE PLACE MYSELF, BUT BETWEEN SCHOOL AND MY INTERNSHIP, THERE JUST HASN'T BEEN ANY FREE TIME.
LIKE I SAID, IT'S NOT MUCH, BUT AT LEAST YOU'LL BE OUT OF SIGHT, WHICH IS WHAT YOU WANT, RIGHT?
LET ME HIT THE LIGHTS.
TA DA!
WALTZ
OH, WOW...
THIS IS...
...AWESOME!
ELECTRONICS
COMICS
COMICS

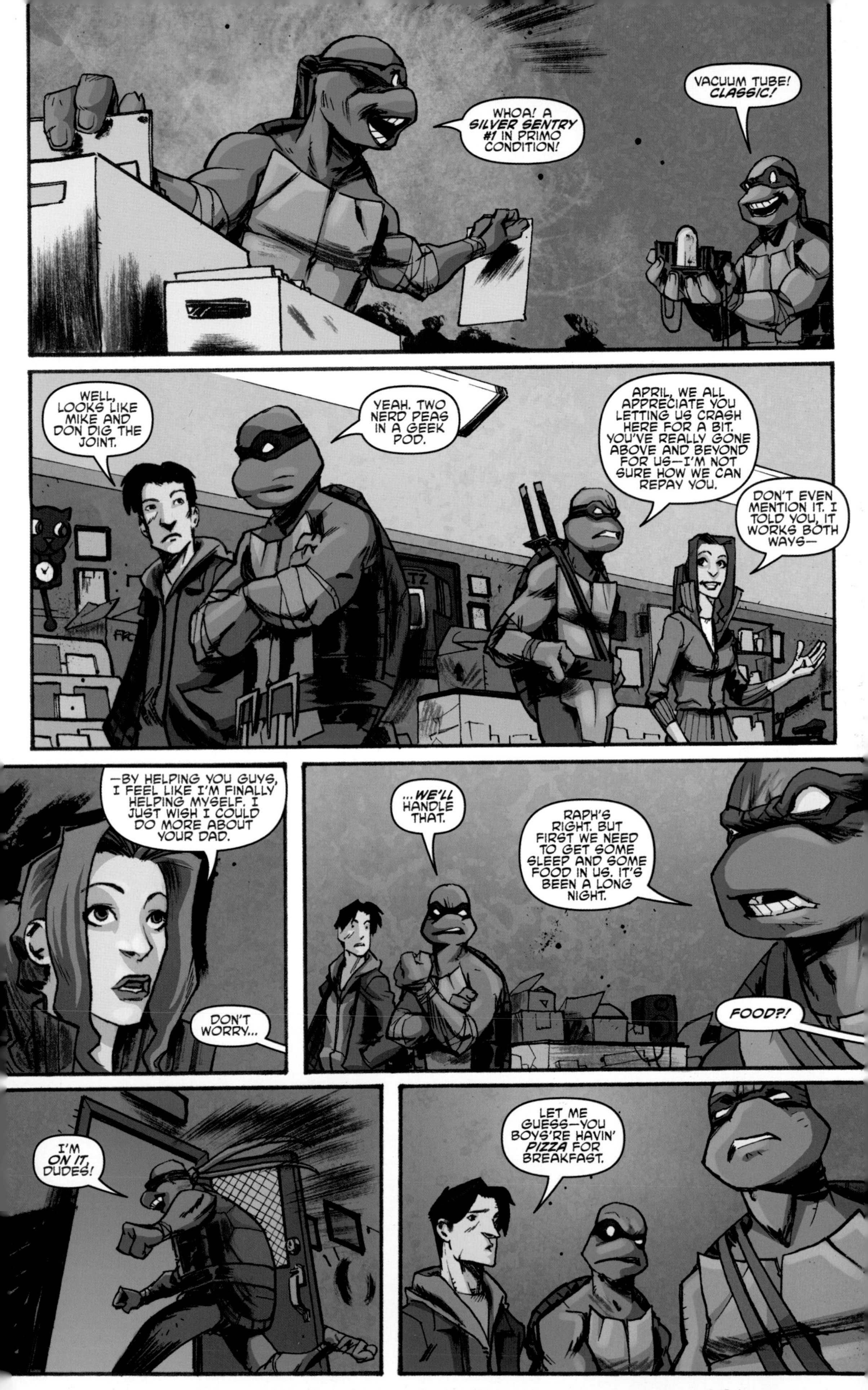
WHOA! A SILVER SENTRY #1 IN PRIMO CONDITION!
VACUUM TUBE! CLASSIC!
WELL, LOOKS LIKE MIKE AND DON DIG THE JOINT.
YEAH. TWO NERD PEAS IN A GEEK POD.
APRIL, WE ALL APPRECIATE YOU LETTING US CRASH HERE FOR A BIT. YOU'VE REALLY GONE ABOVE AND BEYOND FOR US—I'M NOT SURE HOW WE CAN REPAY YOU.
DON'T EVEN MENTION IT. I TOLD YOU, IT WORKS BOTH WAYS—
—BY HELPING YOU GUYS, I FEEL LIKE I'M FINALLY HELPING MYSELF. I JUST WISH I COULD DO MORE ABOUT YOUR DAD.
DON'T WORRY...
...WE'LL HANDLE THAT.
RAPH'S RIGHT. BUT FIRST WE NEED TO GET SOME SLEEP AND SOME FOOD IN US. IT'S BEEN A LONG NIGHT.
FOOD?!
I'M ON IT, DUDES!
LET ME GUESS—YOU BOYS'RE HAVIN' PIZZA FOR BREAKFAST.

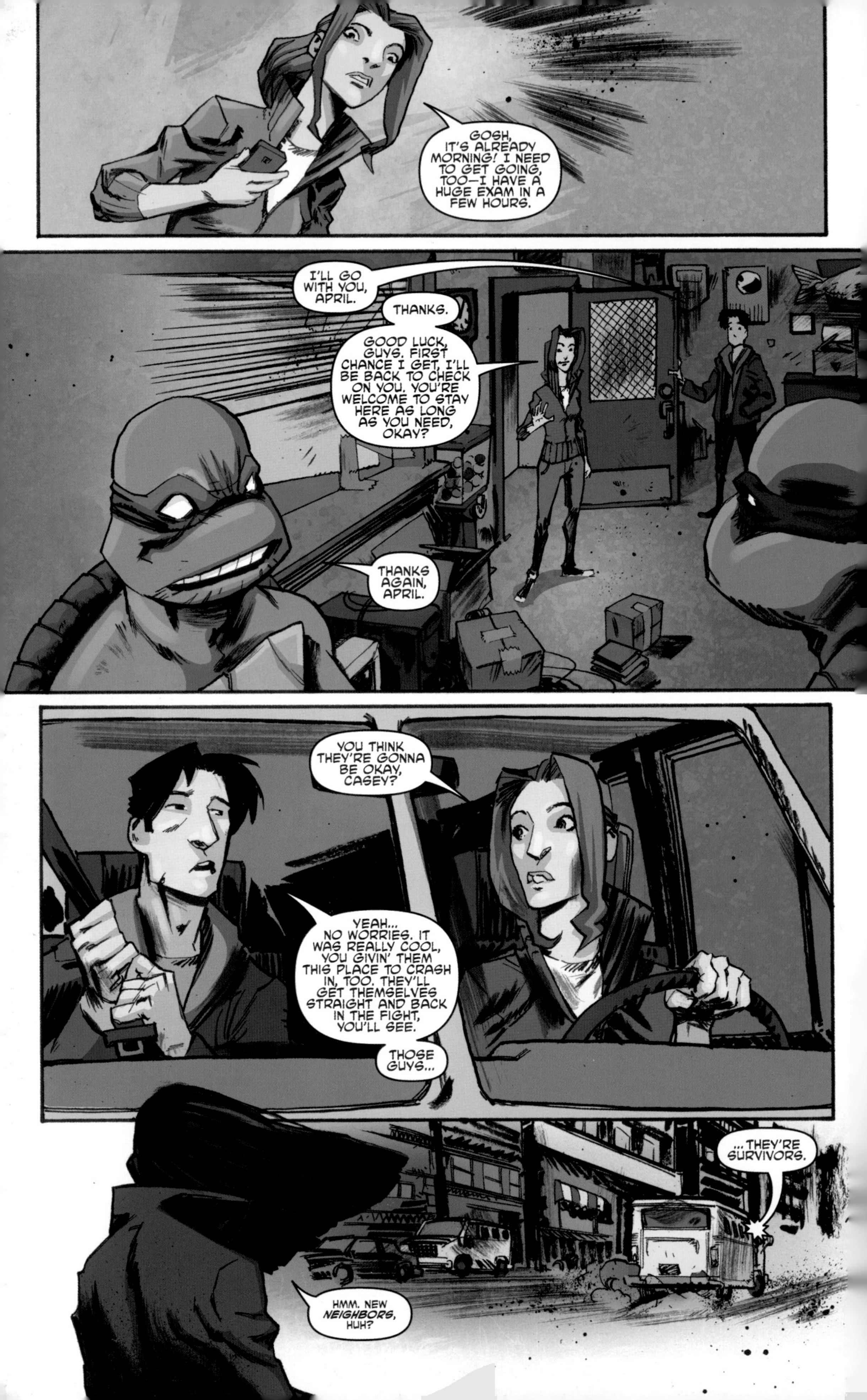
GOSH, IT'S ALREADY MORNING! I NEED TO GET GOING, TOO—I HAVE A HUGE EXAM IN A FEW HOURS.
I'LL GO WITH YOU, APRIL.
THANKS.
GOOD LUCK, GUYS. FIRST CHANCE I GET, I'LL BE BACK TO CHECK ON YOU. YOU'RE WELCOME TO STAY HERE AS LONG AS YOU NEED, OKAY?
THANKS AGAIN, APRIL.
YOU THINK THEY'RE GONNA BE OKAY, CASEY?
YEAH... NO WORRIES. IT WAS REALLY COOL, YOU GIVIN' THEM THIS PLACE TO CRASH IN, TOO. THEY'LL GET THEMSELVES STRAIGHT AND BACK IN THE FIGHT, YOU'LL SEE.
THOSE GUYS...
...THEY'RE SURVIVORS.
HMM. NEW NEIGHBORS, HUH?

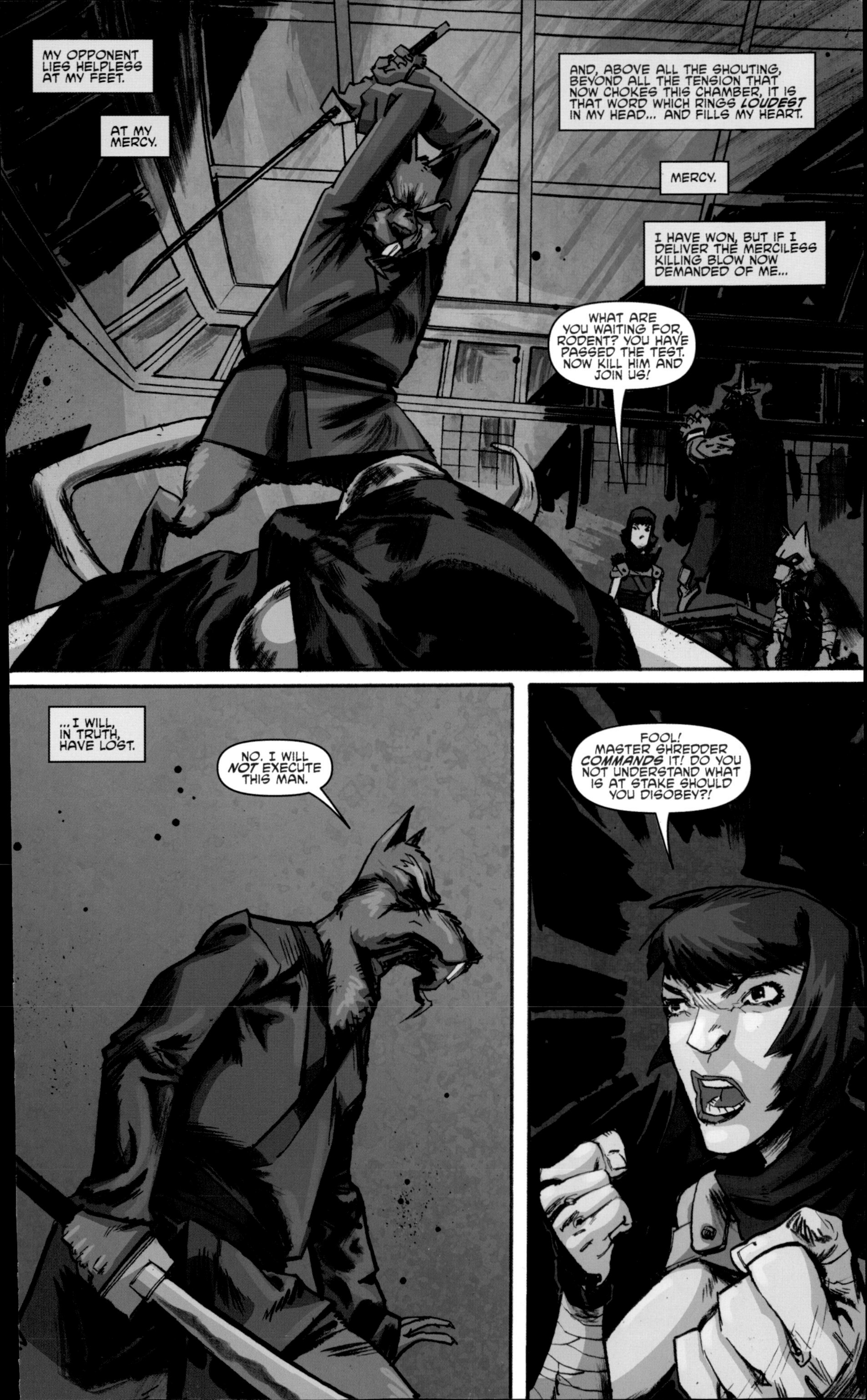

MY OPPONENT LIES HELPLESS AT MY FEET.
AT MY MERCY.
AND, ABOVE ALL THE SHOUTING, BEYOND ALL THE TENSION THAT NOW CHOKES THIS CHAMBER, IT IS THAT WORD WHICH RINGS *LOUDEST* IN MY HEAD... AND FILLS MY HEART.
MERCY.
I HAVE WON, BUT IF I DELIVER THE MERCILESS KILLING BLOW NOW DEMANDED OF ME...
WHAT ARE YOU WAITING FOR, RODENT? YOU HAVE PASSED THE TEST. NOW KILL HIM AND JOIN US!
...I WILL, IN TRUTH, HAVE LOST.
NO. I WILL *NOT* EXECUTE THIS MAN.
FOOL! MASTER SHREDDER *COMMANDS* IT! DO YOU NOT UNDERSTAND WHAT IS AT STAKE SHOULD YOU DISOBEY?!

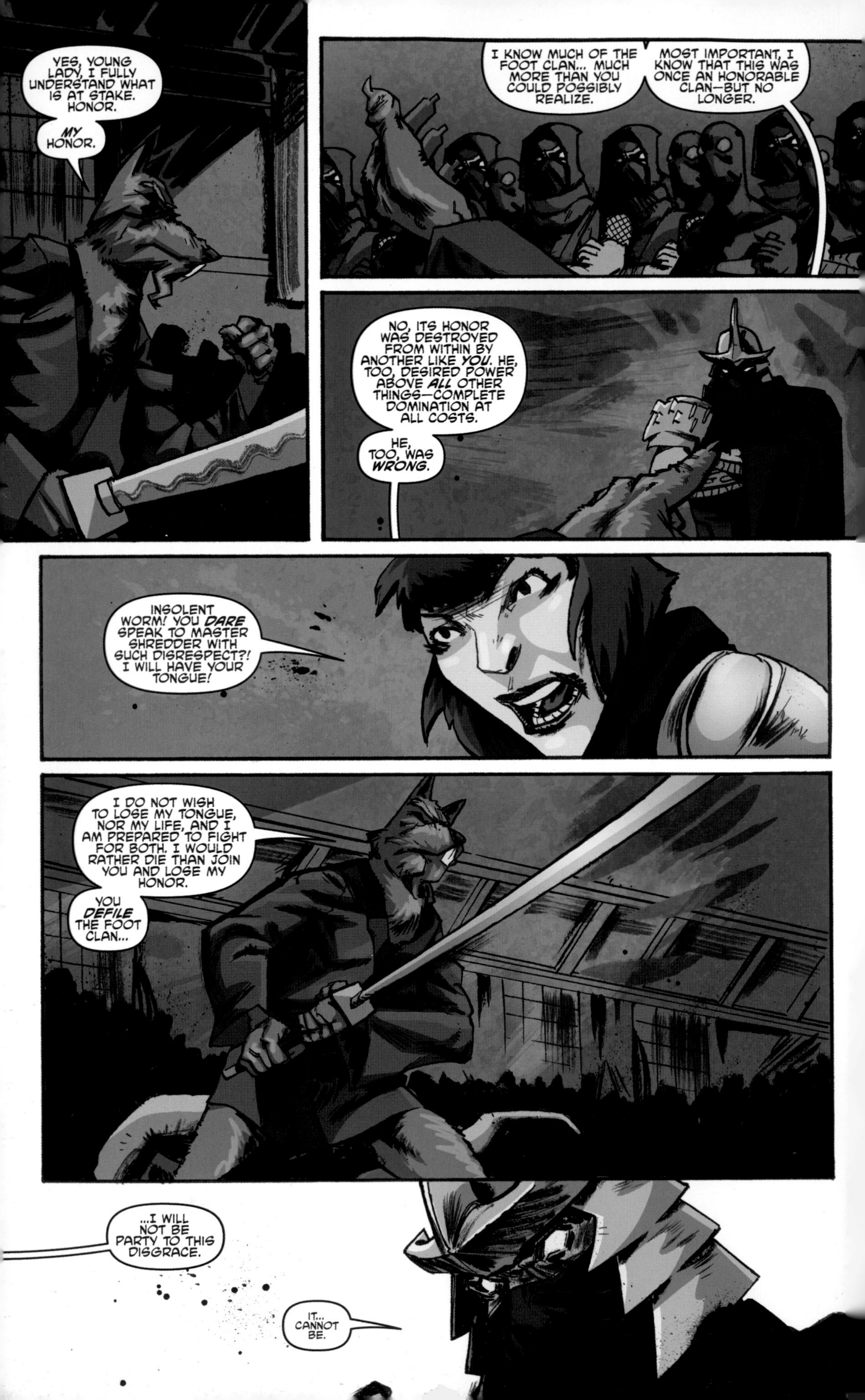
YES, YOUNG LADY, I FULLY UNDERSTAND WHAT IS AT STAKE. HONOR.
MY HONOR.
I KNOW MUCH OF THE FOOT CLAN... MUCH MORE THAN YOU COULD POSSIBLY REALIZE.
MOST IMPORTANT, I KNOW THAT THIS WAS ONCE AN HONORABLE CLAN—BUT NO LONGER.
NO, ITS HONOR WAS DESTROYED FROM WITHIN BY ANOTHER LIKE YOU. HE, TOO, DESIRED POWER ABOVE ALL OTHER THINGS—COMPLETE DOMINATION AT ALL COSTS.
HE, TOO, WAS WRONG.
INSOLENT WORM! YOU DARE SPEAK TO MASTER SHREDDER WITH SUCH DISRESPECT?! I WILL HAVE YOUR TONGUE!
I DO NOT WISH TO LOSE MY TONGUE, NOR MY LIFE, AND I AM PREPARED TO FIGHT FOR BOTH. I WOULD RATHER DIE THAN JOIN YOU AND LOSE MY HONOR.
YOU DEFILE THE FOOT CLAN...
...I WILL NOT BE PARTY TO THIS DISGRACE.
IT... CANNOT BE.

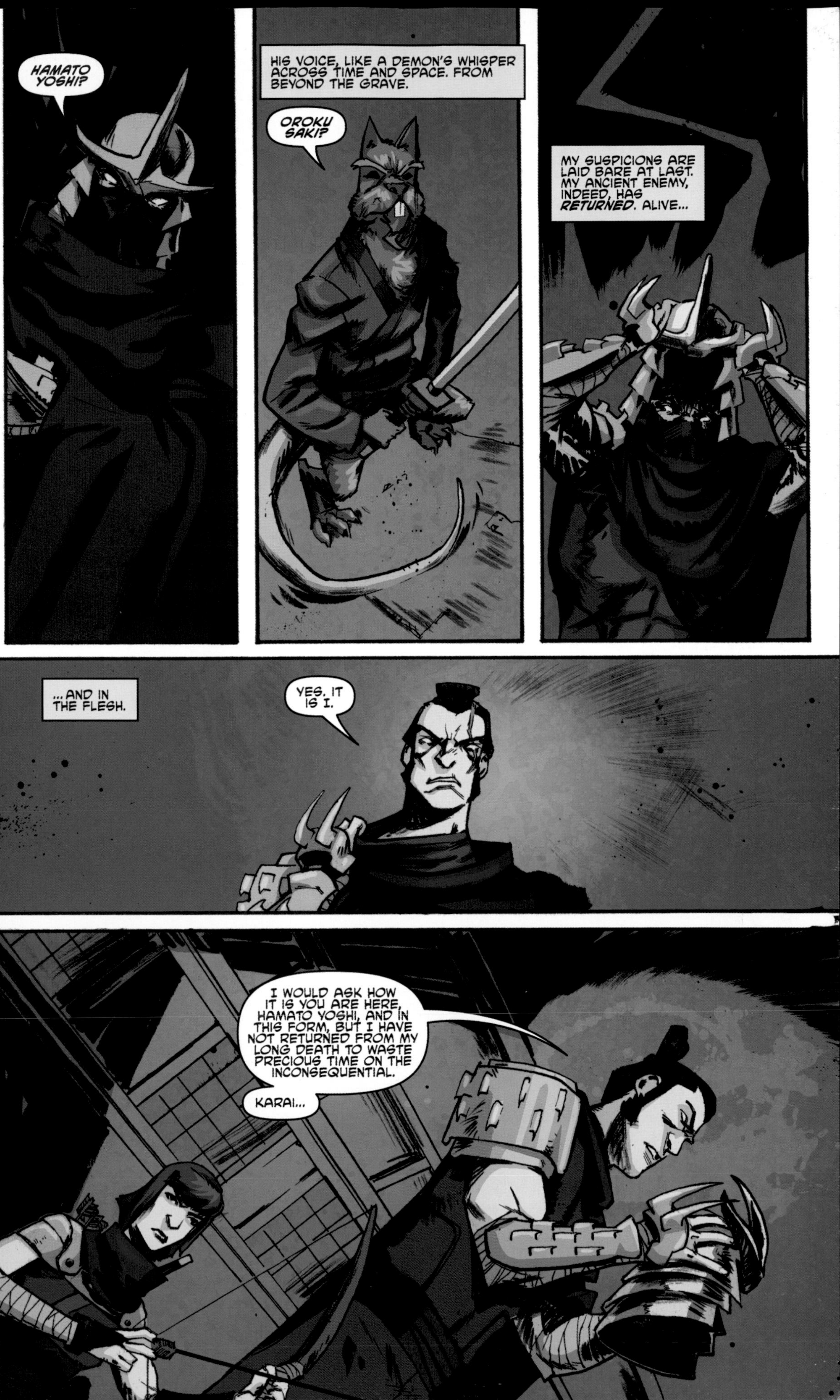
HAMATO YOSHI?
HIS VOICE, LIKE A DEMON'S WHISPER ACROSS TIME AND SPACE. FROM BEYOND THE GRAVE.
OROKU SAKI?
MY SUSPICIONS ARE LAID BARE AT LAST. MY ANCIENT ENEMY, INDEED, HAS RETURNED. ALIVE...
...AND IN THE FLESH.
YES, IT IS I.
I WOULD ASK HOW IT IS YOU ARE HERE, HAMATO YOSHI, AND IN THIS FORM, BUT I HAVE NOT RETURNED FROM MY LONG DEATH TO WASTE PRECIOUS TIME ON THE INCONSEQUENTIAL.
KARAI...

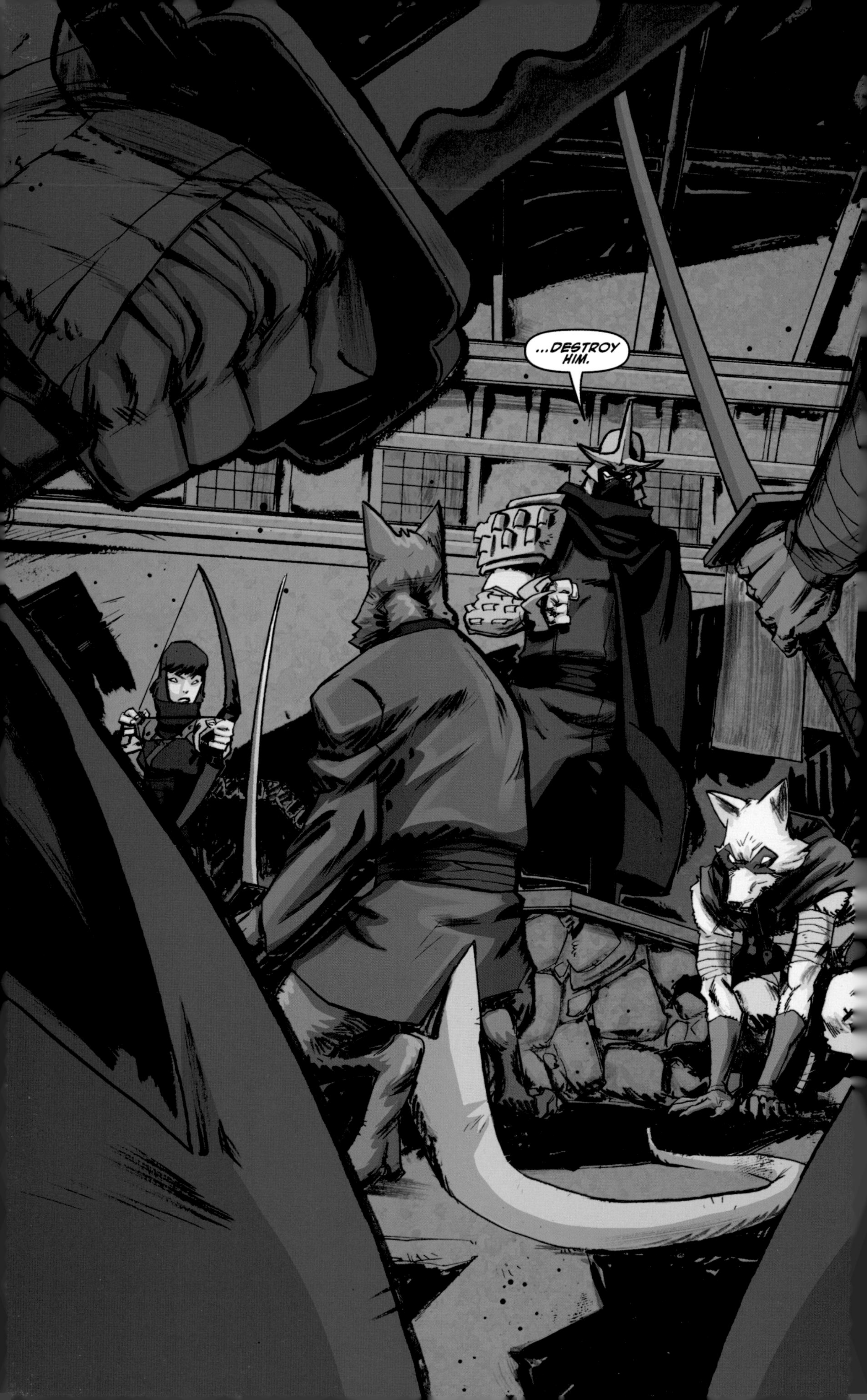
...DESTROY HIM.

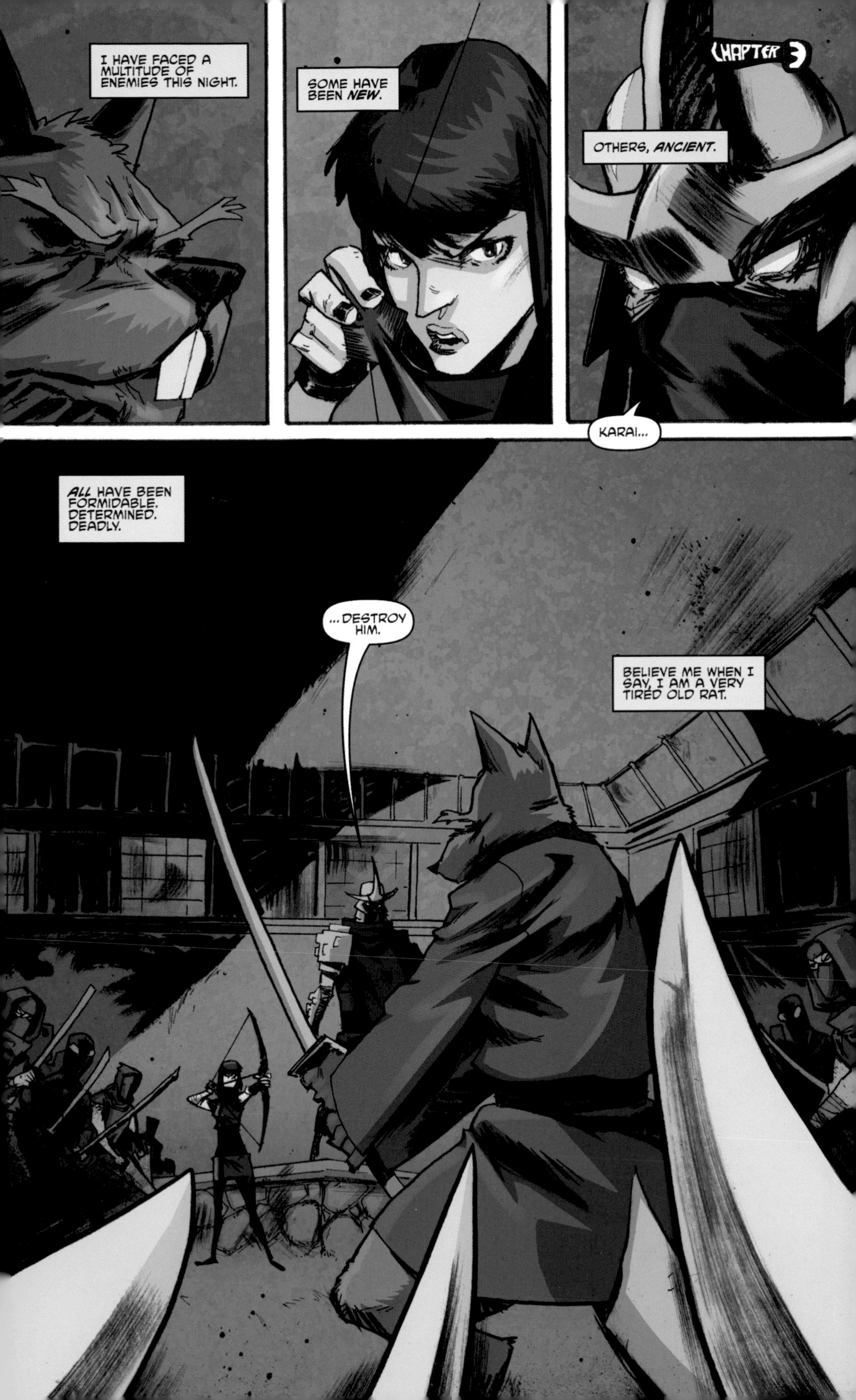
CHAPTER 3
I HAVE FACED A MULTITUDE OF ENEMIES THIS NIGHT.
SOME HAVE BEEN *NEW*.
OTHERS, *ANCIENT*.
KARAI...
ALL HAVE BEEN FORMIDABLE. DETERMINED. DEADLY.
...DESTROY HIM.
BELIEVE ME WHEN I SAY, I AM A VERY TIRED OLD RAT.

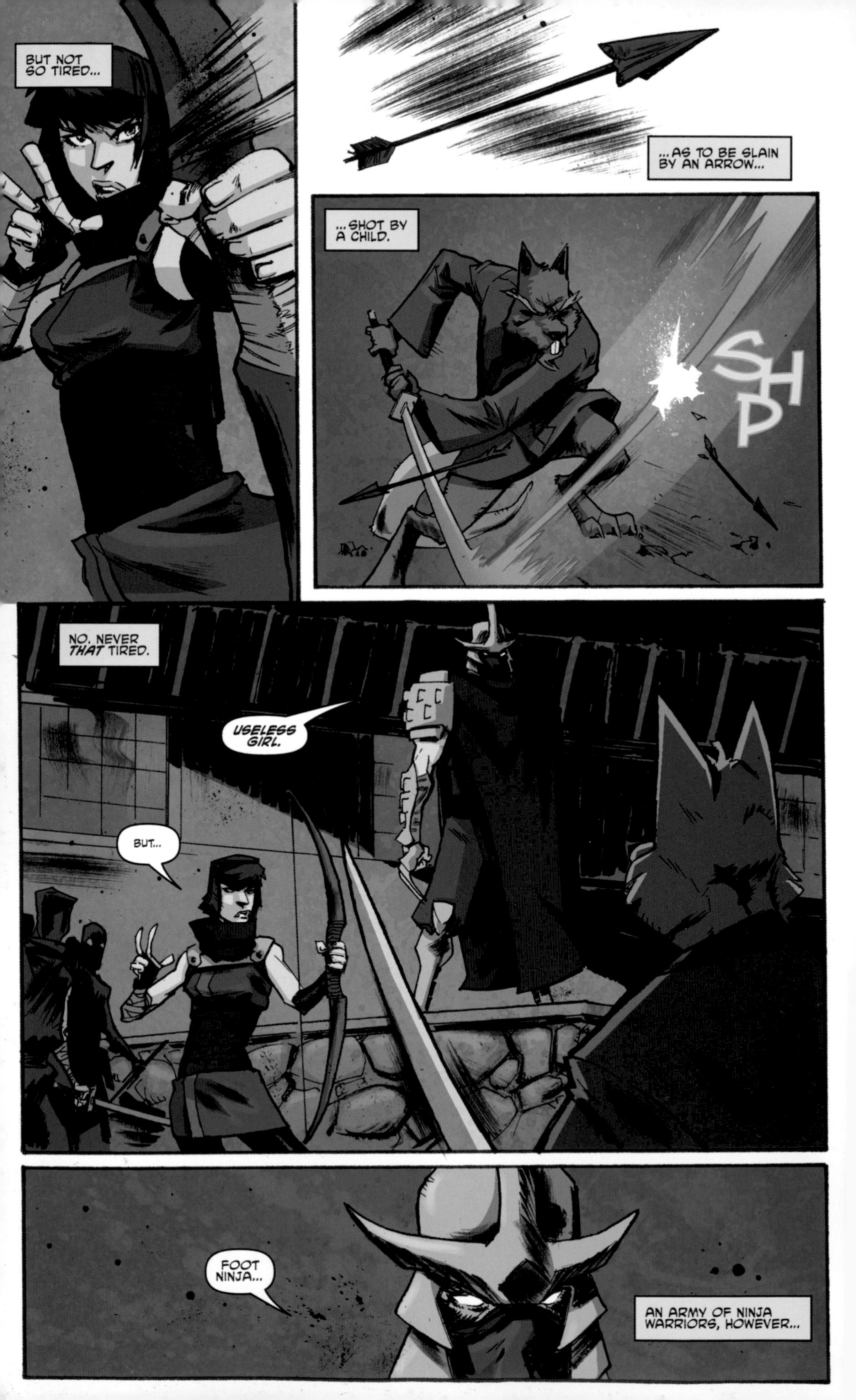
BUT NOT SO TIRED...
...AS TO BE SLAIN BY AN ARROW...
...SHOT BY A CHILD.
SHP
NO. NEVER *THAT* TIRED.
USELESS GIRL.
BUT...
FOOT NINJA...
AN ARMY OF NINJA WARRIORS, HOWEVER...

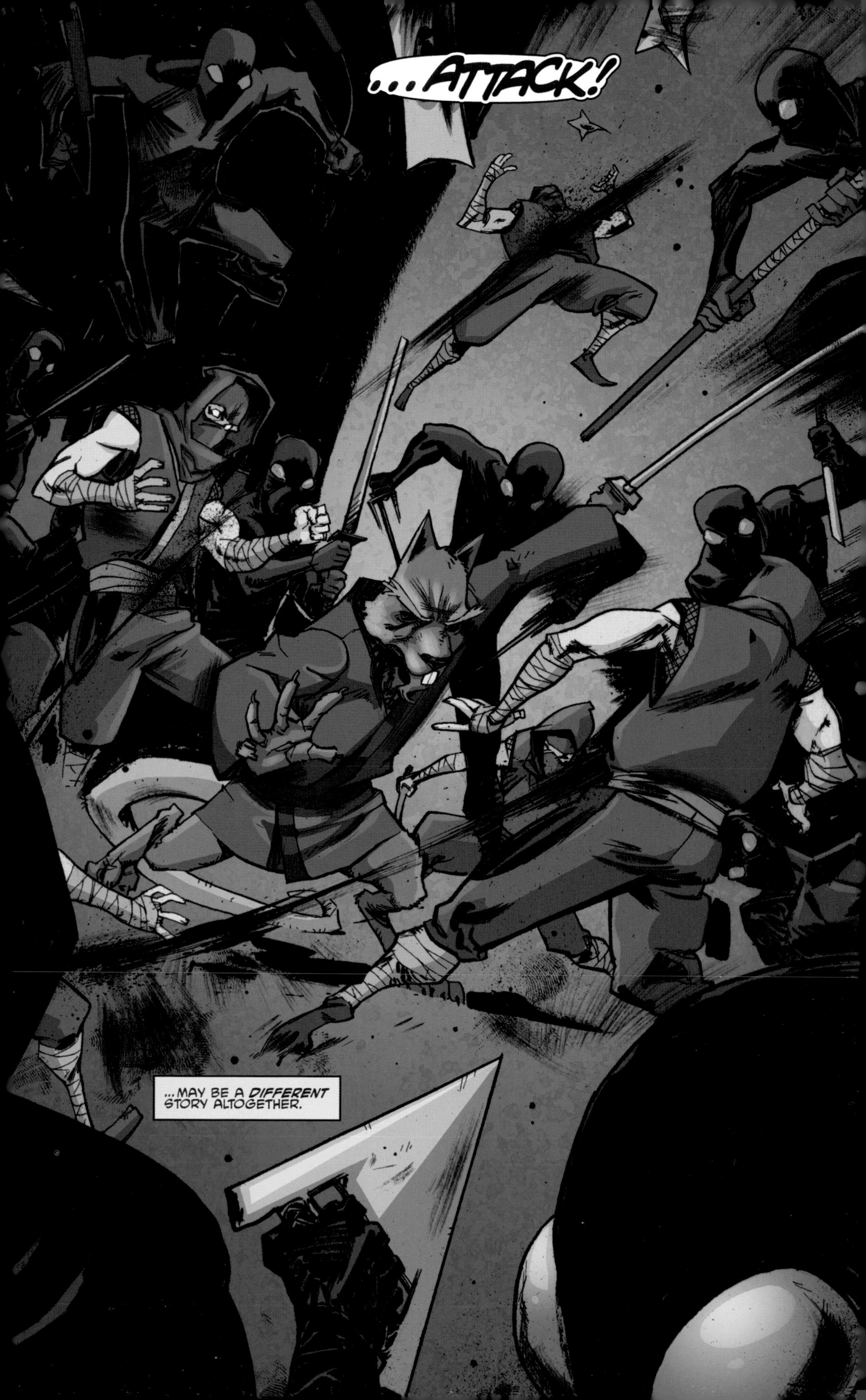
...ATTACK!
...MAY BE A *DIFFERENT* STORY ALTOGETHER.

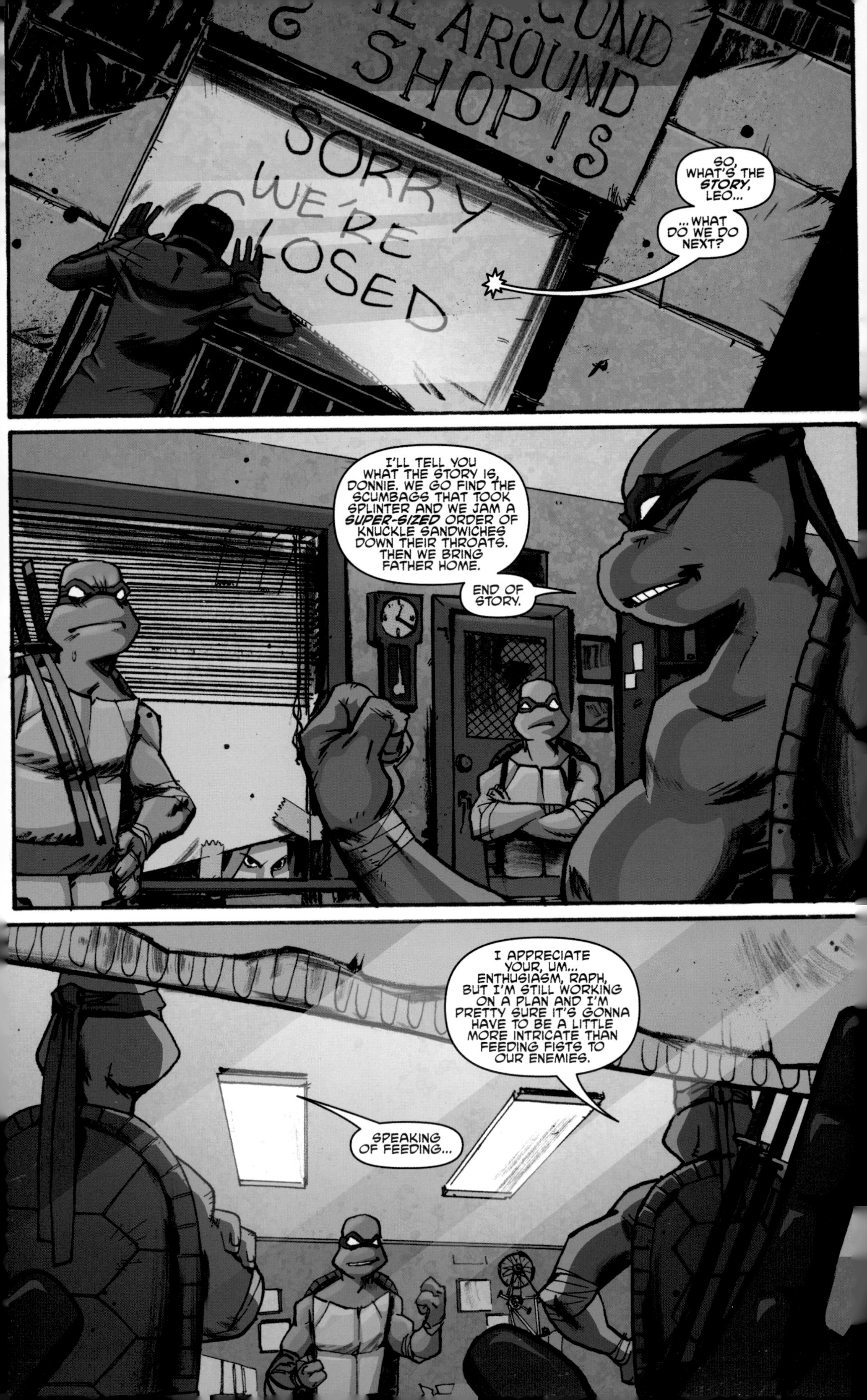

SORRY WE'RE CLOSED
AROUND SHOP!S
SO, WHAT'S THE **STORY,** LEO...
...WHAT DO WE DO NEXT?
I'LL TELL YOU WHAT THE STORY IS, DONNIE. WE GO FIND THE SCUMBAGS THAT TOOK SPLINTER AND WE JAM A **SUPER-SIZED** ORDER OF KNUCKLE SANDWICHES DOWN THEIR THROATS. THEN WE BRING FATHER HOME.
END OF STORY.
I APPRECIATE YOUR, UM... ENTHUSIASM, RAPH, BUT I'M STILL WORKING ON A PLAN AND I'M PRETTY SURE IT'S GONNA HAVE TO BE A LITTLE MORE INTRICATE THAN FEEDING FISTS TO OUR ENEMIES.
SPEAKING OF FEEDING...

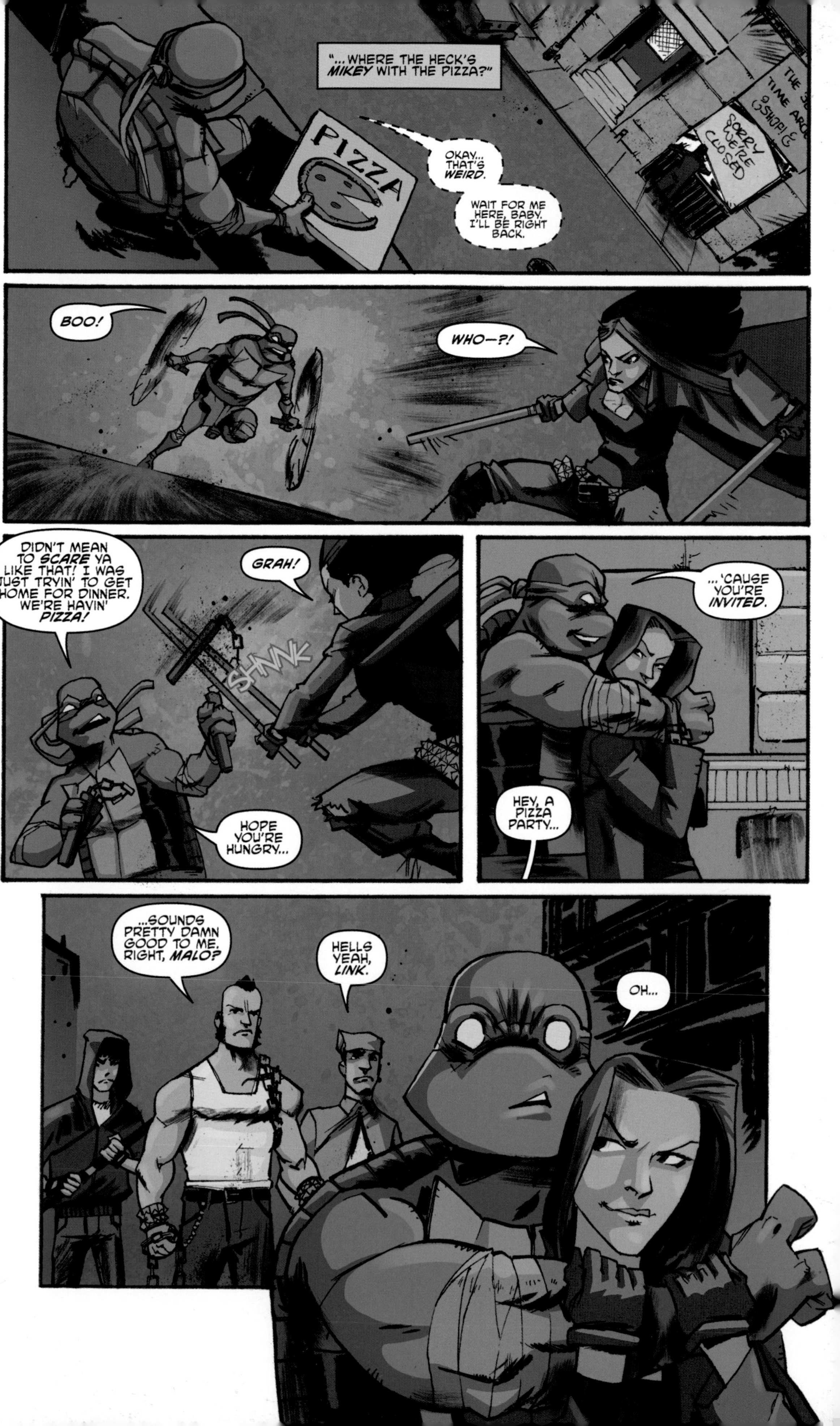
"...WHERE THE HECK'S *MIKEY* WITH THE PIZZA?"
PIZZA
SORRY WE'RE CLOSED
OKAY... THAT'S *WEIRD*.
WAIT FOR ME HERE, BABY. I'LL BE RIGHT BACK.
BOO!
WHO—?!
DIDN'T MEAN TO *SCARE* YA LIKE THAT! I WAS JUST TRYIN' TO GET HOME FOR DINNER. WE'RE HAVIN' *PIZZA!*
GRAH!
SHNNK
HOPE YOU'RE HUNGRY...
...'CAUSE YOU'RE *INVITED*.
HEY, A PIZZA PARTY...
...SOUNDS PRETTY DAMN GOOD TO ME. RIGHT, *MALO?*
HELLS YEAH, *LINK*.
OH...

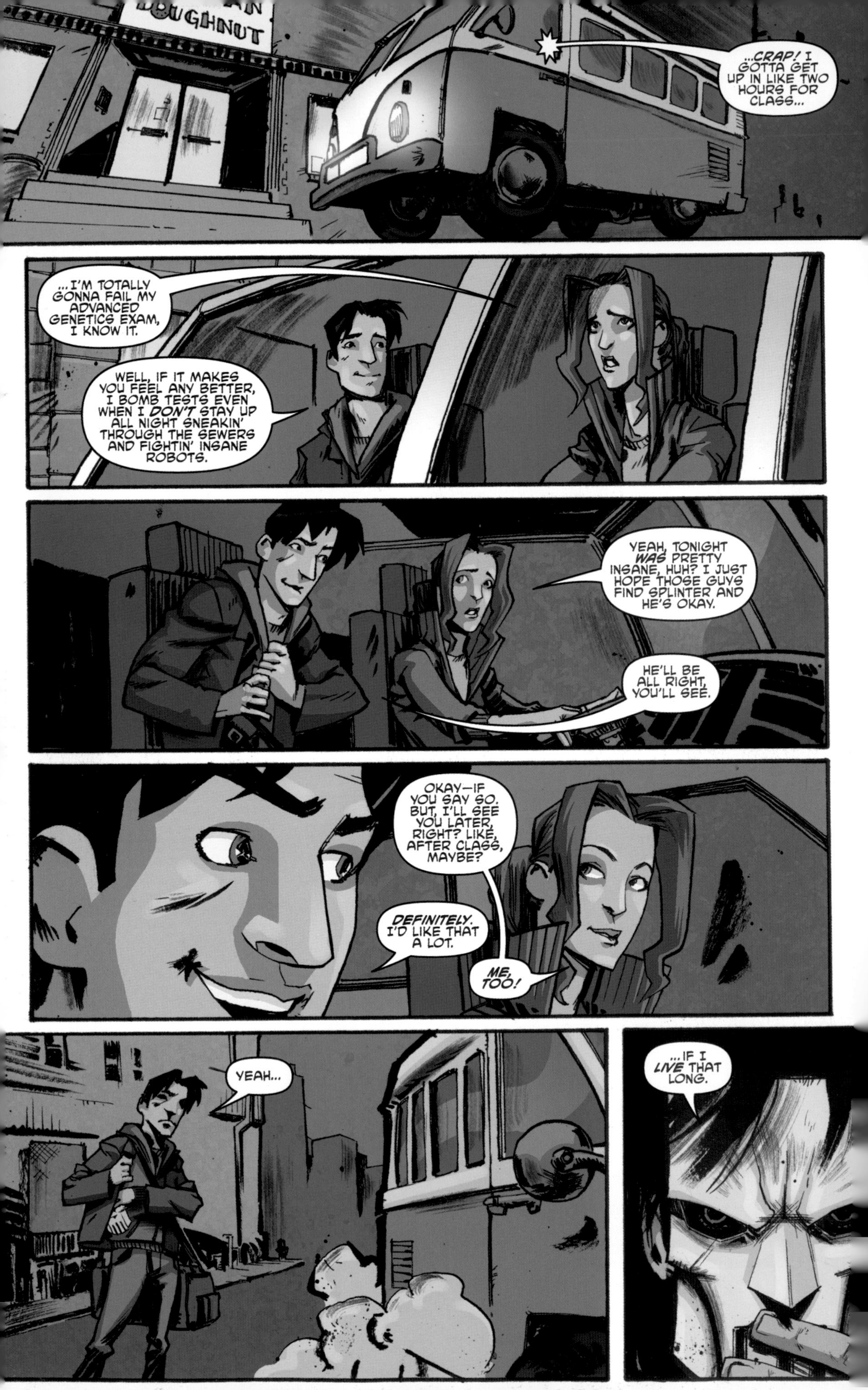
...CRAP! I GOTTA GET UP IN LIKE TWO HOURS FOR CLASS...
...I'M TOTALLY GONNA FAIL MY ADVANCED GENETICS EXAM, I KNOW IT.
WELL, IF IT MAKES YOU FEEL ANY BETTER, I BOMB TESTS EVEN WHEN I DON'T STAY UP ALL NIGHT SNEAKIN' THROUGH THE SEWERS AND FIGHTIN' INSANE ROBOTS.
YEAH, TONIGHT WAS PRETTY INSANE, HUH? I JUST HOPE THOSE GUYS FIND SPLINTER AND HE'S OKAY.
HE'LL BE ALL RIGHT, YOU'LL SEE.
OKAY—IF YOU SAY SO. BUT, I'LL SEE YOU LATER, RIGHT? LIKE, AFTER CLASS, MAYBE?
DEFINITELY. I'D LIKE THAT A LOT.
ME, TOO!
YEAH...
...IF I LIVE THAT LONG.

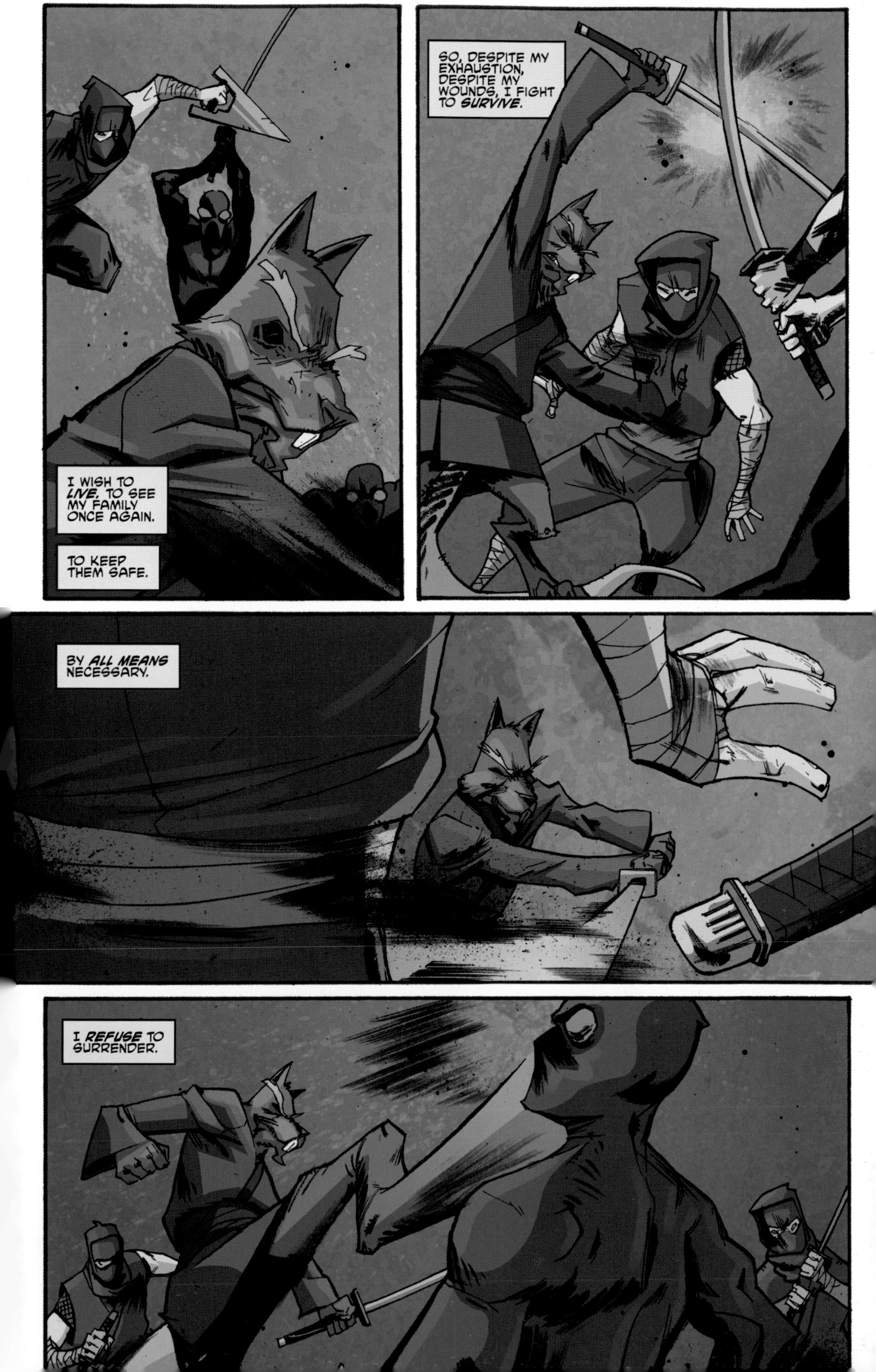
I WISH TO LIVE. TO SEE MY FAMILY ONCE AGAIN.
TO KEEP THEM SAFE.
SO, DESPITE MY EXHAUSTION, DESPITE MY WOUNDS, I FIGHT TO SURVIVE.
BY ALL MEANS NECESSARY.
I REFUSE TO SURRENDER.

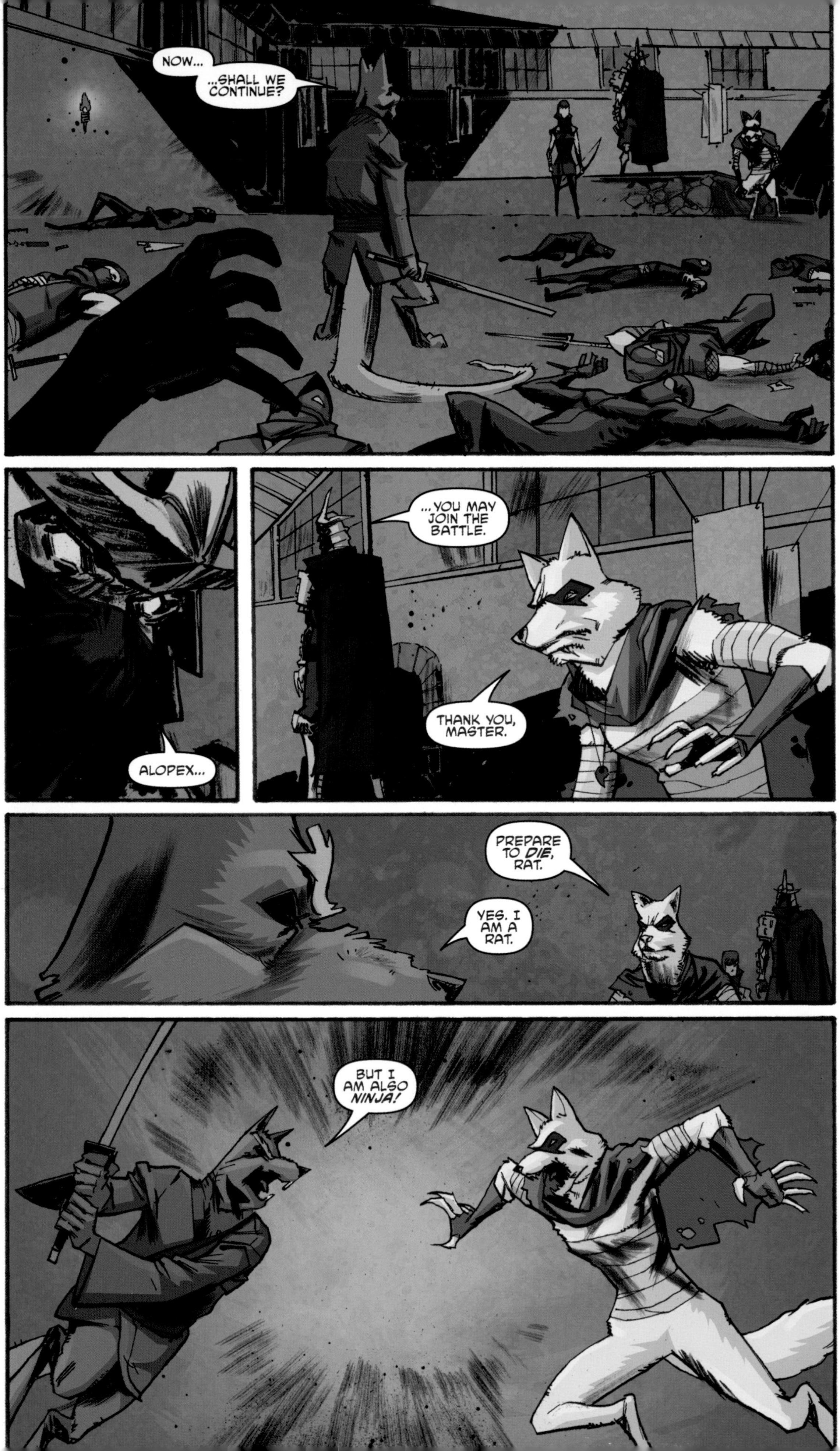
NOW...
...SHALL WE CONTINUE?
ALOPEX...
...YOU MAY JOIN THE BATTLE.
THANK YOU, MASTER.
PREPARE TO *DIE*, RAT.
YES. I AM A RAT.
BUT I AM ALSO *NINJA!*

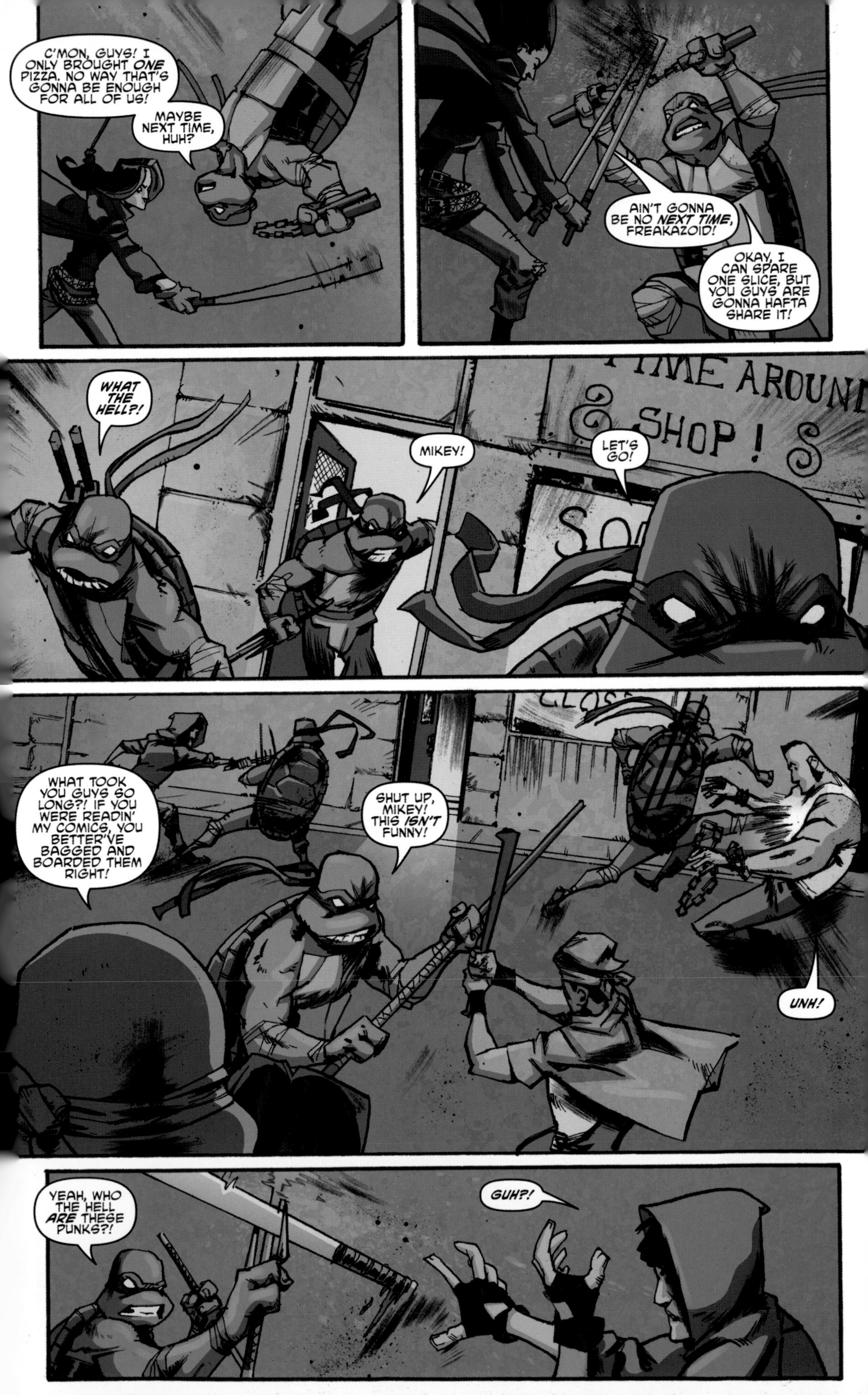
C'MON, GUYS! I ONLY BROUGHT ONE PIZZA. NO WAY THAT'S GONNA BE ENOUGH FOR ALL OF US!
MAYBE NEXT TIME, HUH?
AIN'T GONNA BE NO NEXT TIME, FREAKAZOID!
OKAY, I CAN SPARE ONE SLICE, BUT YOU GUYS ARE GONNA HAFTA SHARE IT!
WHAT THE HELL?!
MIKEY!
LET'S GO!
TIME AROUN
SHOP!
WHAT TOOK YOU GUYS SO LONG?! IF YOU WERE READIN' MY COMICS, YOU BETTER'VE BAGGED AND BOARDED THEM RIGHT!
SHUT UP, MIKEY! THIS ISN'T FUNNY!
UNH!
YEAH, WHO THE HELL ARE THESE PUNKS?!
GUH?!

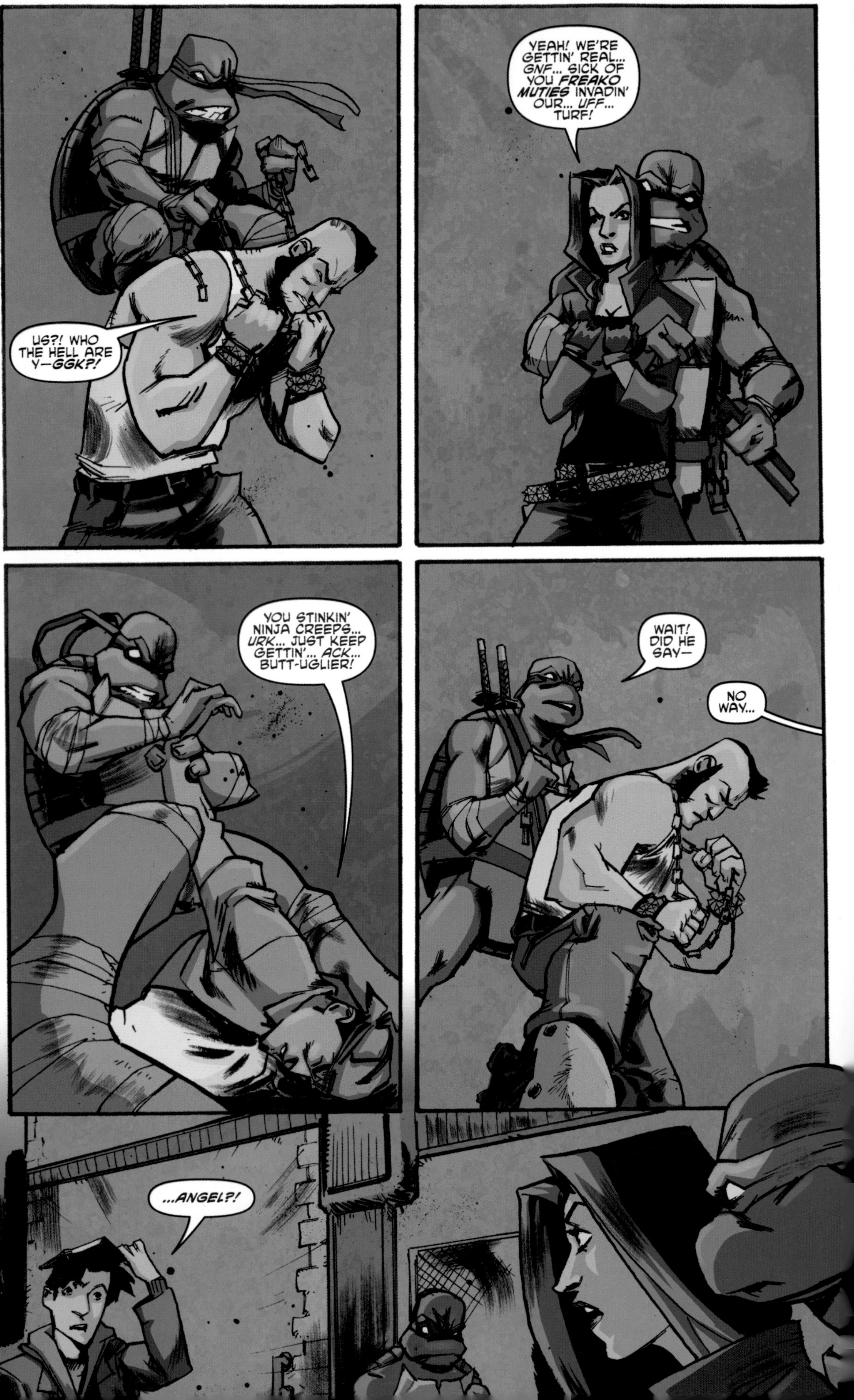
US?! WHO THE HELL ARE Y—*GGK?!*
YEAH! WE'RE GETTIN' REAL... GNF... SICK OF YOU *FREAKO MUTIES* INVADIN' OUR... *UFF*... TURF!
YOU STINKIN' NINJA CREEPS... *URK*... JUST KEEP GETTIN'... *ACK*... BUTT-UGLIER!
WAIT! DID HE SAY—
NO WAY...
...ANGEL?!

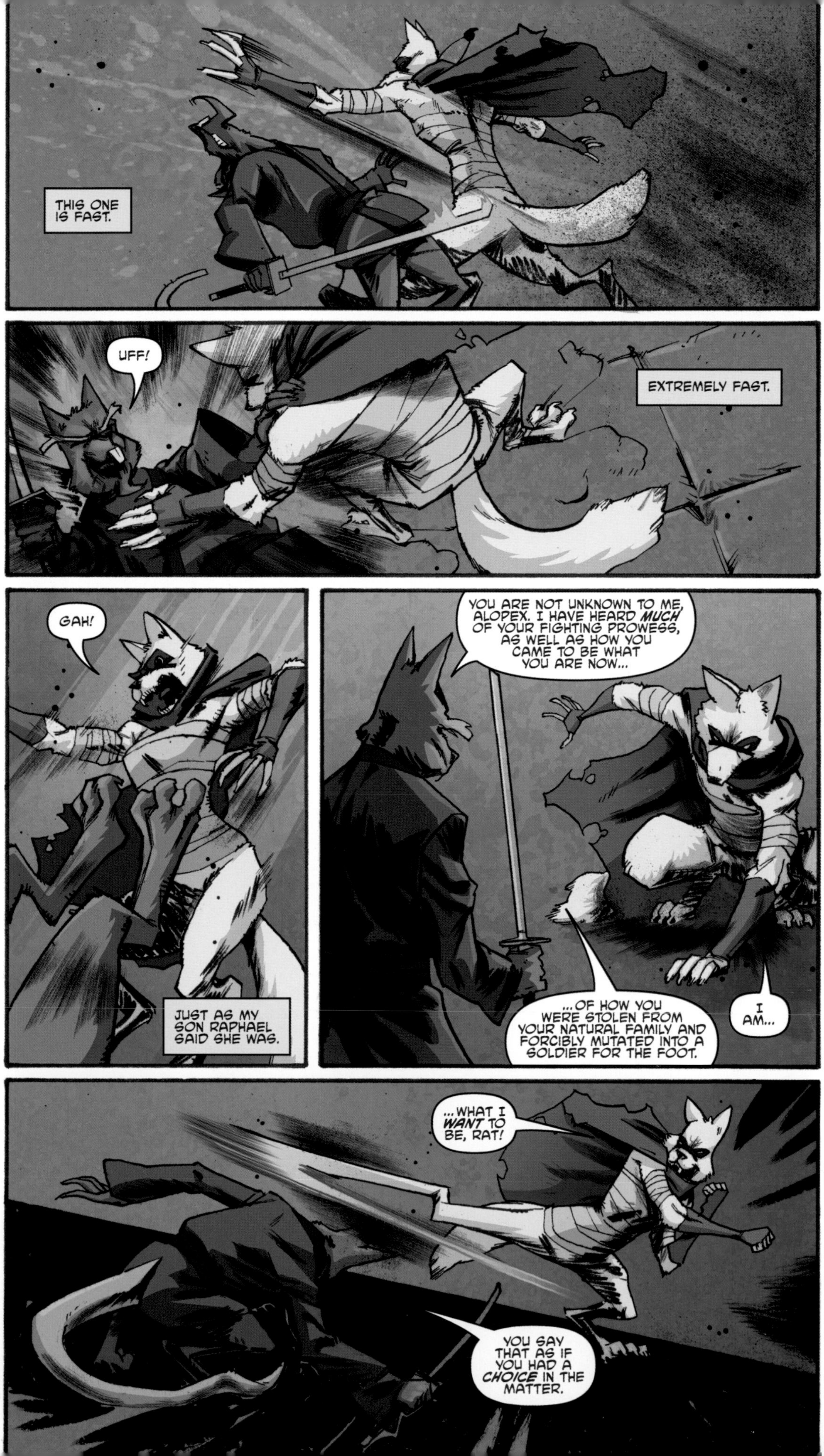
THIS ONE IS FAST.
UFF!
EXTREMELY FAST.
GAH!
JUST AS MY SON RAPHAEL SAID SHE WAS.
YOU ARE NOT UNKNOWN TO ME, ALOPEX. I HAVE HEARD MUCH OF YOUR FIGHTING PROWESS, AS WELL AS HOW YOU CAME TO BE WHAT YOU ARE NOW...
...OF HOW YOU WERE STOLEN FROM YOUR NATURAL FAMILY AND FORCIBLY MUTATED INTO A SOLDIER FOR THE FOOT.
I AM...
...WHAT I WANT TO BE, RAT!
YOU SAY THAT AS IF YOU HAD A CHOICE IN THE MATTER.

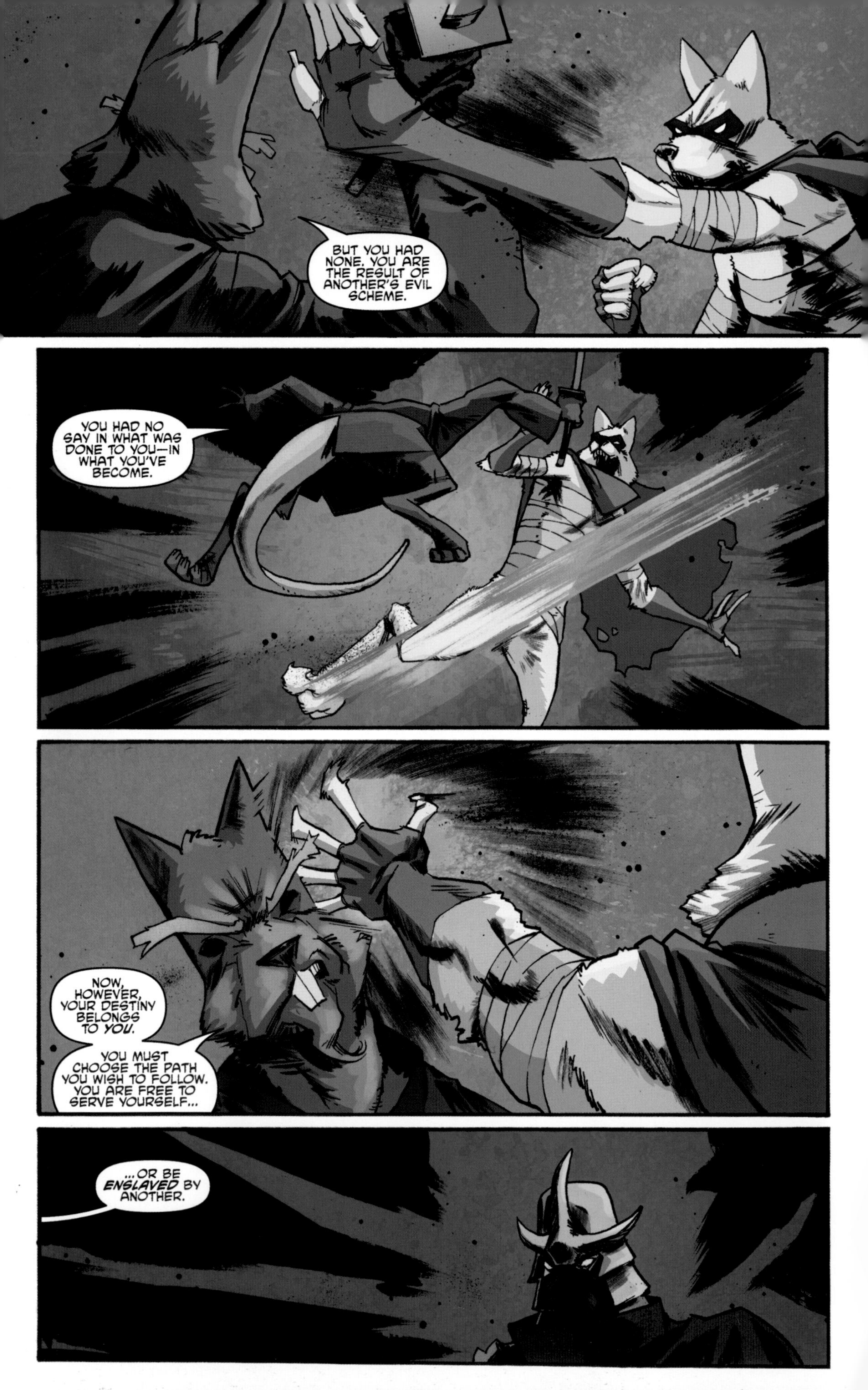
BUT YOU HAD NONE. YOU ARE THE RESULT OF ANOTHER'S EVIL SCHEME.
YOU HAD NO SAY IN WHAT WAS DONE TO YOU—IN WHAT YOU'VE BECOME.
NOW, HOWEVER, YOUR DESTINY BELONGS TO *YOU*.
YOU MUST CHOOSE THE PATH YOU WISH TO FOLLOW. YOU ARE FREE TO SERVE YOURSELF...
...OR BE *ENSLAVED* BY ANOTHER.

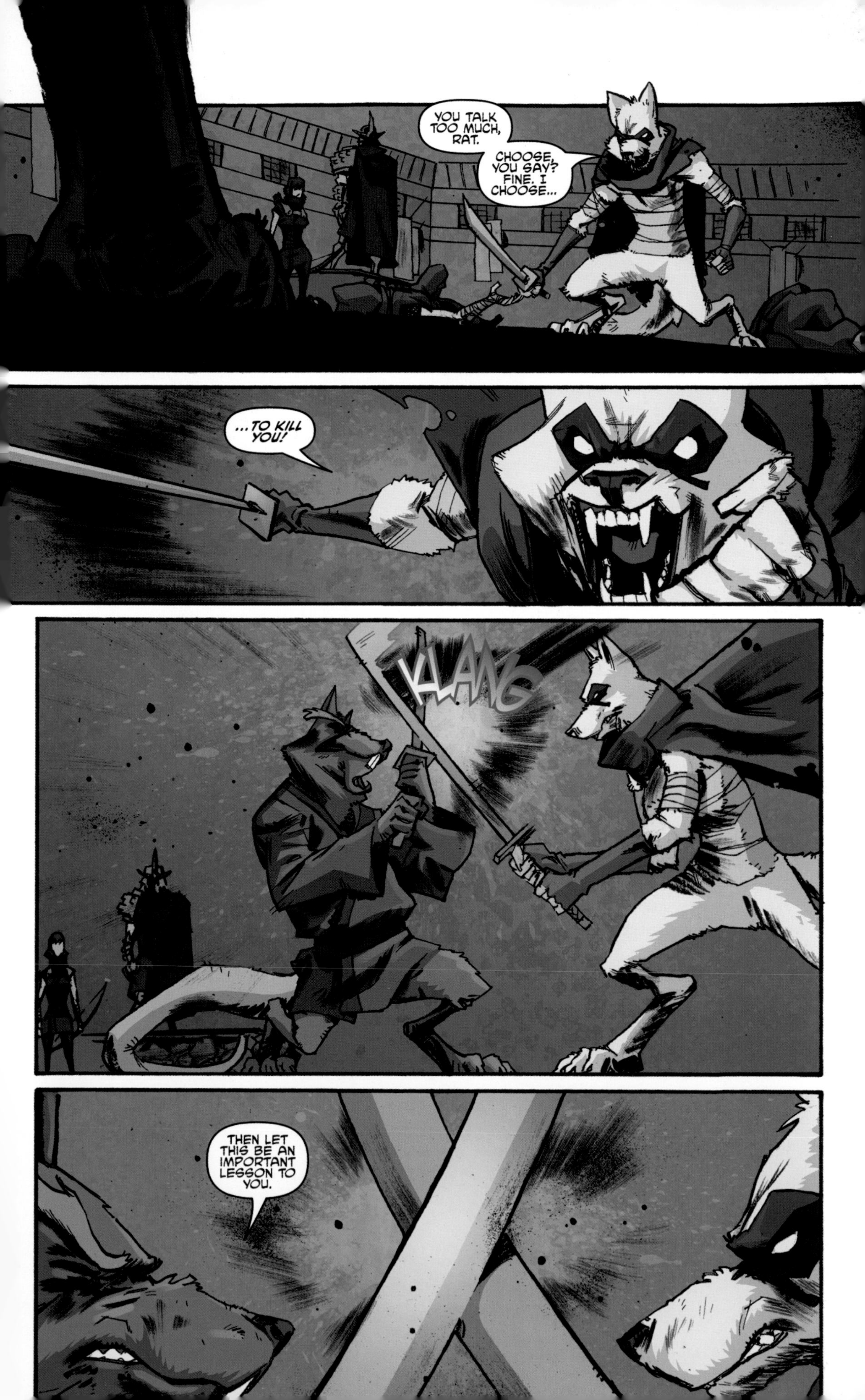
YOU TALK TOO MUCH, RAT.
CHOOSE, YOU SAY? FINE. I CHOOSE...
...TO KILL YOU!
KLANG
THEN LET THIS BE AN IMPORTANT LESSON TO YOU.

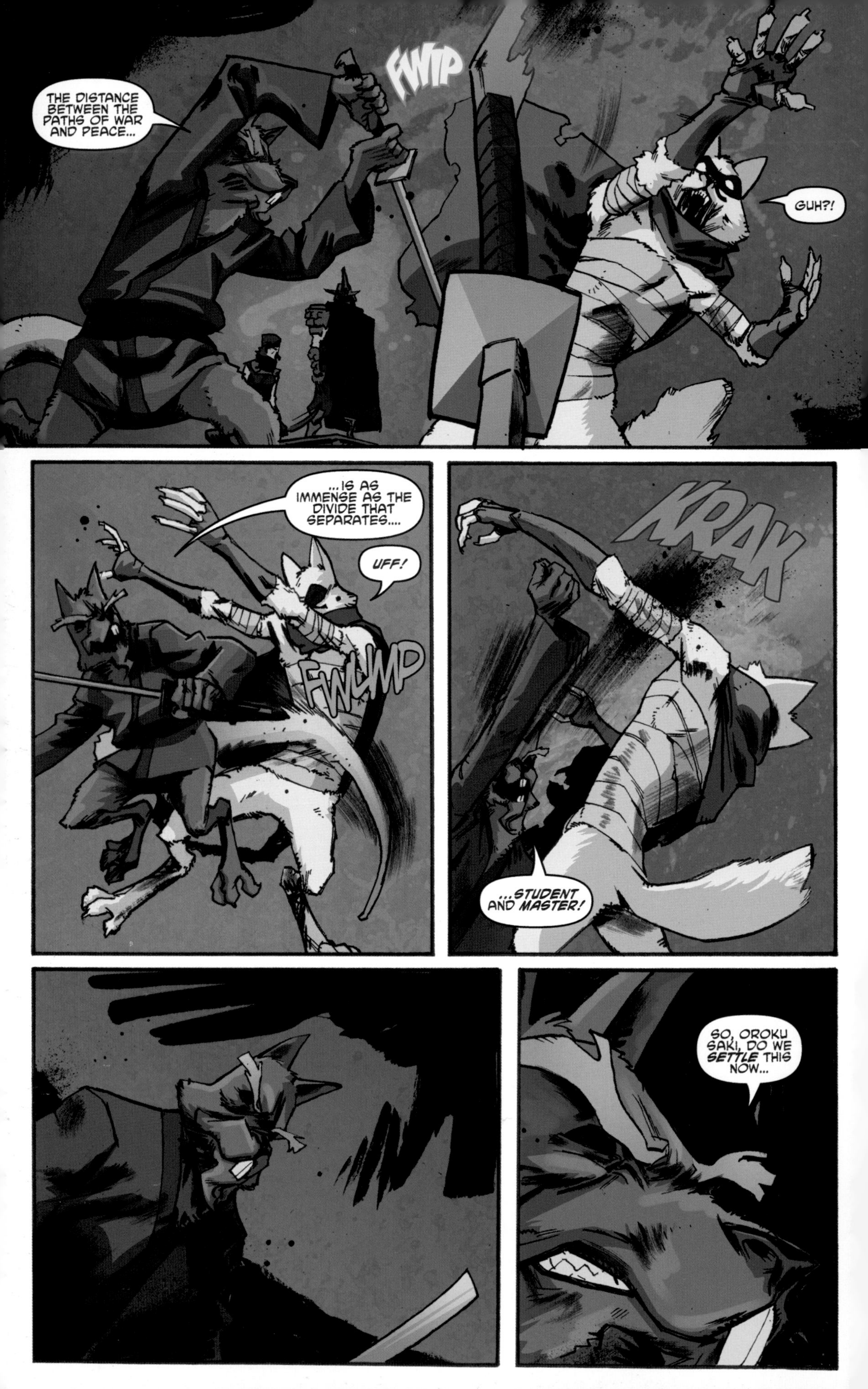
THE DISTANCE BETWEEN THE PATHS OF WAR AND PEACE...
FWIP
GUH?!
...IS AS IMMENSE AS THE DIVIDE THAT SEPARATES....
UFF!
FWUMP
KRAK
...STUDENT AND MASTER!
SO, OROKU SAKI, DO WE SETTLE THIS NOW...

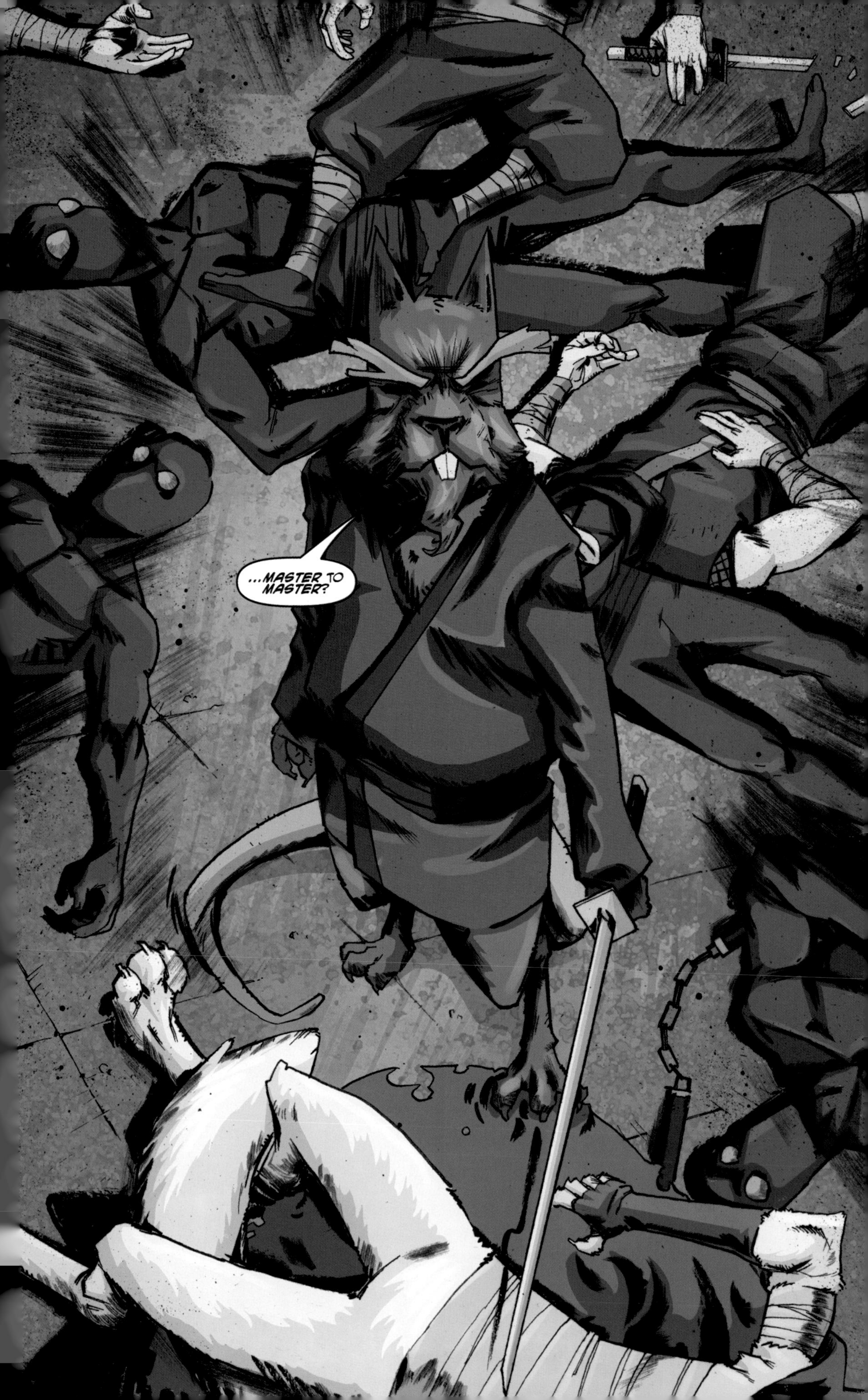
...MASTER TO MASTER?

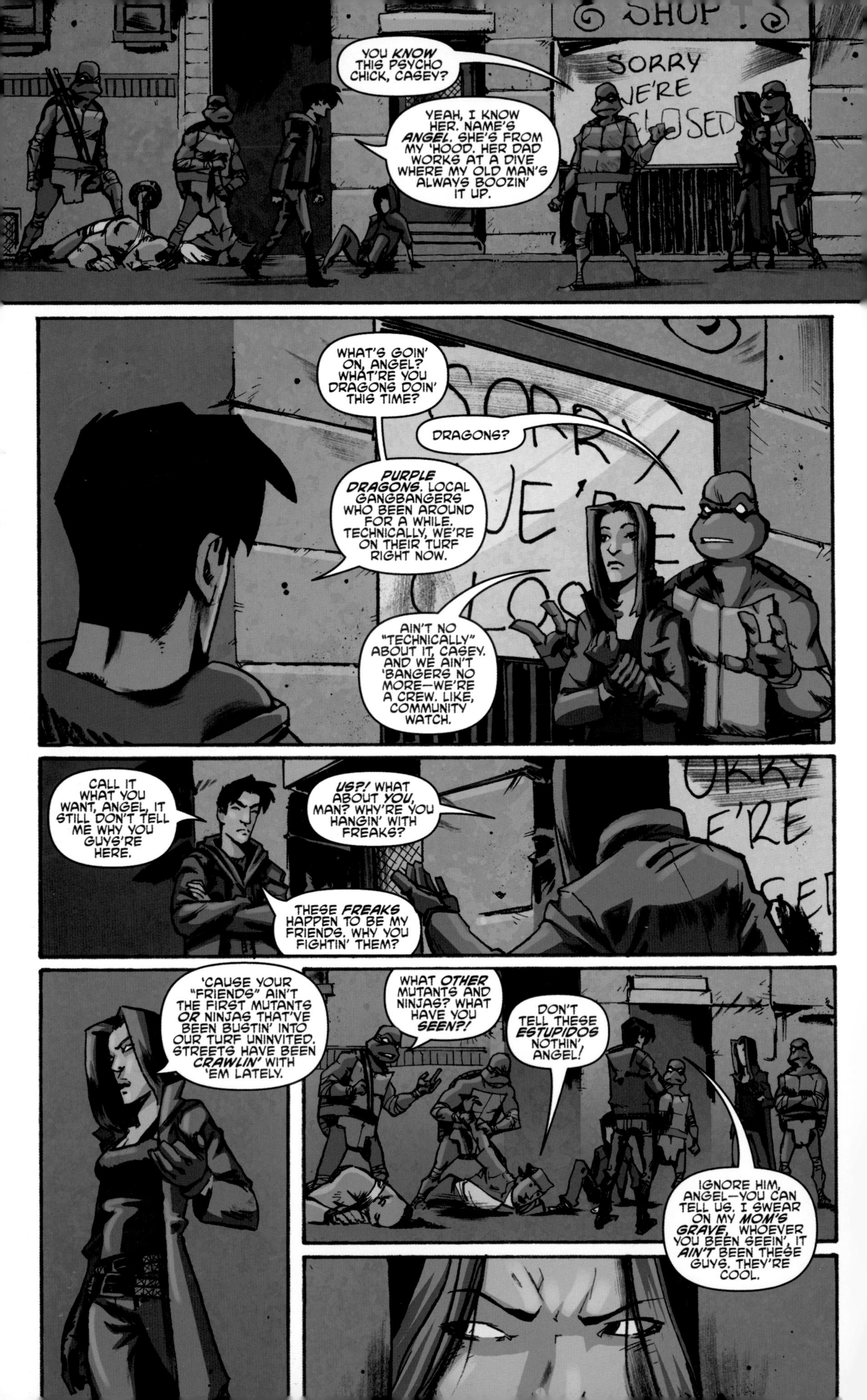
SHOP!
SORRY WE'RE CLOSED
YOU KNOW THIS PSYCHO CHICK, CASEY?
YEAH, I KNOW HER. NAME'S ANGEL. SHE'S FROM MY 'HOOD. HER DAD WORKS AT A DIVE WHERE MY OLD MAN'S ALWAYS BOOZIN' IT UP.
WHAT'S GOIN' ON, ANGEL? WHAT'RE YOU DRAGONS DOIN' THIS TIME?
DRAGONS?
PURPLE DRAGONS. LOCAL GANGBANGERS WHO BEEN AROUND FOR A WHILE. TECHNICALLY, WE'RE ON THEIR TURF RIGHT NOW.
AIN'T NO "TECHNICALLY" ABOUT IT, CASEY. AND WE AIN'T 'BANGERS NO MORE—WE'RE A CREW. LIKE, COMMUNITY WATCH.
CALL IT WHAT YOU WANT, ANGEL, IT STILL DON'T TELL ME WHY YOU GUYS'RE HERE.
US?! WHAT ABOUT YOU, MAN? WHY'RE YOU HANGIN' WITH FREAKS?
THESE FREAKS HAPPEN TO BE MY FRIENDS. WHY YOU FIGHTIN' THEM?
'CAUSE YOUR "FRIENDS" AIN'T THE FIRST MUTANTS OR NINJAS THAT'VE BEEN BUSTIN' INTO OUR TURF UNINVITED. STREETS HAVE BEEN CRAWLIN' WITH 'EM LATELY.
WHAT OTHER MUTANTS AND NINJAS? WHAT HAVE YOU SEEN?!
DON'T TELL THESE ESTUPIDOS NOTHIN', ANGEL!
IGNORE HIM, ANGEL—YOU CAN TELL US. I SWEAR ON MY MOM'S GRAVE, WHOEVER YOU BEEN SEEIN', IT AIN'T BEEN THESE GUYS. THEY'RE COOL.

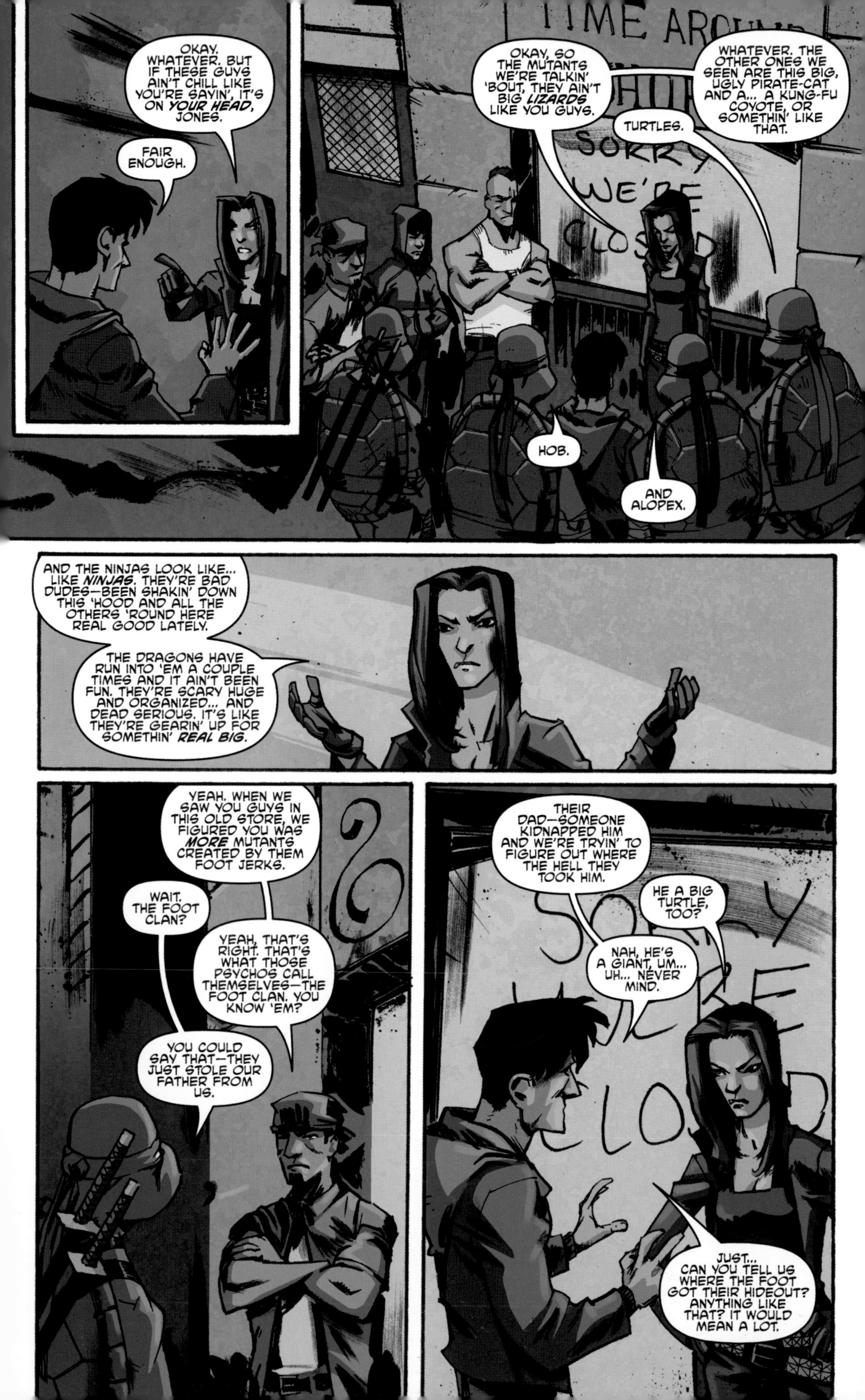
OKAY. WHATEVER. BUT IF THESE GUYS AIN'T CHILL LIKE YOU'RE SAYIN', IT'S ON YOUR HEAD, JONES.
FAIR ENOUGH.
TIME AROUN
OKAY, SO THE MUTANTS WE'RE TALKIN' 'BOUT, THEY AIN'T BIG LIZARDS LIKE YOU GUYS.
TURTLES.
WHATEVER. THE OTHER ONES WE SEEN ARE THIS BIG, UGLY PIRATE-CAT AND A... A KUNG-FU COYOTE, OR SOMETHIN' LIKE THAT.
SORRY WE'RE CLOSED
HOB.
AND ALOPEX.
AND THE NINJAS LOOK LIKE... LIKE NINJAS. THEY'RE BAD DUDES—BEEN SHAKIN' DOWN THIS 'HOOD AND ALL THE OTHERS 'ROUND HERE REAL GOOD LATELY.
THE DRAGONS HAVE RUN INTO 'EM A COUPLE TIMES AND IT AIN'T BEEN FUN. THEY'RE SCARY HUGE AND ORGANIZED... AND DEAD SERIOUS. IT'S LIKE THEY'RE GEARIN' UP FOR SOMETHIN' REAL BIG.
YEAH. WHEN WE SAW YOU GUYS IN THIS OLD STORE, WE FIGURED YOU WAS MORE MUTANTS CREATED BY THEM FOOT JERKS.
WAIT. THE FOOT CLAN?
YEAH, THAT'S RIGHT. THAT'S WHAT THOSE PSYCHOS CALL THEMSELVES—THE FOOT CLAN. YOU KNOW 'EM?
YOU COULD SAY THAT—THEY JUST STOLE OUR FATHER FROM US.
THEIR DAD—SOMEONE KIDNAPPED HIM AND WE'RE TRYIN' TO FIGURE OUT WHERE THE HELL THEY TOOK HIM.
HE A BIG TURTLE, TOO?
NAH, HE'S A GIANT, UM... UH... NEVER MIND.
JUST... CAN YOU TELL US WHERE THE FOOT GOT THEIR HIDEOUT? ANYTHING LIKE THAT? IT WOULD MEAN A LOT.

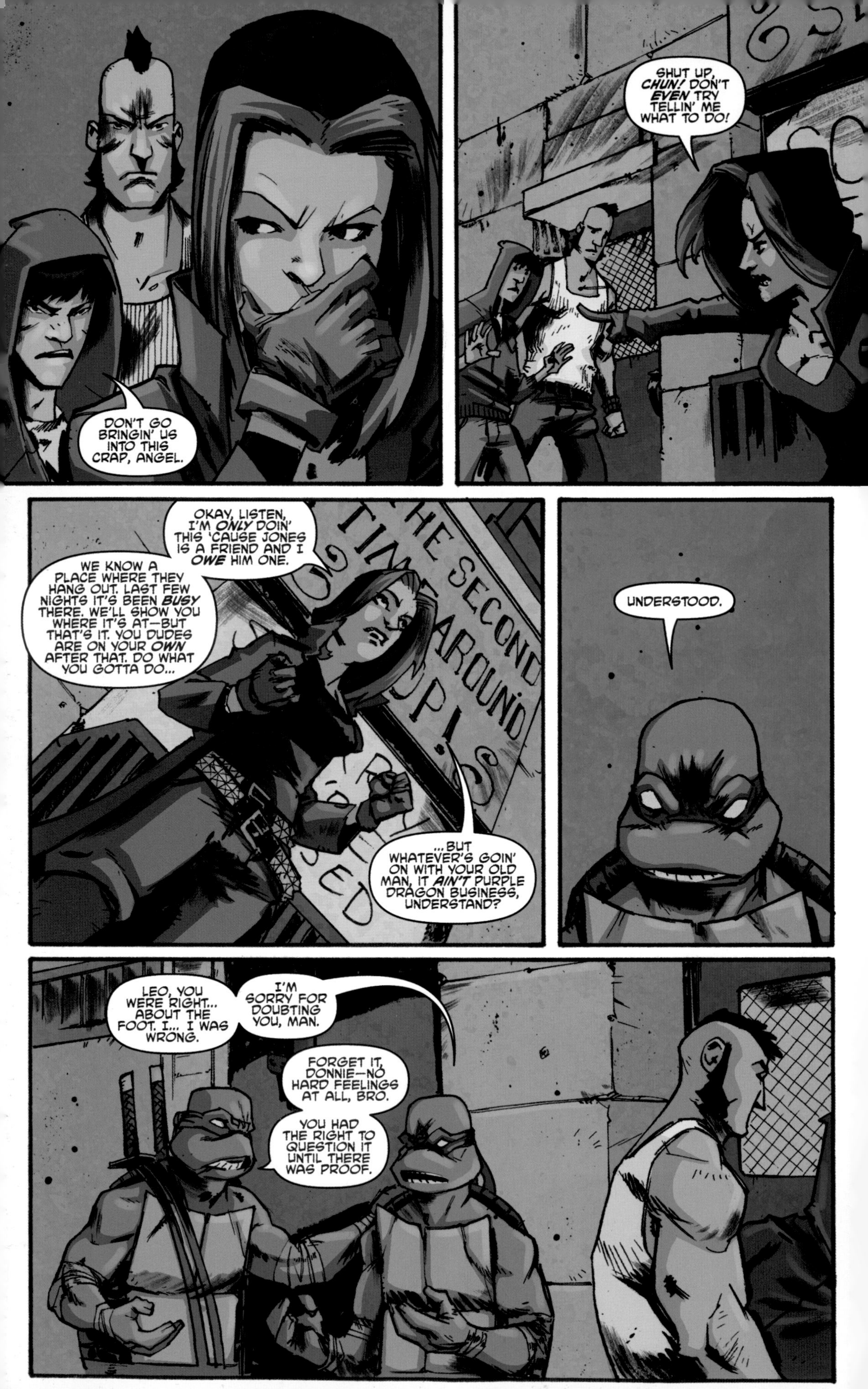
DON'T GO BRINGIN' US INTO THIS CRAP, ANGEL.
SHUT UP, CHUN! DON'T EVEN TRY TELLIN' ME WHAT TO DO!
OKAY, LISTEN, I'M ONLY DOIN' THIS 'CAUSE JONES IS A FRIEND AND I OWE HIM ONE.
WE KNOW A PLACE WHERE THEY HANG OUT. LAST FEW NIGHTS IT'S BEEN BUSY THERE. WE'LL SHOW YOU WHERE IT'S AT—BUT THAT'S IT. YOU DUDES ARE ON YOUR OWN AFTER THAT. DO WHAT YOU GOTTA DO...
...BUT WHATEVER'S GOIN' ON WITH YOUR OLD MAN, IT AIN'T PURPLE DRAGON BUSINESS, UNDERSTAND?
UNDERSTOOD.
LEO, YOU WERE RIGHT... ABOUT THE FOOT. I... I WAS WRONG.
I'M SORRY FOR DOUBTING YOU, MAN.
FORGET IT, DONNIE—NO HARD FEELINGS AT ALL, BRO.
YOU HAD THE RIGHT TO QUESTION IT UNTIL THERE WAS PROOF.

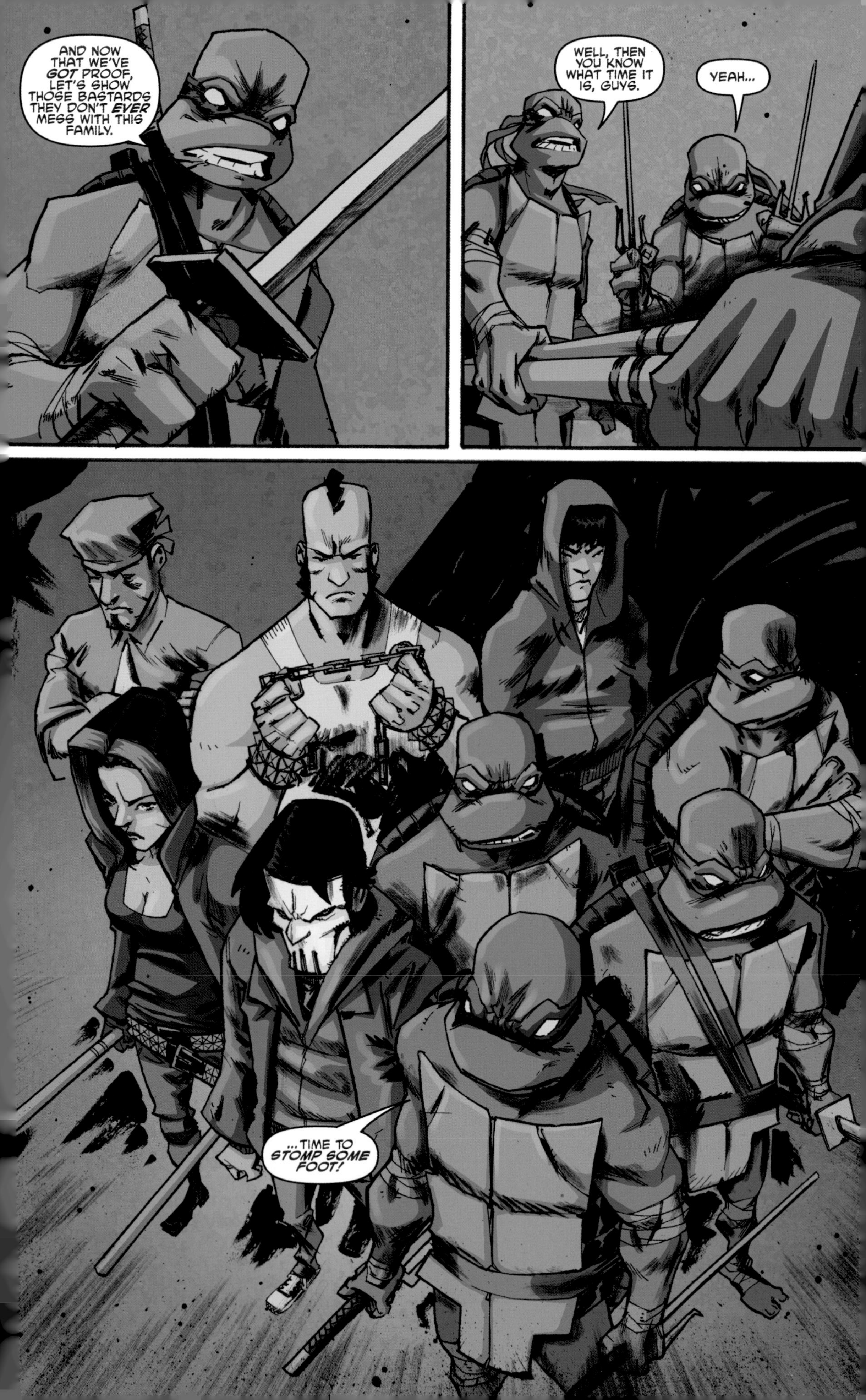
AND NOW THAT WE'VE *GOT* PROOF, LET'S SHOW THOSE BASTARDS THEY DON'T *EVER* MESS WITH THIS FAMILY.
WELL, THEN YOU KNOW WHAT TIME IT IS, GUYS.
YEAH...
...TIME TO *STOMP SOME FOOT!*

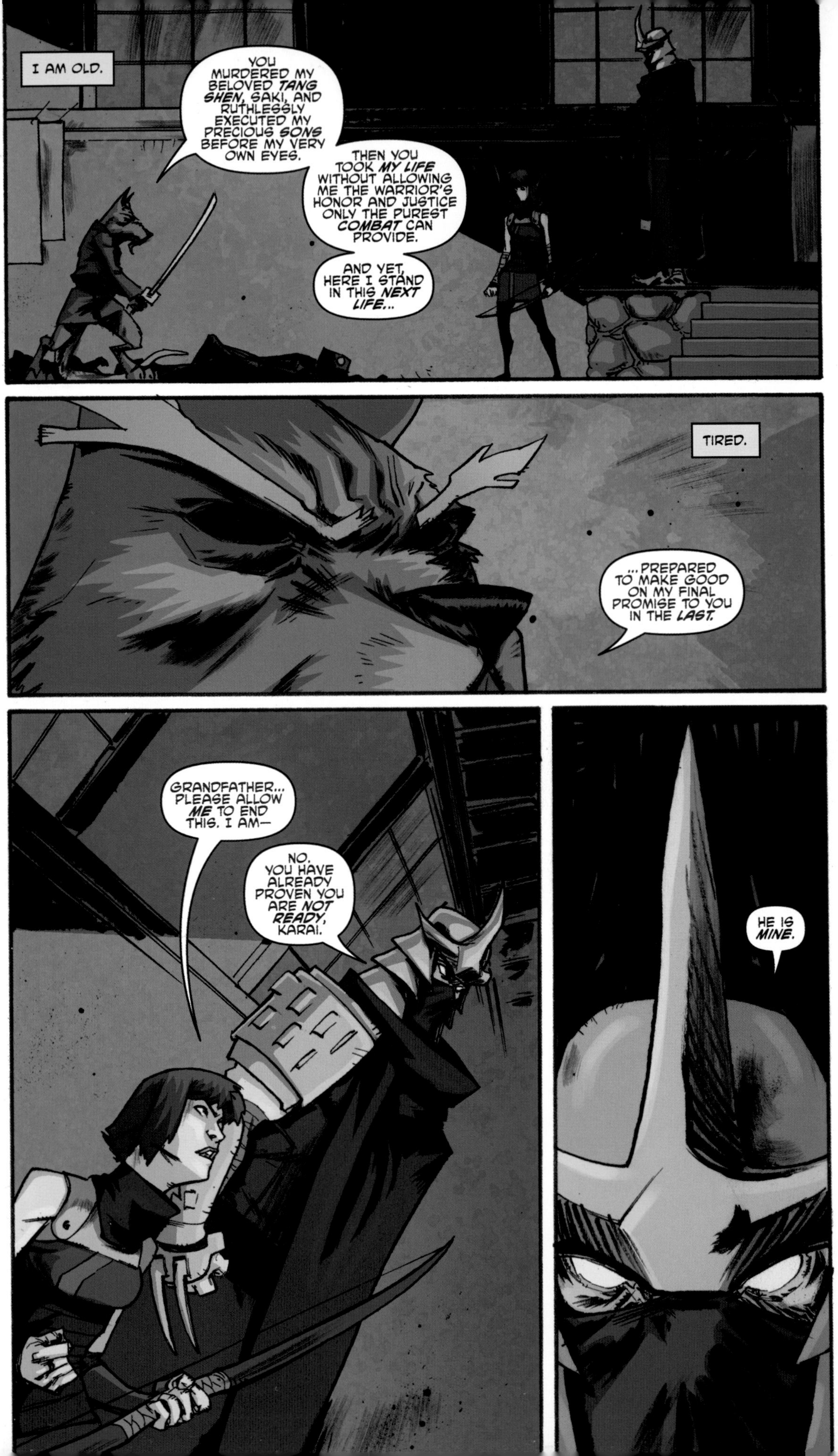
I AM OLD.
YOU MURDERED MY BELOVED TANG SHEN, SAKI, AND RUTHLESSLY EXECUTED MY PRECIOUS SONS BEFORE MY VERY OWN EYES.
THEN YOU TOOK MY LIFE WITHOUT ALLOWING ME THE WARRIOR'S HONOR AND JUSTICE ONLY THE PUREST COMBAT CAN PROVIDE.
AND YET, HERE I STAND IN THIS NEXT LIFE...
TIRED.
...PREPARED TO MAKE GOOD ON MY FINAL PROMISE TO YOU IN THE LAST.
GRANDFATHER... PLEASE ALLOW ME TO END THIS. I AM—
NO. YOU HAVE ALREADY PROVEN YOU ARE NOT READY, KARAI.
HE IS MINE.

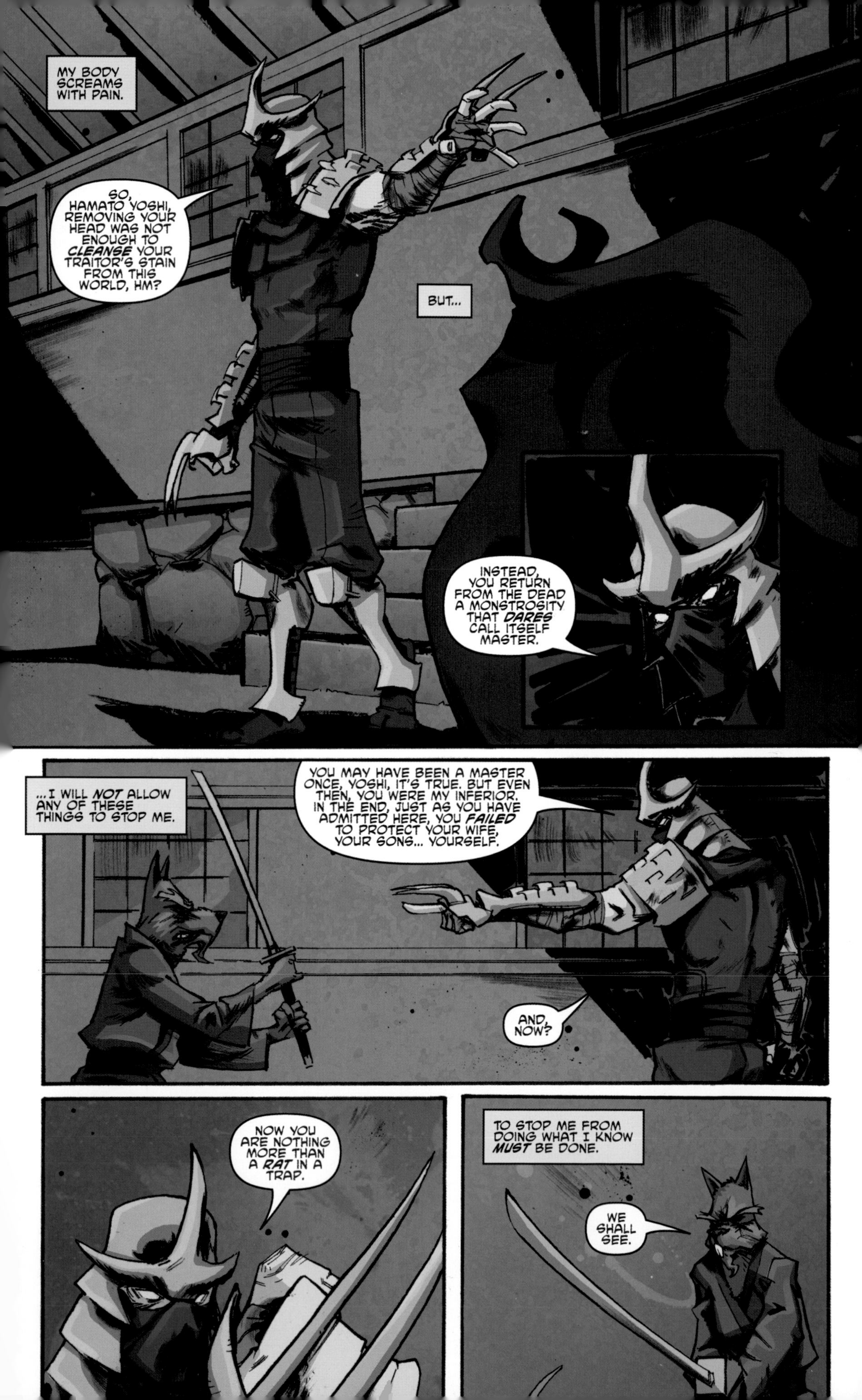
MY BODY SCREAMS WITH PAIN.
SO, HAMATO YOSHI, REMOVING YOUR HEAD WAS NOT ENOUGH TO CLEANSE YOUR TRAITOR'S STAIN FROM THIS WORLD, HM?
BUT...
INSTEAD, YOU RETURN FROM THE DEAD A MONSTROSITY THAT DARES CALL ITSELF MASTER.
...I WILL NOT ALLOW ANY OF THESE THINGS TO STOP ME.
YOU MAY HAVE BEEN A MASTER ONCE, YOSHI, IT'S TRUE. BUT EVEN THEN, YOU WERE MY INFERIOR. IN THE END, JUST AS YOU HAVE ADMITTED HERE, YOU FAILED TO PROTECT YOUR WIFE, YOUR SONS... YOURSELF.
AND, NOW?
NOW YOU ARE NOTHING MORE THAN A RAT IN A TRAP.
TO STOP ME FROM DOING WHAT I KNOW MUST BE DONE.
WE SHALL SEE.

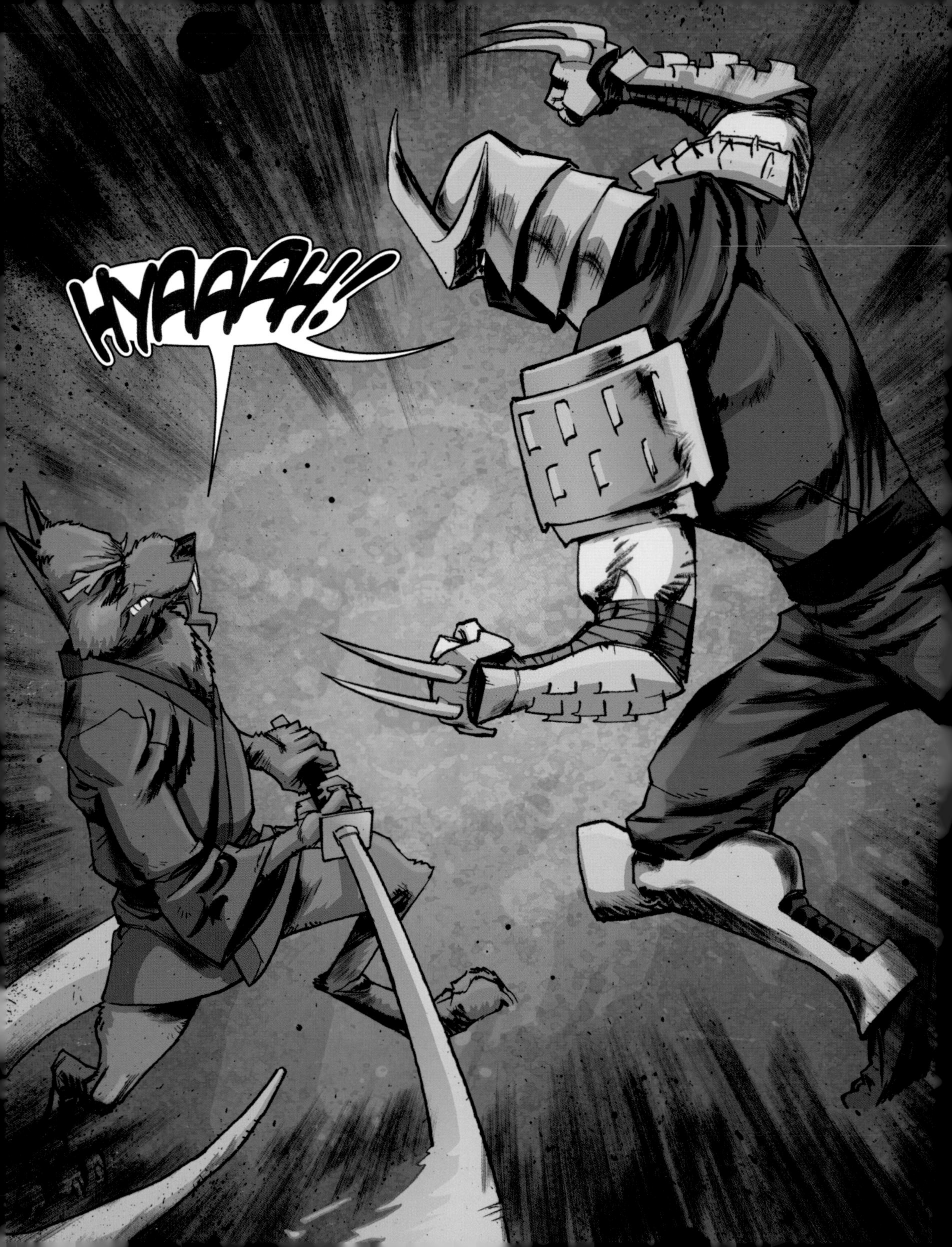
HYAAAH!!

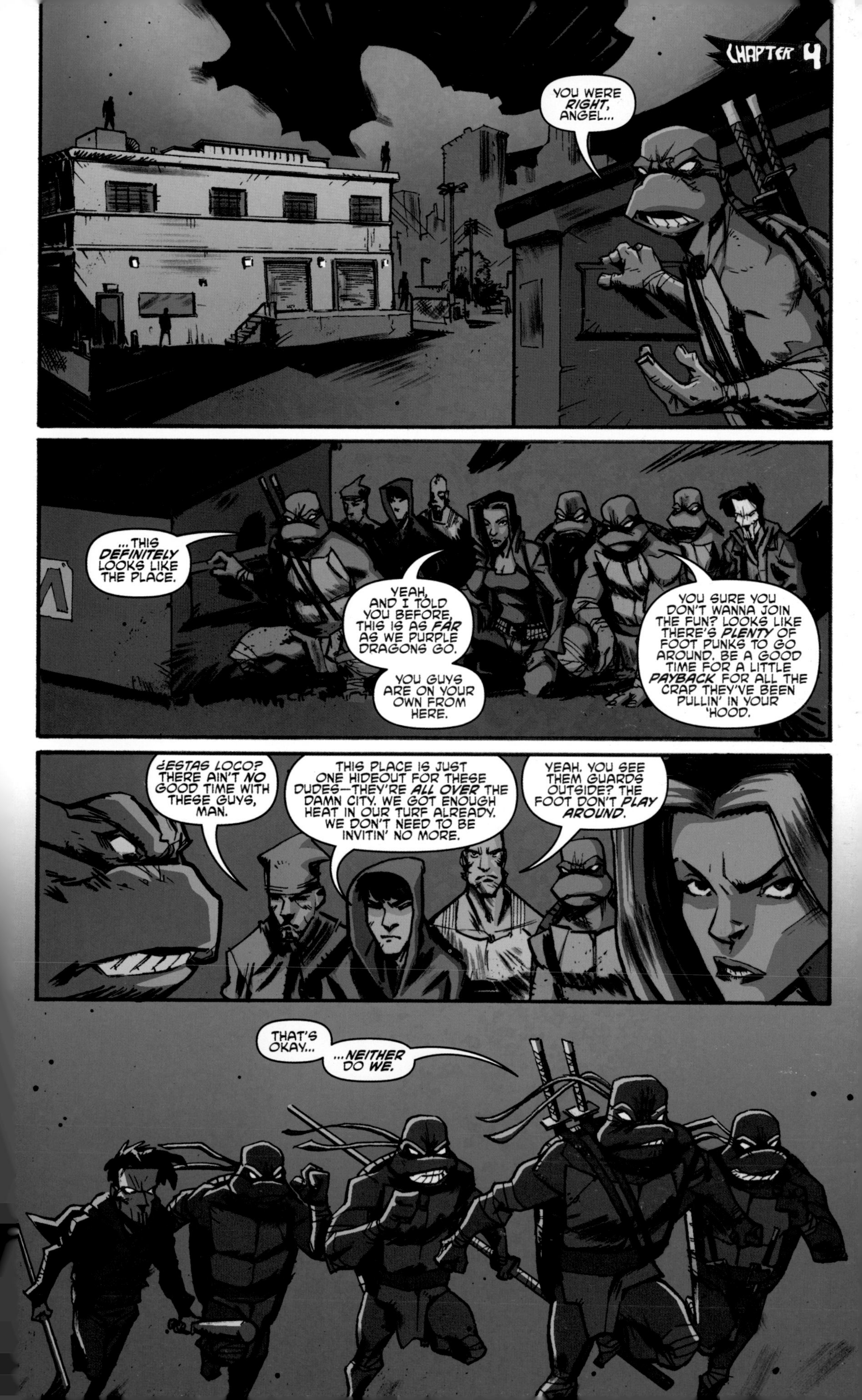
CHAPTER 4
YOU WERE RIGHT, ANGEL...
...THIS DEFINITELY LOOKS LIKE THE PLACE.
YEAH, AND I TOLD YOU BEFORE, THIS IS AS FAR AS WE PURPLE DRAGONS GO.
YOU GUYS ARE ON YOUR OWN FROM HERE.
YOU SURE YOU DON'T WANNA JOIN THE FUN? LOOKS LIKE THERE'S PLENTY OF FOOT PUNKS TO GO AROUND. BE A GOOD TIME FOR A LITTLE PAYBACK FOR ALL THE CRAP THEY'VE BEEN PULLIN' IN YOUR 'HOOD.
¿ESTAS LOCO? THERE AIN'T NO GOOD TIME WITH THESE GUYS, MAN.
THIS PLACE IS JUST ONE HIDEOUT FOR THESE DUDES--THEY'RE ALL OVER THE DAMN CITY. WE GOT ENOUGH HEAT IN OUR TURF ALREADY. WE DON'T NEED TO BE INVITIN' NO MORE.
YEAH. YOU SEE THEM GUARDS OUTSIDE? THE FOOT DON'T PLAY AROUND.
THAT'S OKAY...
...NEITHER DO WE.

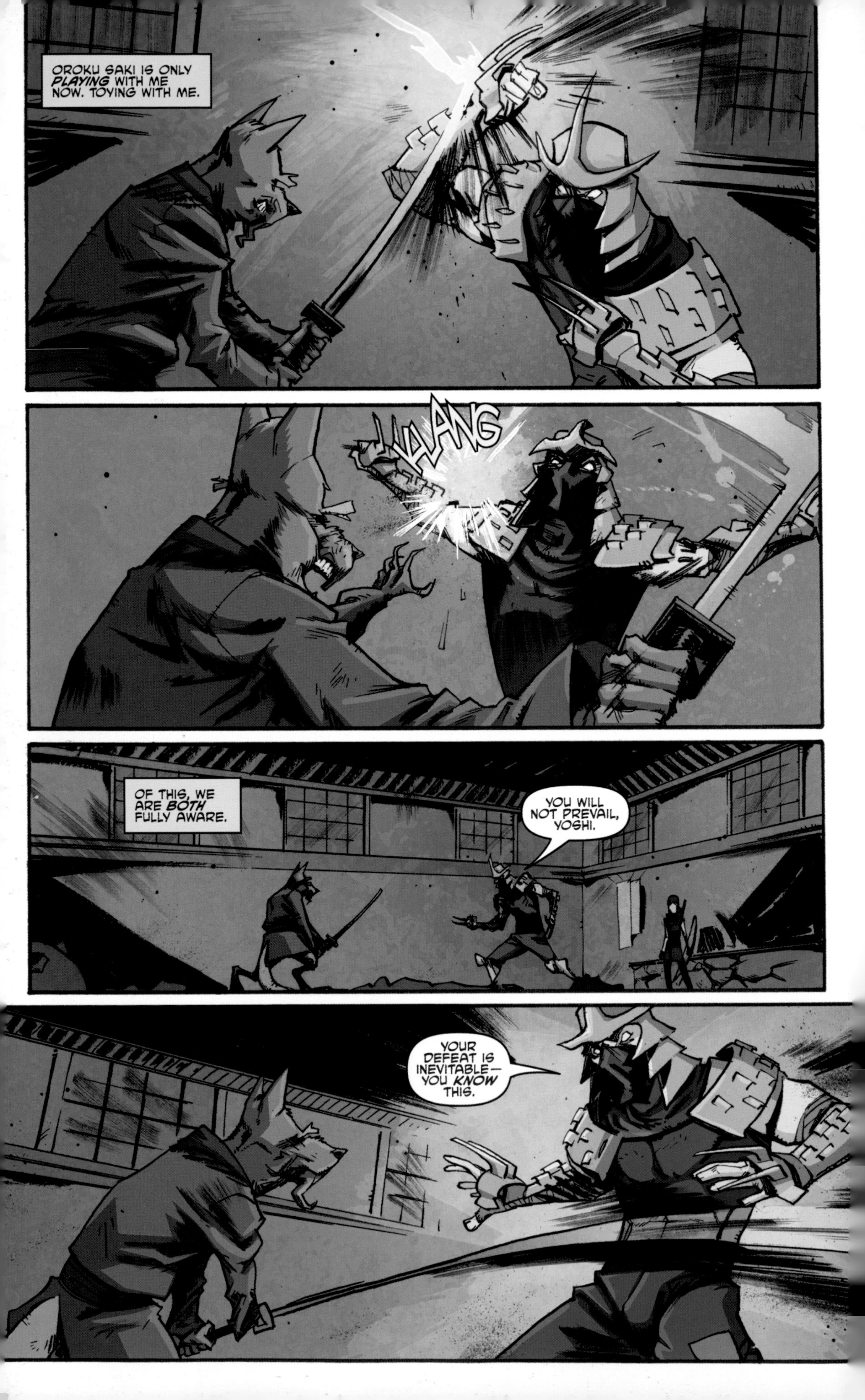
OROKU SAKI IS ONLY *PLAYING* WITH ME NOW. TOYING WITH ME.
WHANG
OF THIS, WE ARE *BOTH* FULLY AWARE.
YOU WILL NOT PREVAIL, YOSHI.
YOUR DEFEAT IS INEVITABLE— YOU *KNOW* THIS.

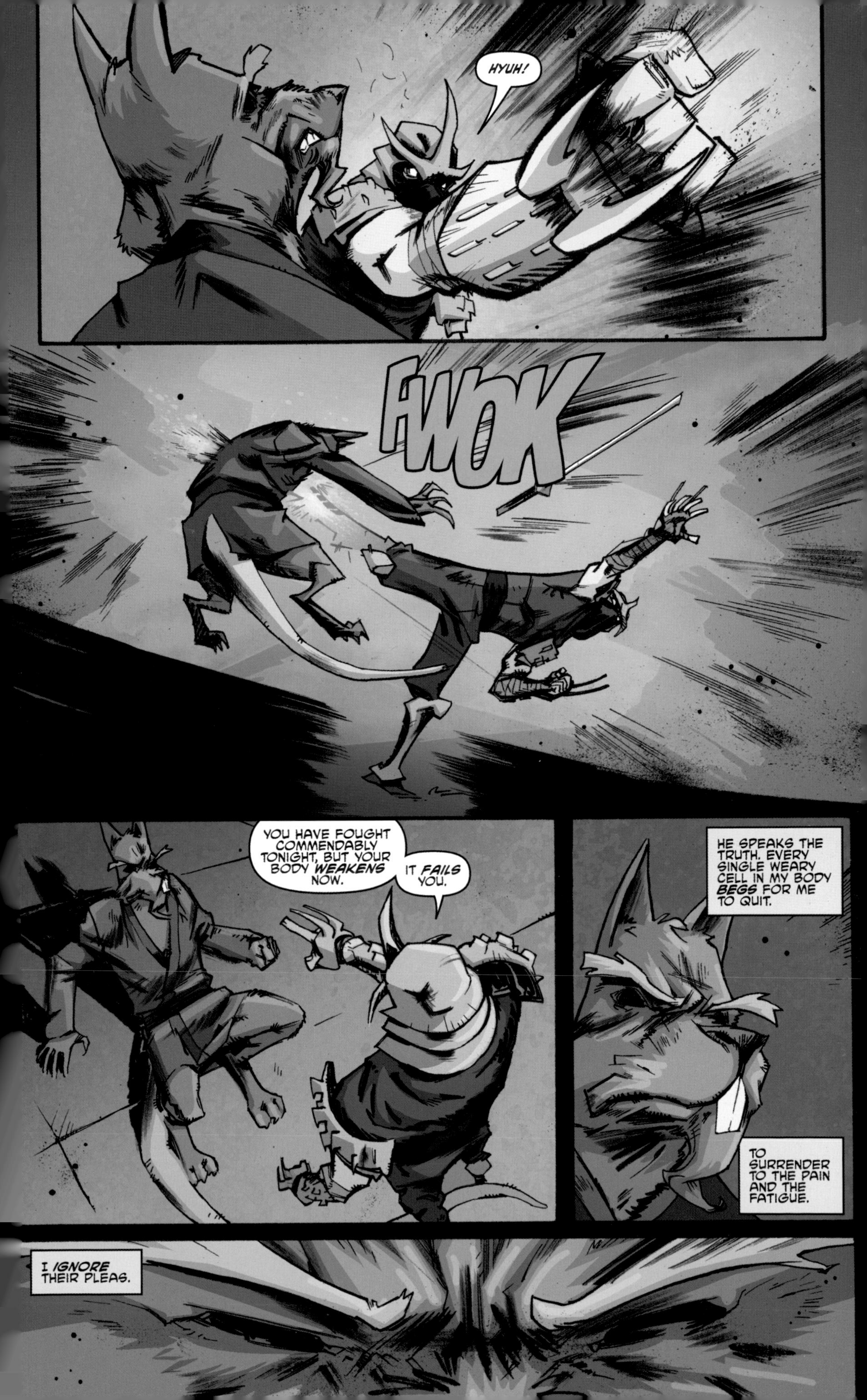
HYUH!
FWOK
YOU HAVE FOUGHT COMMENDABLY TONIGHT, BUT YOUR BODY WEAKENS NOW.
IT FAILS YOU.
HE SPEAKS THE TRUTH. EVERY SINGLE WEARY CELL IN MY BODY BEGS FOR ME TO QUIT.
TO SURRENDER TO THE PAIN AND THE FATIGUE.
I IGNORE THEIR PLEAS.

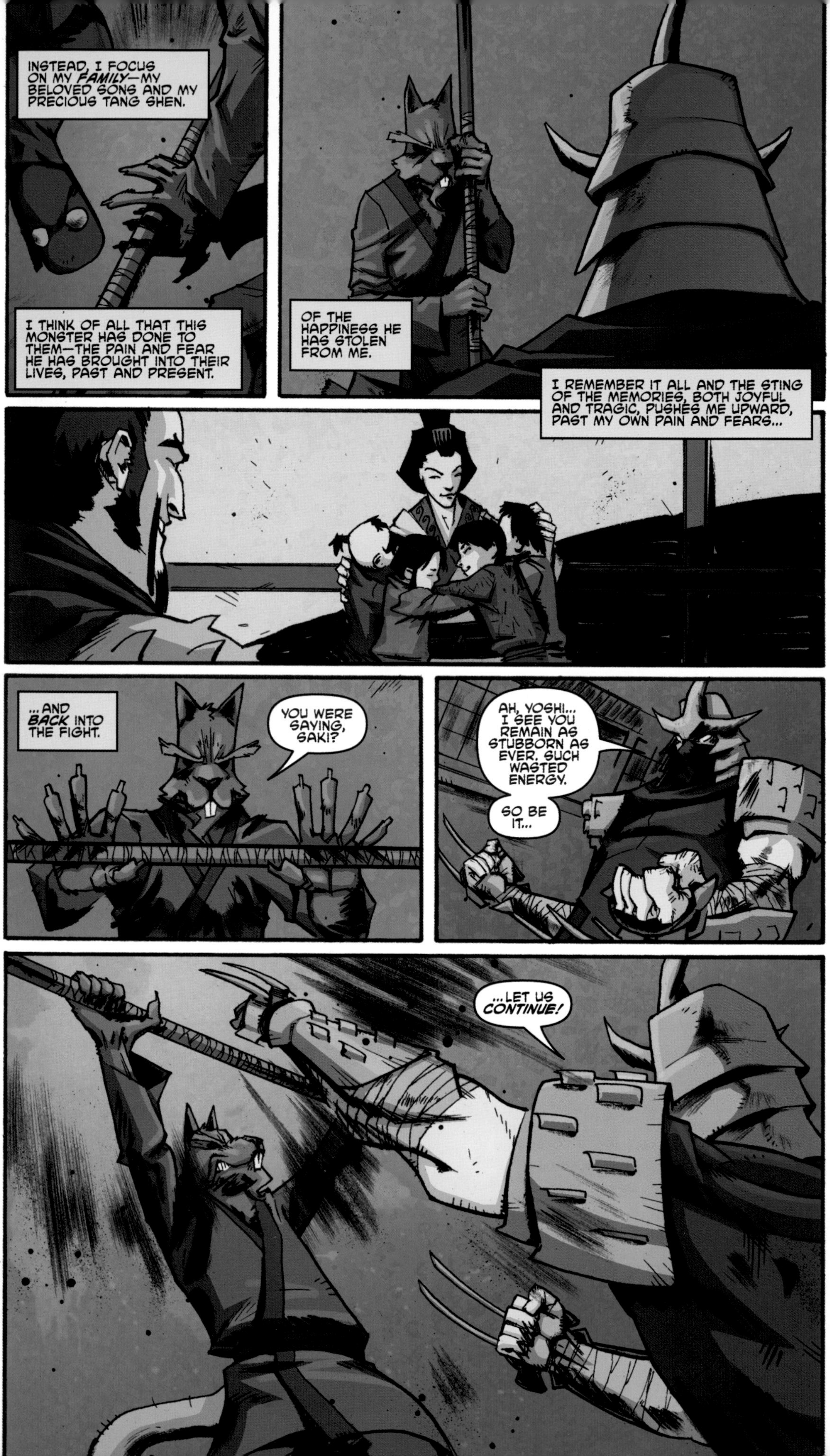
INSTEAD, I FOCUS ON MY FAMILY—MY BELOVED SONS AND MY PRECIOUS TANG SHEN.
I THINK OF ALL THAT THIS MONSTER HAS DONE TO THEM—THE PAIN AND FEAR HE HAS BROUGHT INTO THEIR LIVES, PAST AND PRESENT.
OF THE HAPPINESS HE HAS STOLEN FROM ME.
I REMEMBER IT ALL AND THE STING OF THE MEMORIES, BOTH JOYFUL AND TRAGIC, PUSHES ME UPWARD, PAST MY OWN PAIN AND FEARS...
...AND BACK INTO THE FIGHT.
YOU WERE SAYING, SAKI?
AH, YOSHI... I SEE YOU REMAIN AS STUBBORN AS EVER. SUCH WASTED ENERGY.
SO BE IT...
...LET US CONTINUE!

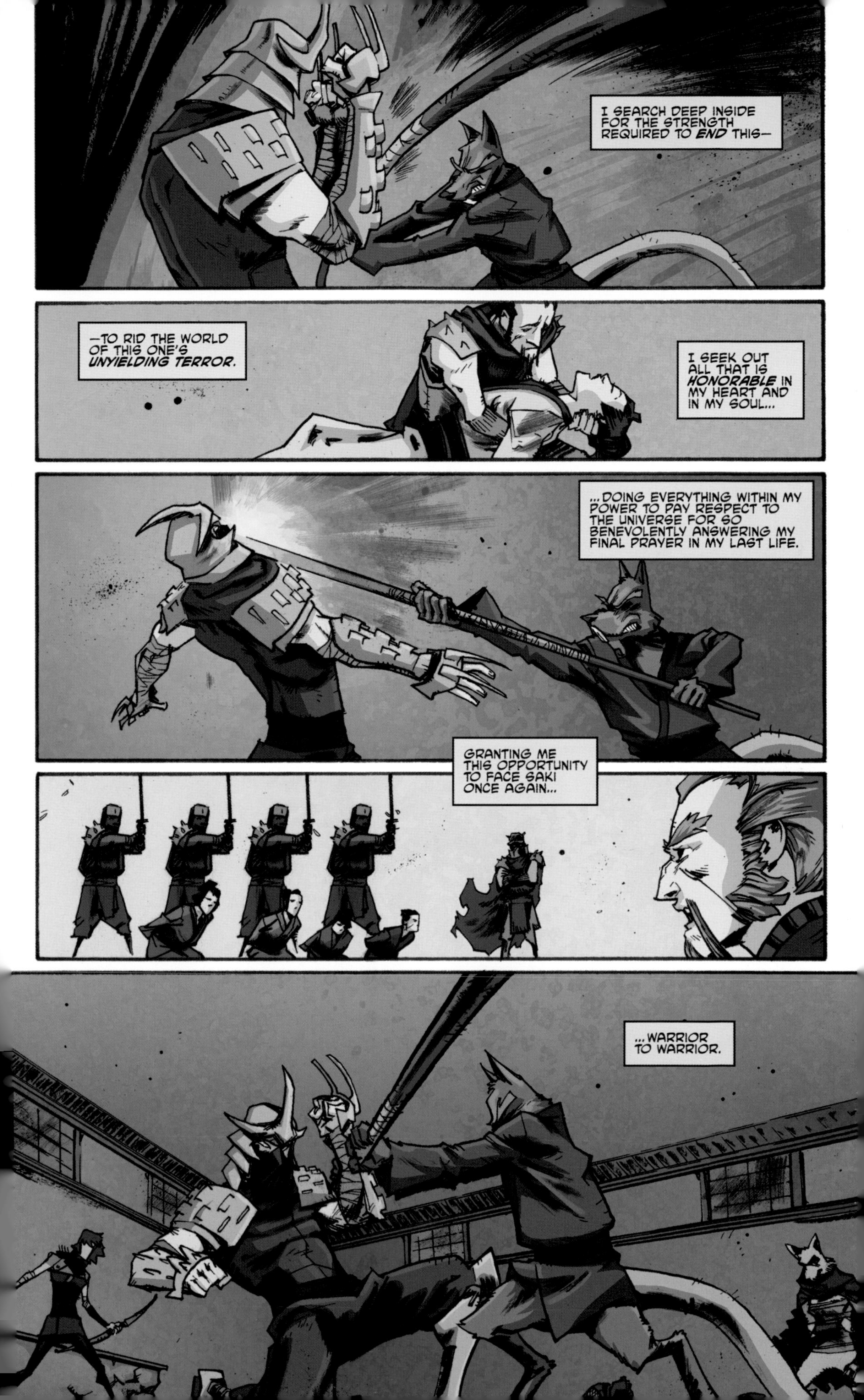
I SEARCH DEEP INSIDE FOR THE STRENGTH REQUIRED TO *END* THIS—
—TO RID THE WORLD OF THIS ONE'S *UNYIELDING TERROR*.
I SEEK OUT ALL THAT IS *HONORABLE* IN MY HEART AND IN MY SOUL...
...DOING EVERYTHING WITHIN MY POWER TO PAY RESPECT TO THE UNIVERSE FOR SO BENEVOLENTLY ANSWERING MY FINAL PRAYER IN MY LAST LIFE.
GRANTING ME THIS OPPORTUNITY TO FACE SAKI ONCE AGAIN...
...WARRIOR TO WARRIOR.

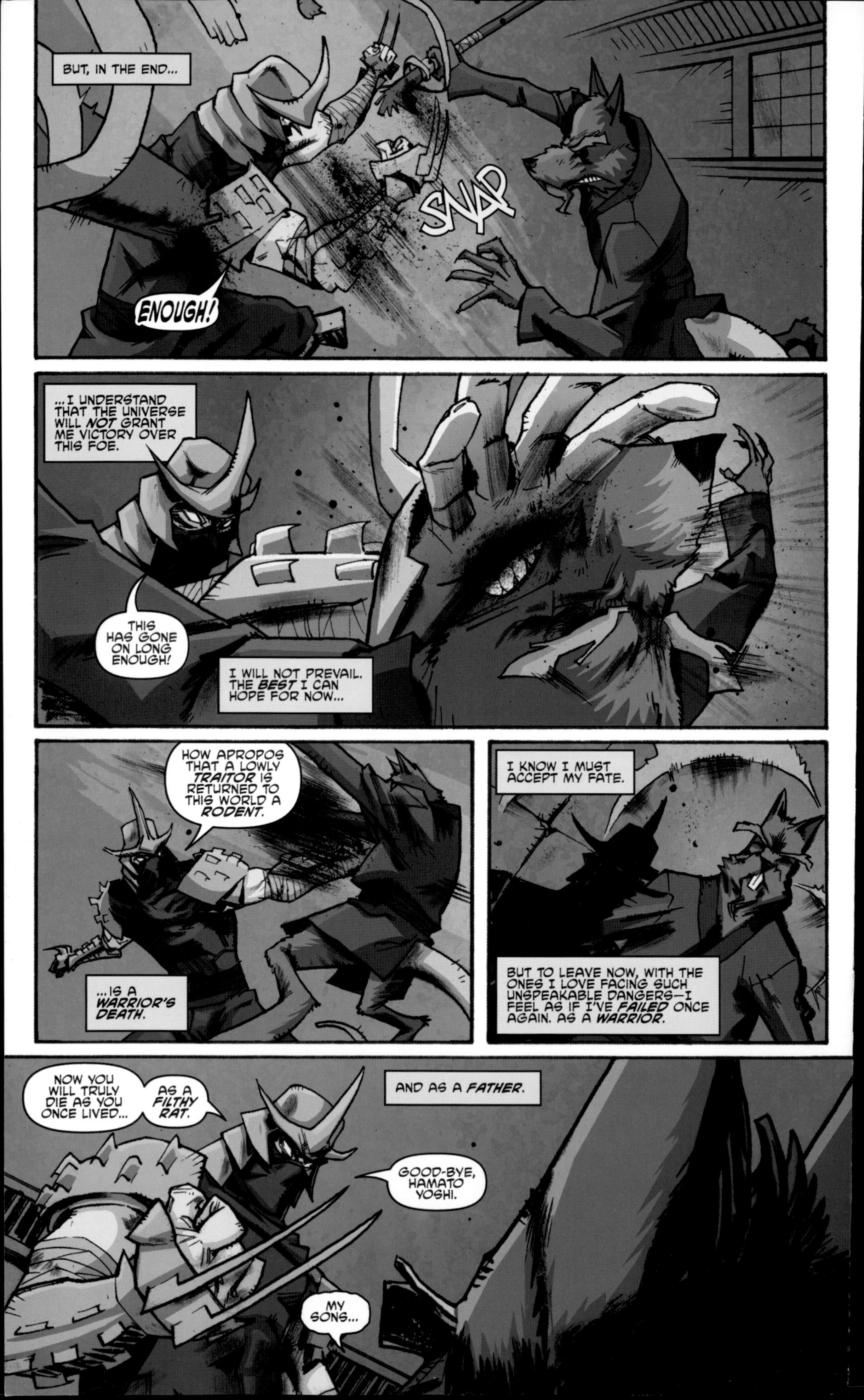

BUT, IN THE END...
SNAP
ENOUGH!
...I UNDERSTAND THAT THE UNIVERSE WILL NOT GRANT ME VICTORY OVER THIS FOE.
THIS HAS GONE ON LONG ENOUGH!
I WILL NOT PREVAIL. THE BEST I CAN HOPE FOR NOW...
HOW APROPOS THAT A LOWLY TRAITOR IS RETURNED TO THIS WORLD A RODENT.
...IS A WARRIOR'S DEATH.
I KNOW I MUST ACCEPT MY FATE.
BUT TO LEAVE NOW, WITH THE ONES I LOVE FACING SUCH UNSPEAKABLE DANGERS—I FEEL AS IF I'VE FAILED ONCE AGAIN. AS A WARRIOR.
NOW YOU WILL TRULY DIE AS YOU ONCE LIVED...
AS A FILTHY RAT.
AND AS A FATHER.
GOOD-BYE, HAMATO YOSHI.
MY SONS...

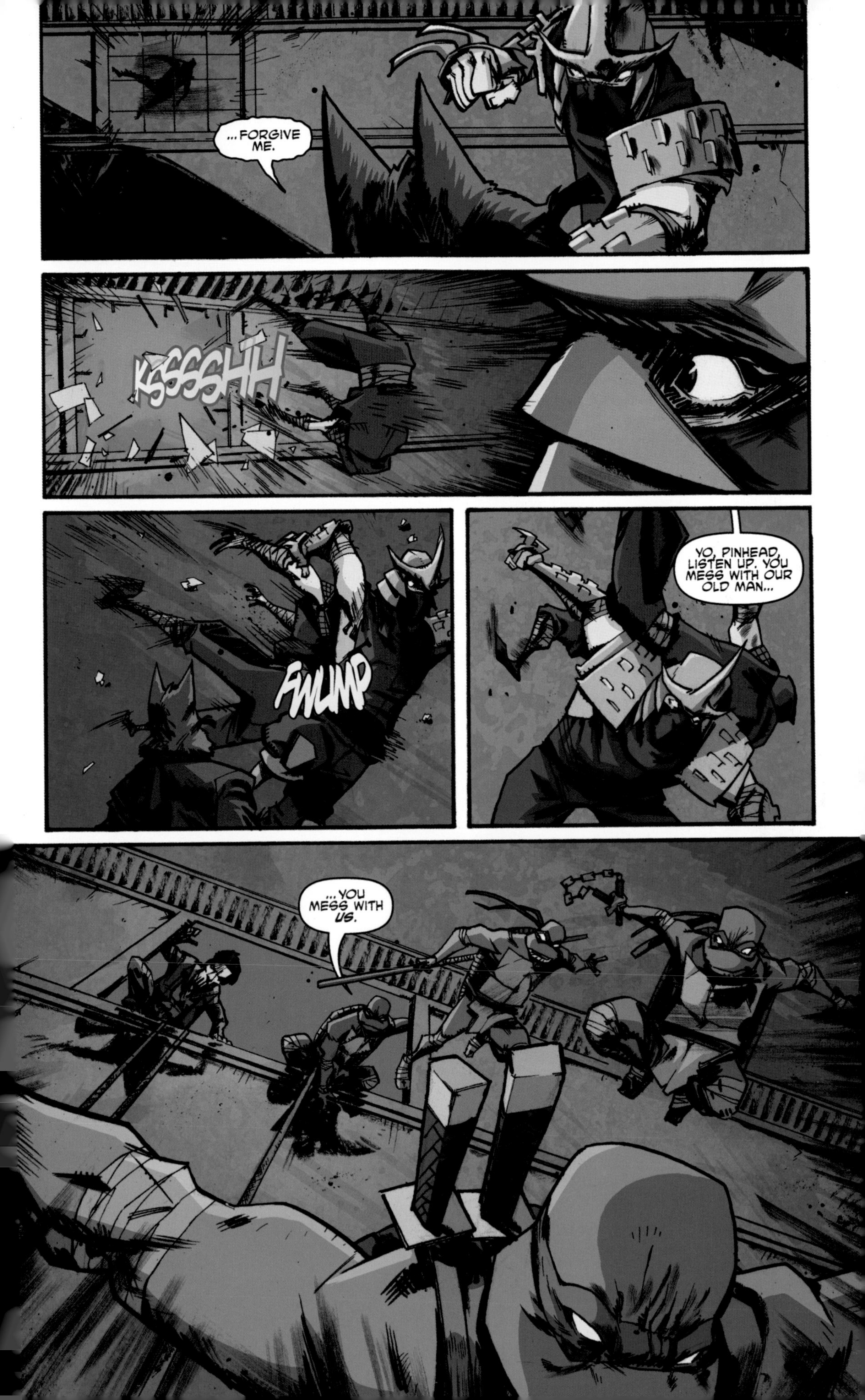
...FORGIVE ME.
KSSSSHH
FWUMP
YO, PINHEAD, LISTEN UP. YOU MESS WITH OUR OLD MAN...
...YOU MESS WITH *US*.

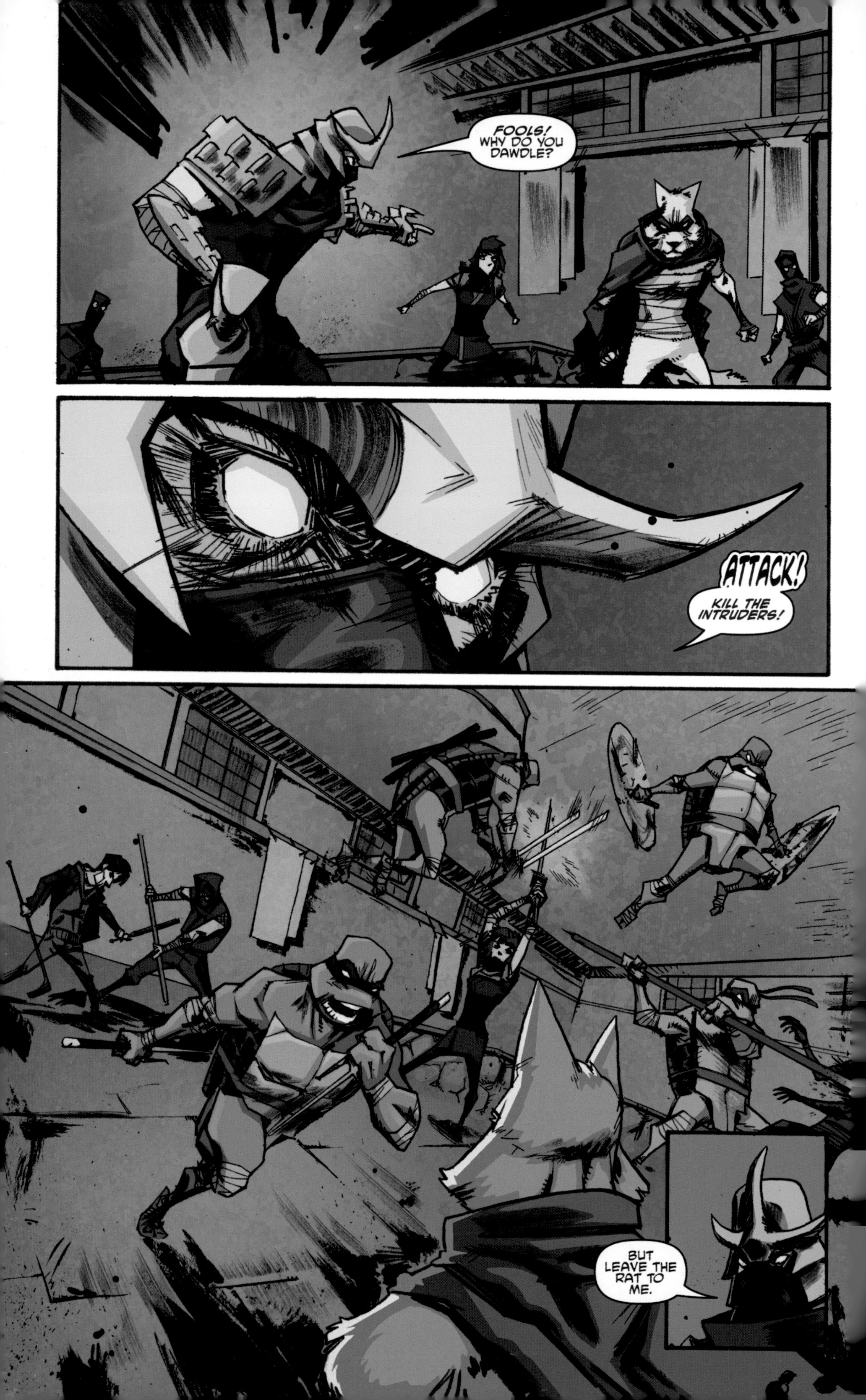
FOOLS! WHY DO YOU DAWDLE?
ATTACK!
KILL THE INTRUDERS!
BUT LEAVE THE RAT TO ME.

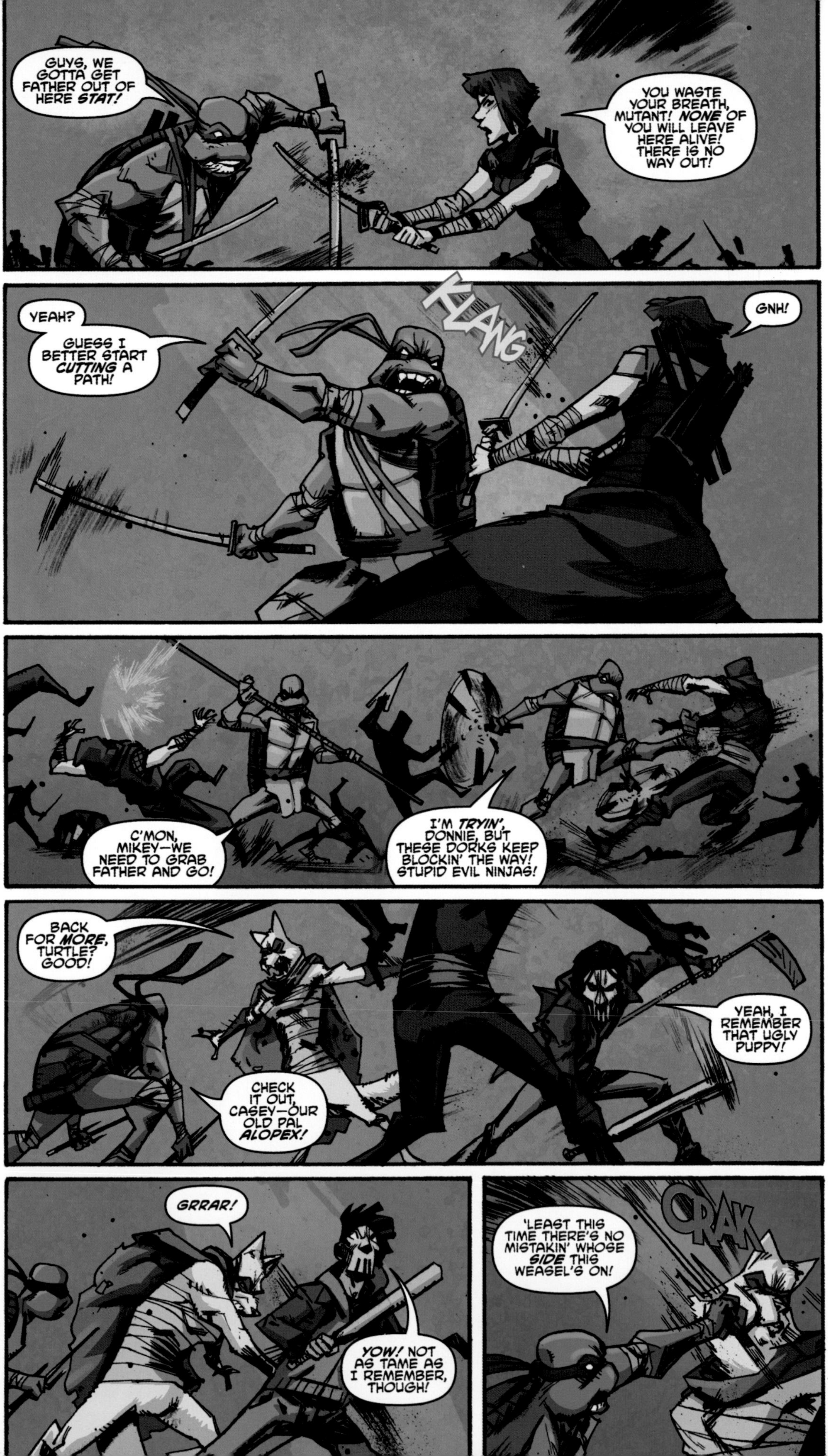
GUYS, WE GOTTA GET FATHER OUT OF HERE STAT!
YOU WASTE YOUR BREATH, MUTANT! NONE OF YOU WILL LEAVE HERE ALIVE! THERE IS NO WAY OUT!
YEAH?
GUESS I BETTER START CUTTING A PATH!
KLANG
GNH!
C'MON, MIKEY—WE NEED TO GRAB FATHER AND GO!
I'M TRYIN', DONNIE, BUT THESE DORKS KEEP BLOCKIN' THE WAY! STUPID EVIL NINJAS!
BACK FOR MORE, TURTLE? GOOD!
CHECK IT OUT, CASEY—OUR OLD PAL ALOPEX!
YEAH, I REMEMBER THAT UGLY PUPPY!
GRRAR!
YOW! NOT AS TAME AS I REMEMBER, THOUGH!
'LEAST THIS TIME THERE'S NO MISTAKIN' WHOSE SIDE THIS WEASEL'S ON!
CRAK

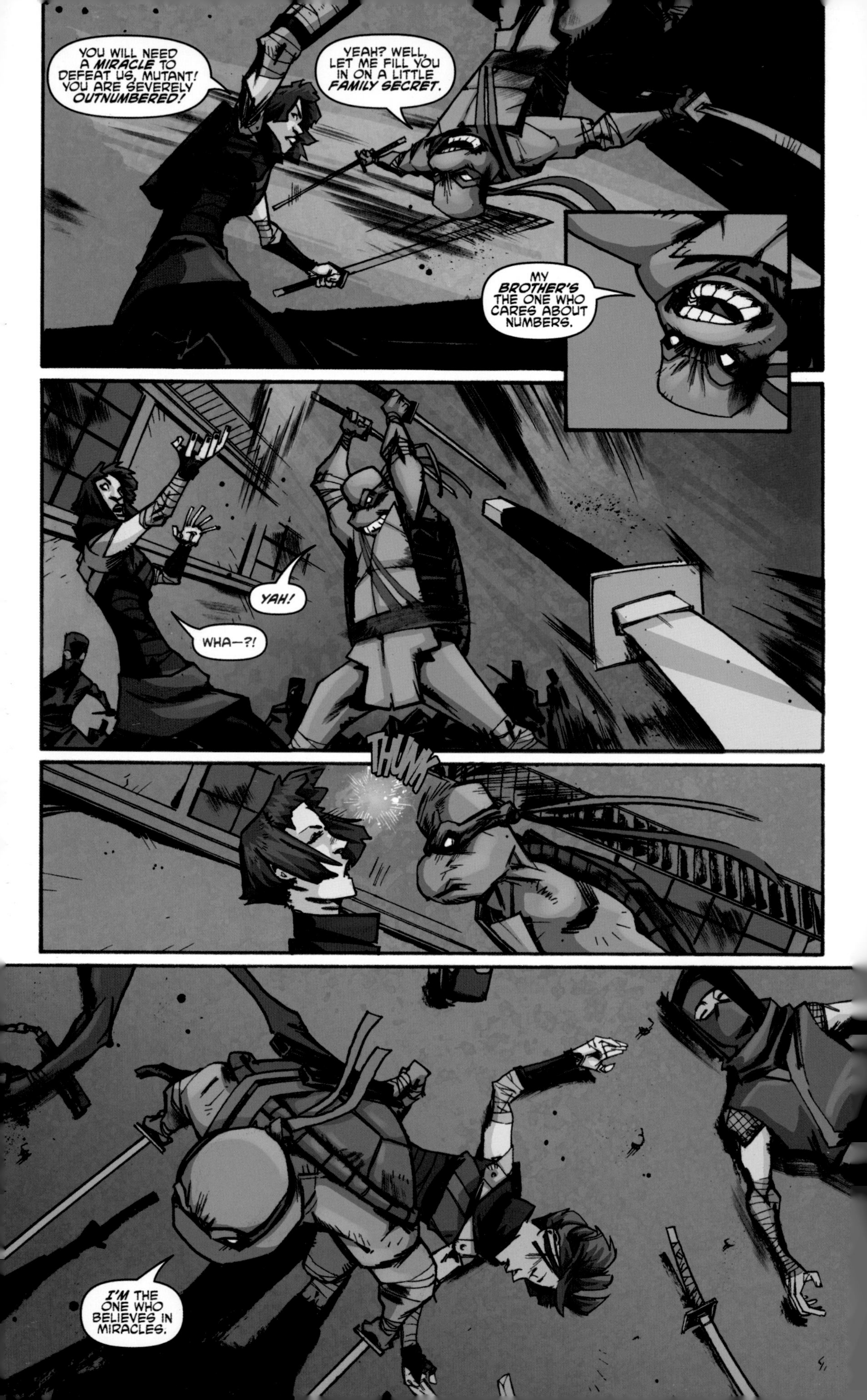
YOU WILL NEED A MIRACLE TO DEFEAT US, MUTANT! YOU ARE SEVERELY OUTNUMBERED!
YEAH? WELL, LET ME FILL YOU IN ON A LITTLE FAMILY SECRET.
MY BROTHER'S THE ONE WHO CARES ABOUT NUMBERS.
YAH!
WHA--?!
THUNK
I'M THE ONE WHO BELIEVES IN MIRACLES.

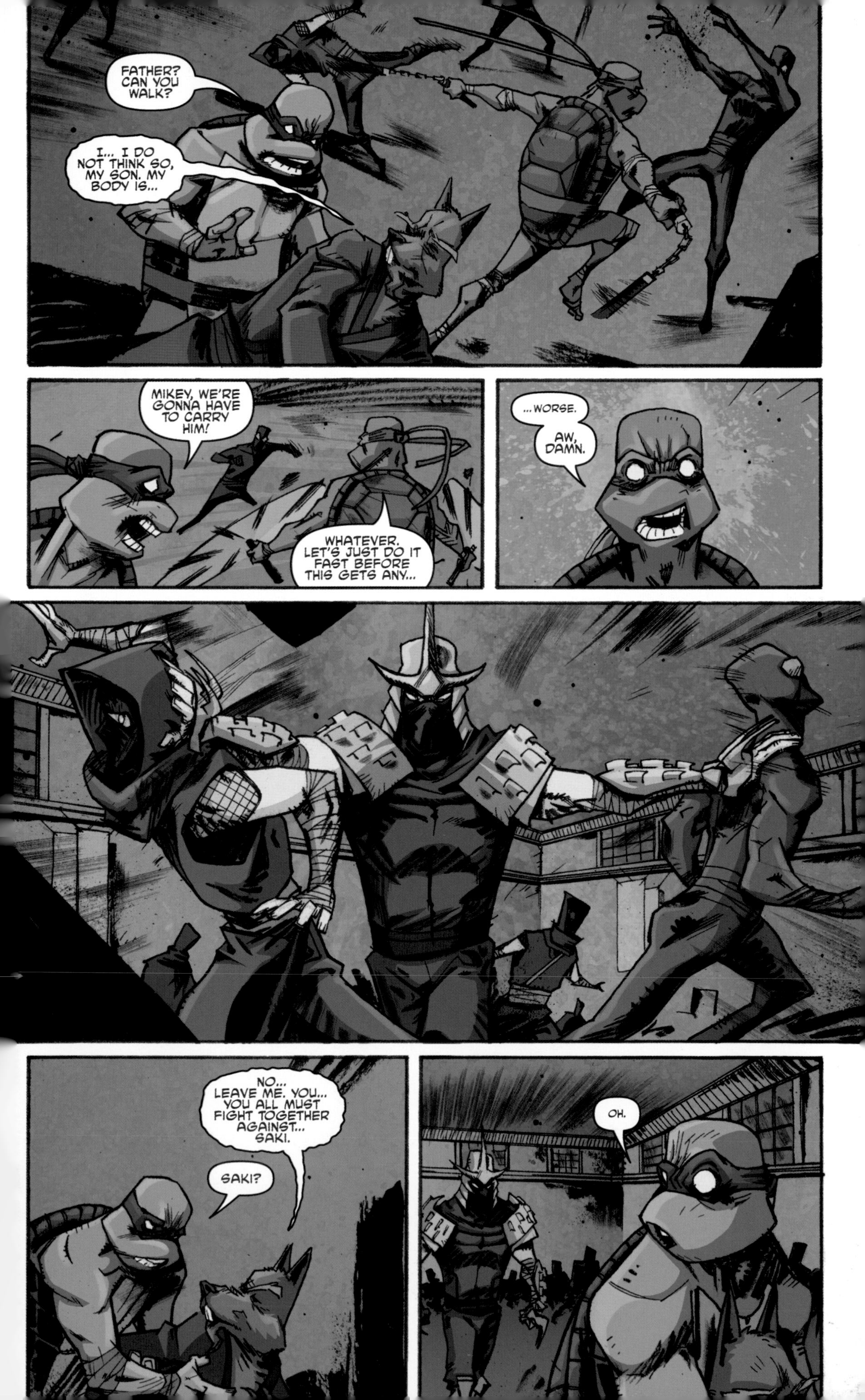
FATHER? CAN YOU WALK?
I... I DO NOT THINK SO, MY SON. MY BODY IS...
MIKEY, WE'RE GONNA HAVE TO CARRY HIM!
WHATEVER. LET'S JUST DO IT FAST BEFORE THIS GETS ANY...
...WORSE.
AW, DAMN.
NO... LEAVE ME. YOU... YOU ALL MUST FIGHT TOGETHER AGAINST... SAKI.
SAKI?
OH.

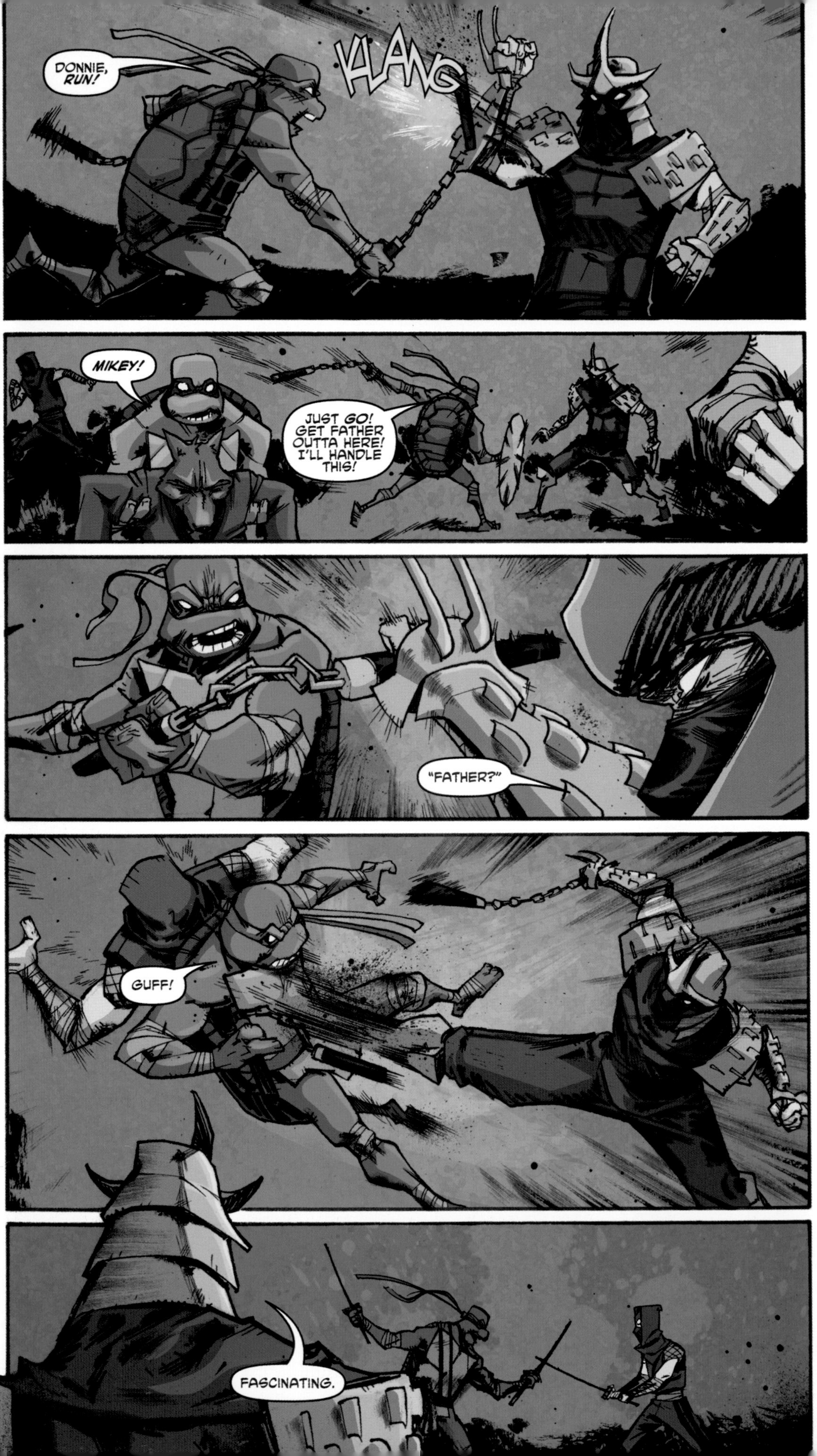
DONNIE, RUN!
KLANG
MIKEY!
JUST GO! GET FATHER OUTTA HERE! I'LL HANDLE THIS!
"FATHER?"
GUFF!
FASCINATING.

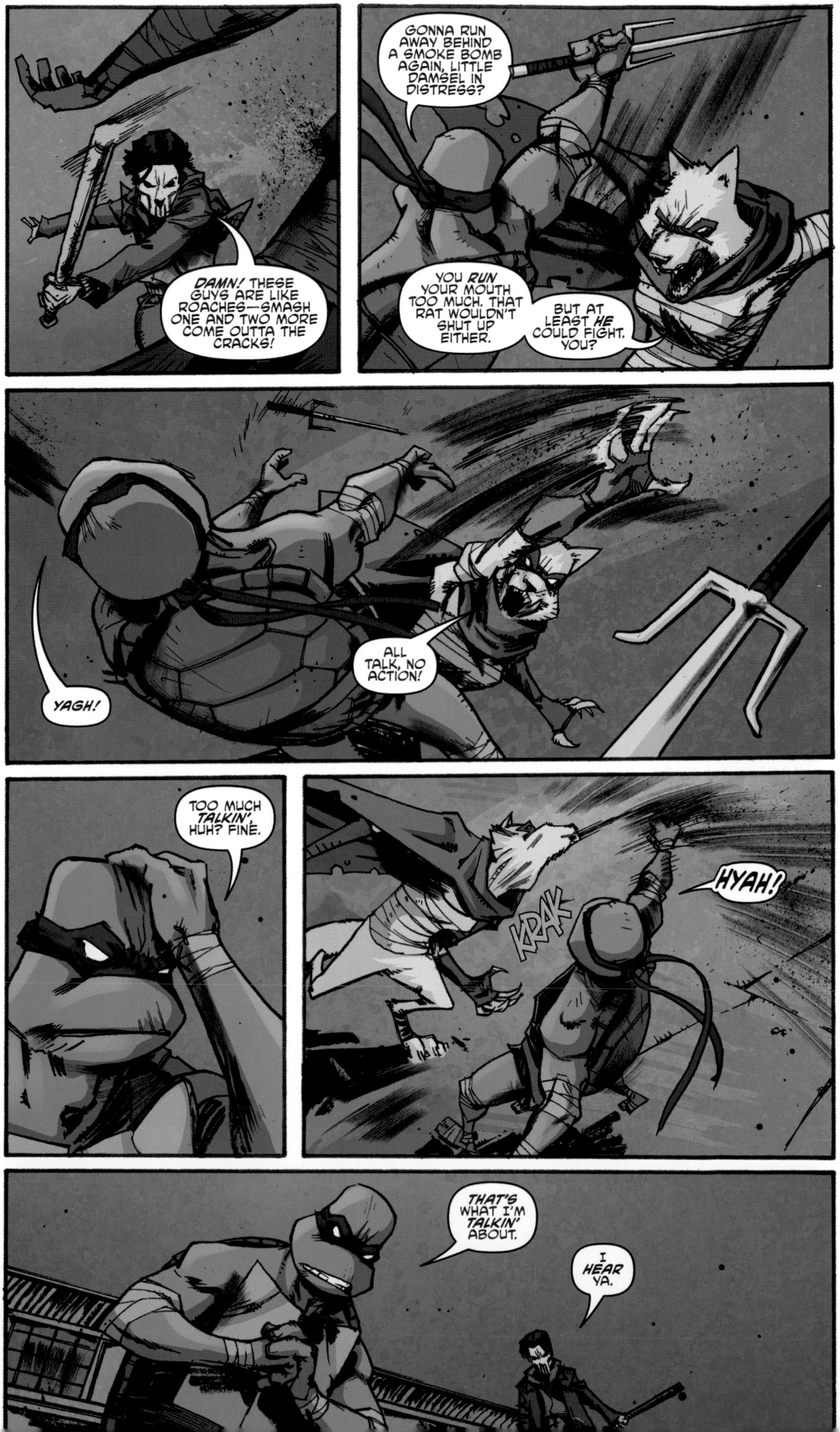
DAMN! THESE GUYS ARE LIKE ROACHES—SMASH ONE AND TWO MORE COME OUTTA THE CRACKS!
GONNA RUN AWAY BEHIND A SMOKE BOMB AGAIN, LITTLE DAMSEL IN DISTRESS?
YOU RUN YOUR MOUTH TOO MUCH. THAT RAT WOULDN'T SHUT UP EITHER.
BUT AT LEAST HE COULD FIGHT. YOU?
YAGH!
ALL TALK, NO ACTION!
TOO MUCH TALKIN' HUH? FINE.
KRAK
HYAH!
THAT'S WHAT I'M TALKIN' ABOUT.
I HEAR YA.

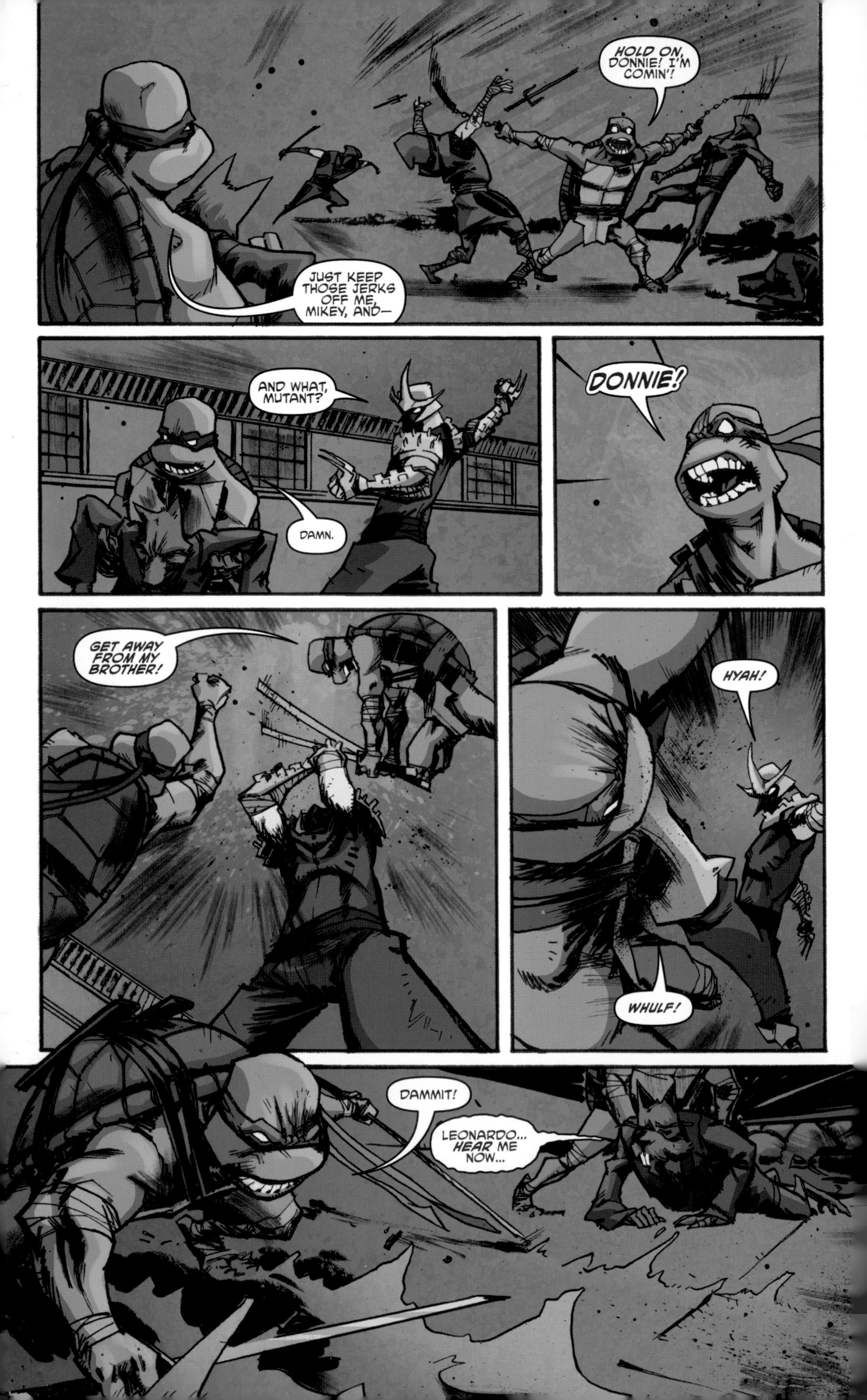
HOLD ON, DONNIE! I'M COMIN'!
JUST KEEP THOSE JERKS OFF ME, MIKEY, AND—
AND WHAT, MUTANT?
DAMN.
DONNIE!
GET AWAY FROM MY BROTHER!
HYAH!
WHULF!
DAMMIT!
LEONARDO... HEAR ME NOW...

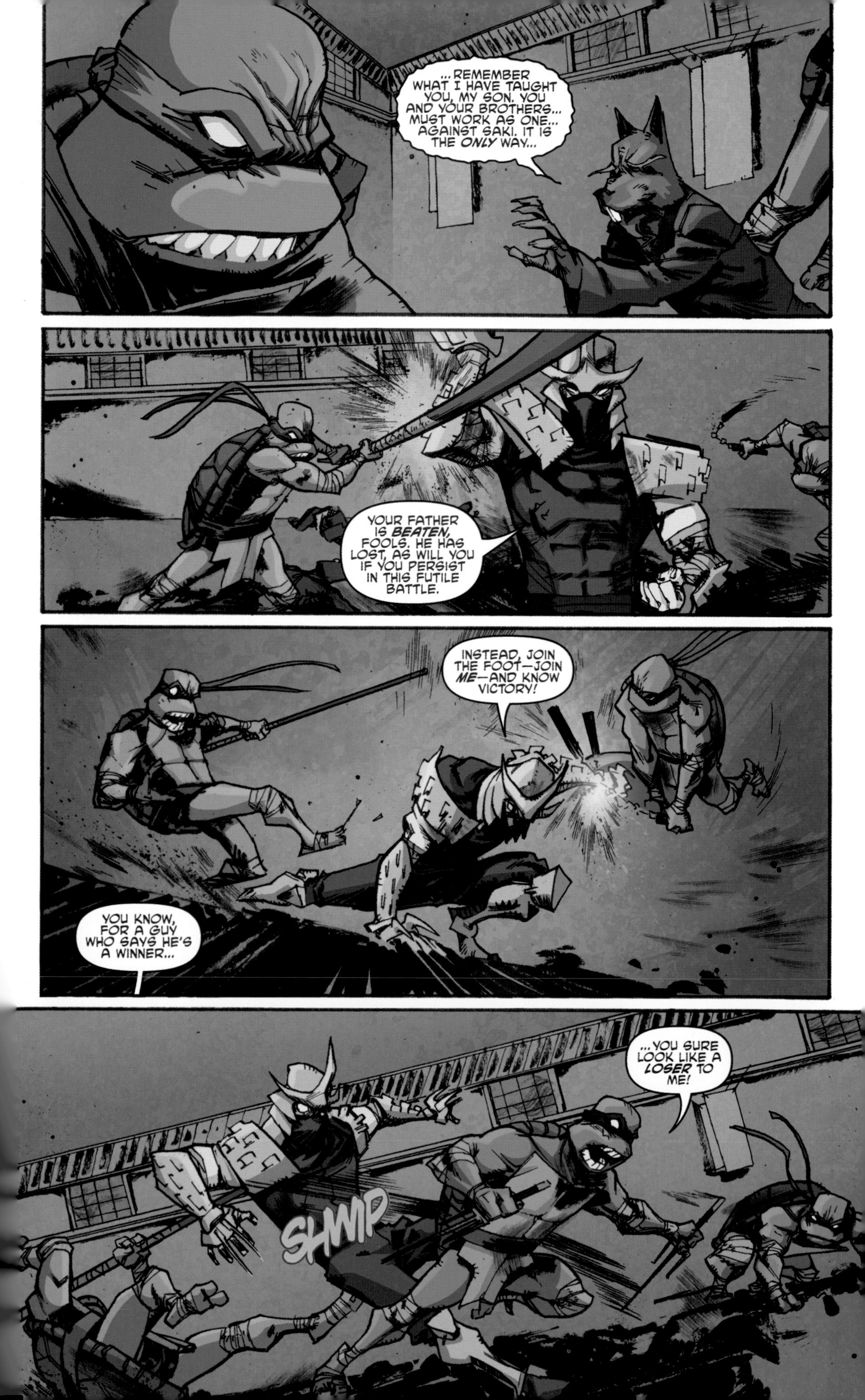
...REMEMBER WHAT I HAVE TAUGHT YOU, MY SON. YOU AND YOUR BROTHERS... MUST WORK AS ONE... AGAINST SAKI. IT IS THE *ONLY* WAY...
YOUR FATHER IS *BEATEN*, FOOLS. HE HAS LOST, AS WILL YOU IF YOU PERSIST IN THIS FUTILE BATTLE.
INSTEAD, JOIN THE FOOT—JOIN *ME*—AND KNOW VICTORY!
YOU KNOW, FOR A GUY WHO SAYS HE'S A WINNER...
...YOU SURE LOOK LIKE A *LOSER* TO ME!
SHWIP

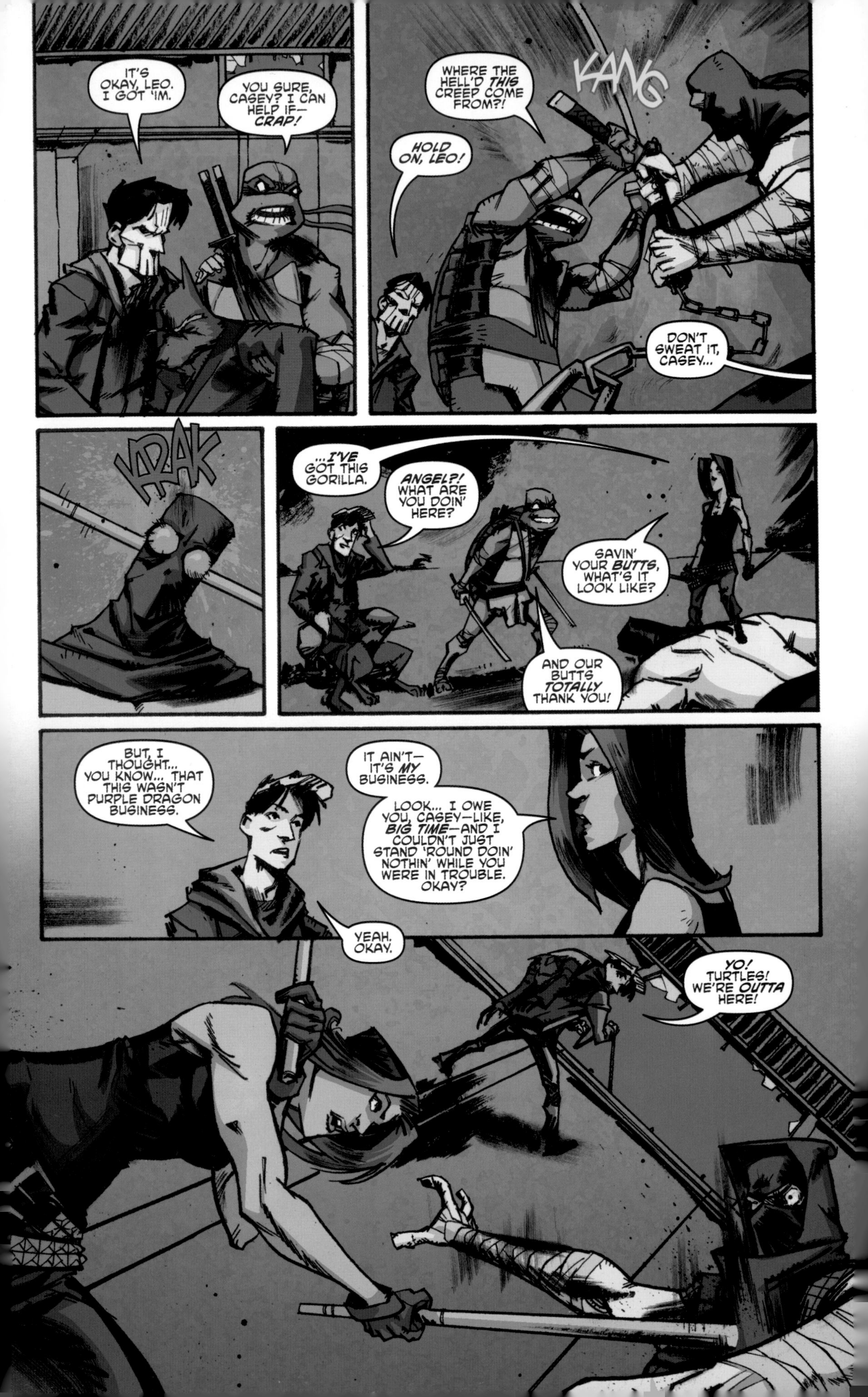
IT'S OKAY, LEO. I GOT 'IM.
YOU SURE, CASEY? I CAN HELP IF— CRAP!
WHERE THE HELL'D THIS CREEP COME FROM?!
KANG
HOLD ON, LEO!
DON'T SWEAT IT, CASEY...
KRAK
...I'VE GOT THIS GORILLA.
ANGEL?! WHAT ARE YOU DOIN' HERE?
SAVIN' YOUR BUTTS, WHAT'S IT LOOK LIKE?
AND OUR BUTTS TOTALLY THANK YOU!
BUT, I THOUGHT... YOU KNOW... THAT THIS WASN'T PURPLE DRAGON BUSINESS.
IT AIN'T— IT'S MY BUSINESS.
LOOK... I OWE YOU, CASEY—LIKE, BIG TIME—AND I COULDN'T JUST STAND 'ROUND DOIN' NOTHIN' WHILE YOU WERE IN TROUBLE. OKAY?
YEAH. OKAY.
YO! TURTLES! WE'RE OUTTA HERE!

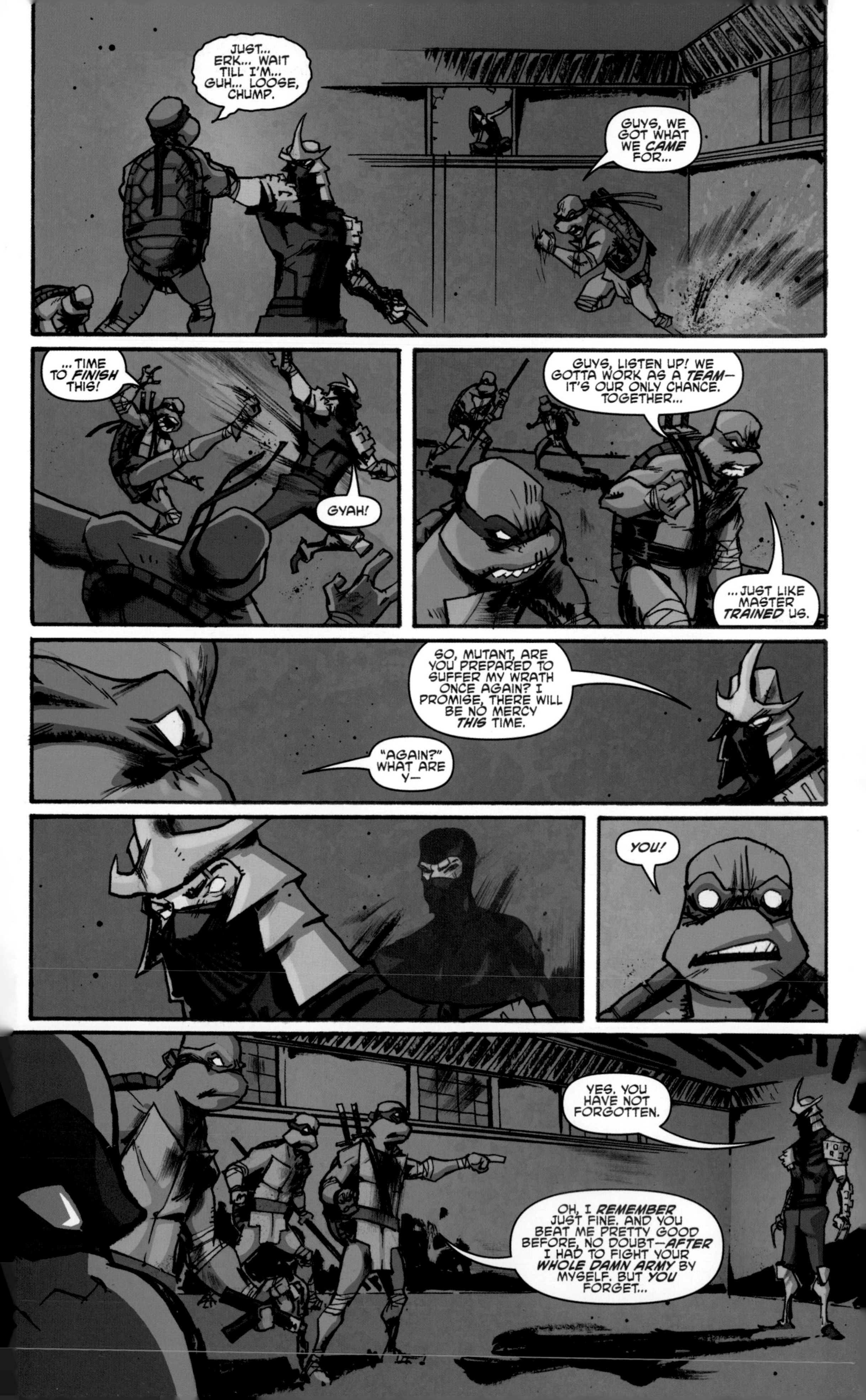
JUST... ERK... WAIT TILL I'M... GUH... LOOSE, CHUMP.
GUYS, WE GOT WHAT WE CAME FOR...
...TIME TO FINISH THIS!
GYAH!
GUYS, LISTEN UP! WE GOTTA WORK AS A TEAM— IT'S OUR ONLY CHANCE. TOGETHER...
...JUST LIKE MASTER TRAINED US.
SO, MUTANT, ARE YOU PREPARED TO SUFFER MY WRATH ONCE AGAIN? I PROMISE, THERE WILL BE NO MERCY THIS TIME.
"AGAIN?" WHAT ARE Y—
YOU!
YES. YOU HAVE NOT FORGOTTEN.
OH, I REMEMBER JUST FINE. AND YOU BEAT ME PRETTY GOOD BEFORE, NO DOUBT—AFTER I HAD TO FIGHT YOUR WHOLE DAMN ARMY BY MYSELF. BUT YOU FORGET...

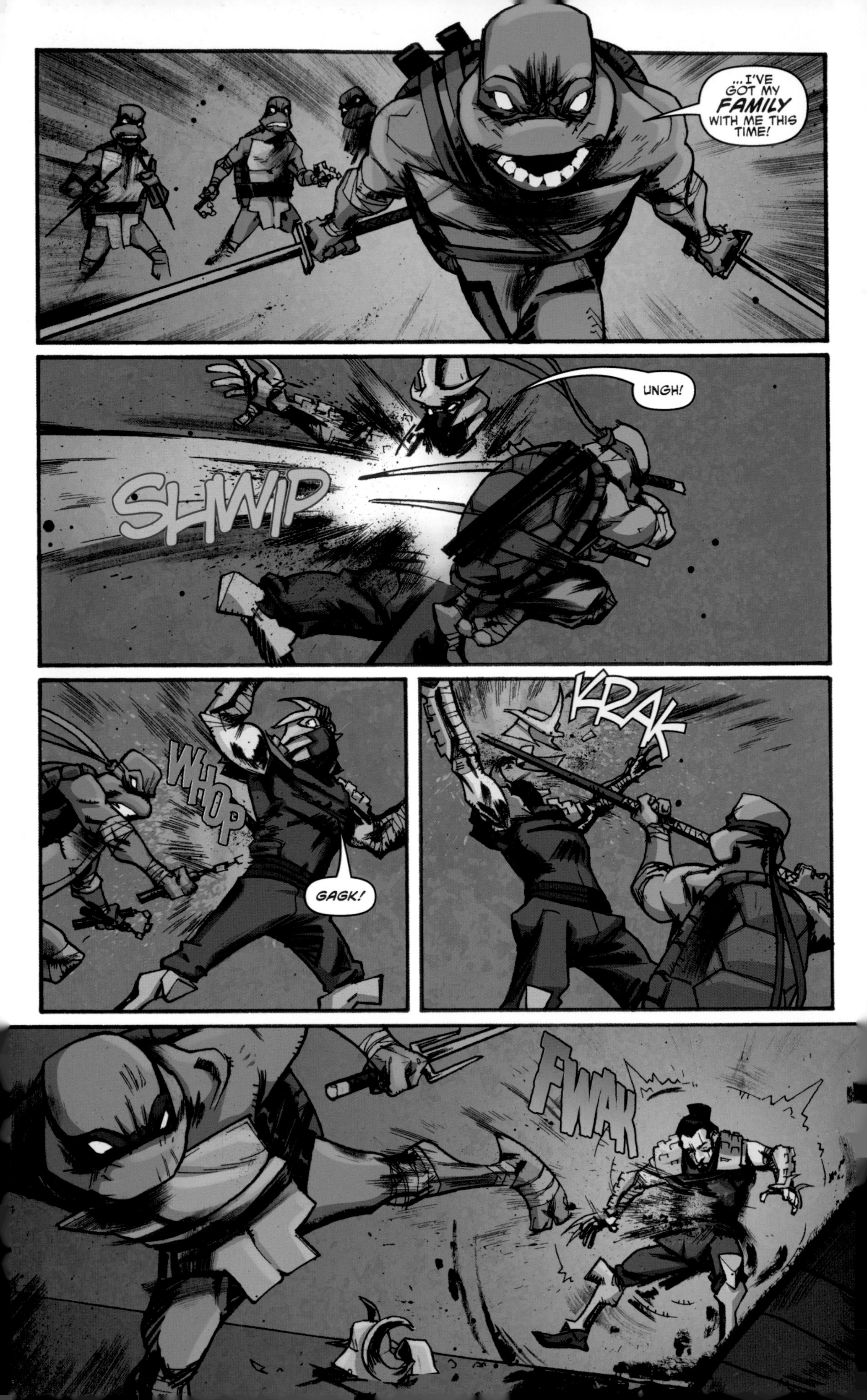
...I'VE GOT MY FAMILY WITH ME THIS TIME!
UNGH!
SHWIP
WHOP
GAGK!
KRAK
F-WAK

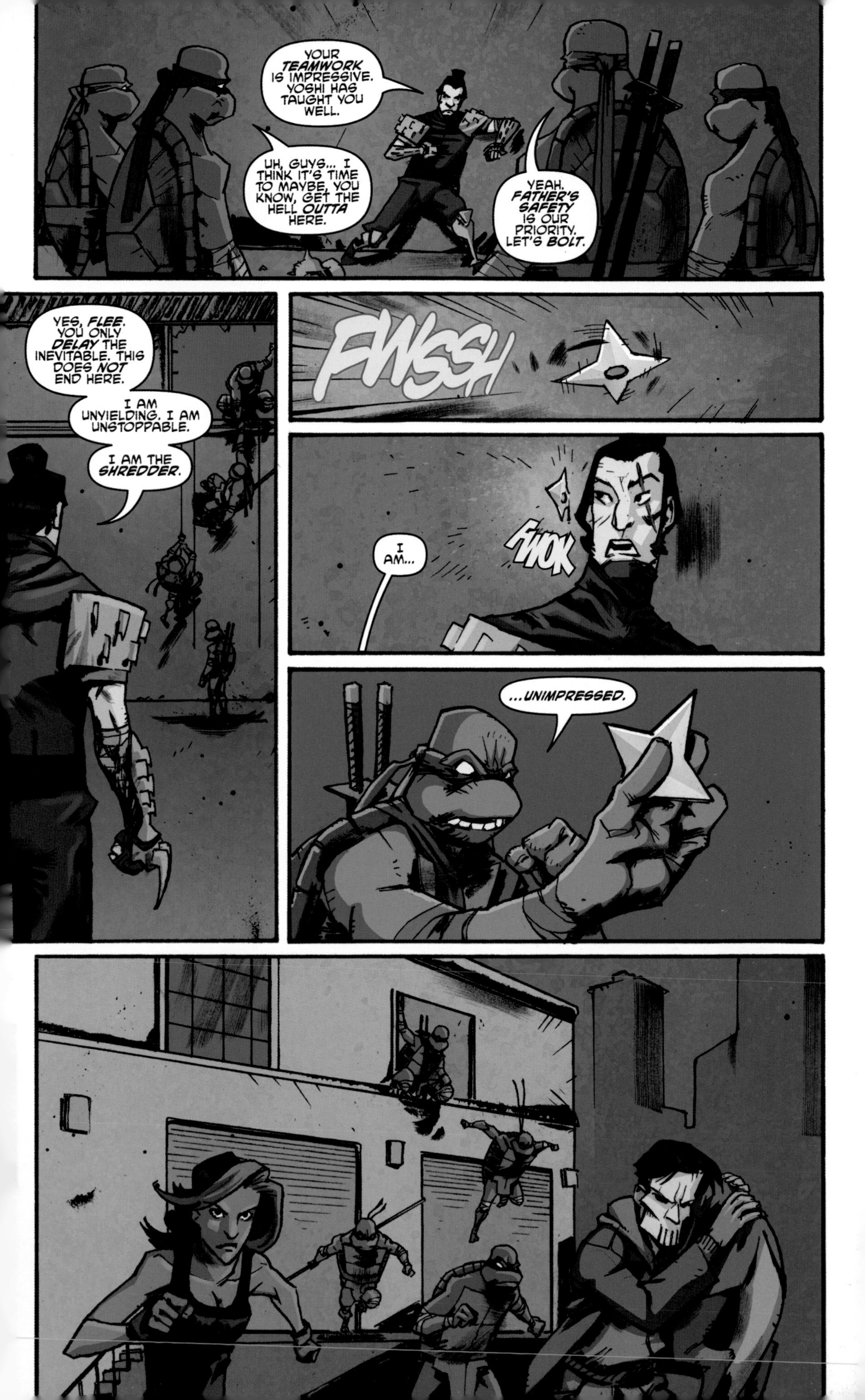
YOUR TEAMWORK IS IMPRESSIVE. YOSHI HAS TAUGHT YOU WELL.
UH, GUYS... I THINK IT'S TIME TO MAYBE, YOU KNOW, GET THE HELL OUTTA HERE.
YEAH. FATHER'S SAFETY IS OUR PRIORITY. LET'S BOLT.
YES, FLEE. YOU ONLY DELAY THE INEVITABLE. THIS DOES NOT END HERE.
I AM UNYIELDING. I AM UNSTOPPABLE.
I AM THE SHREDDER.
FWSSH
I AM...
FWOK
...UNIMPRESSED.

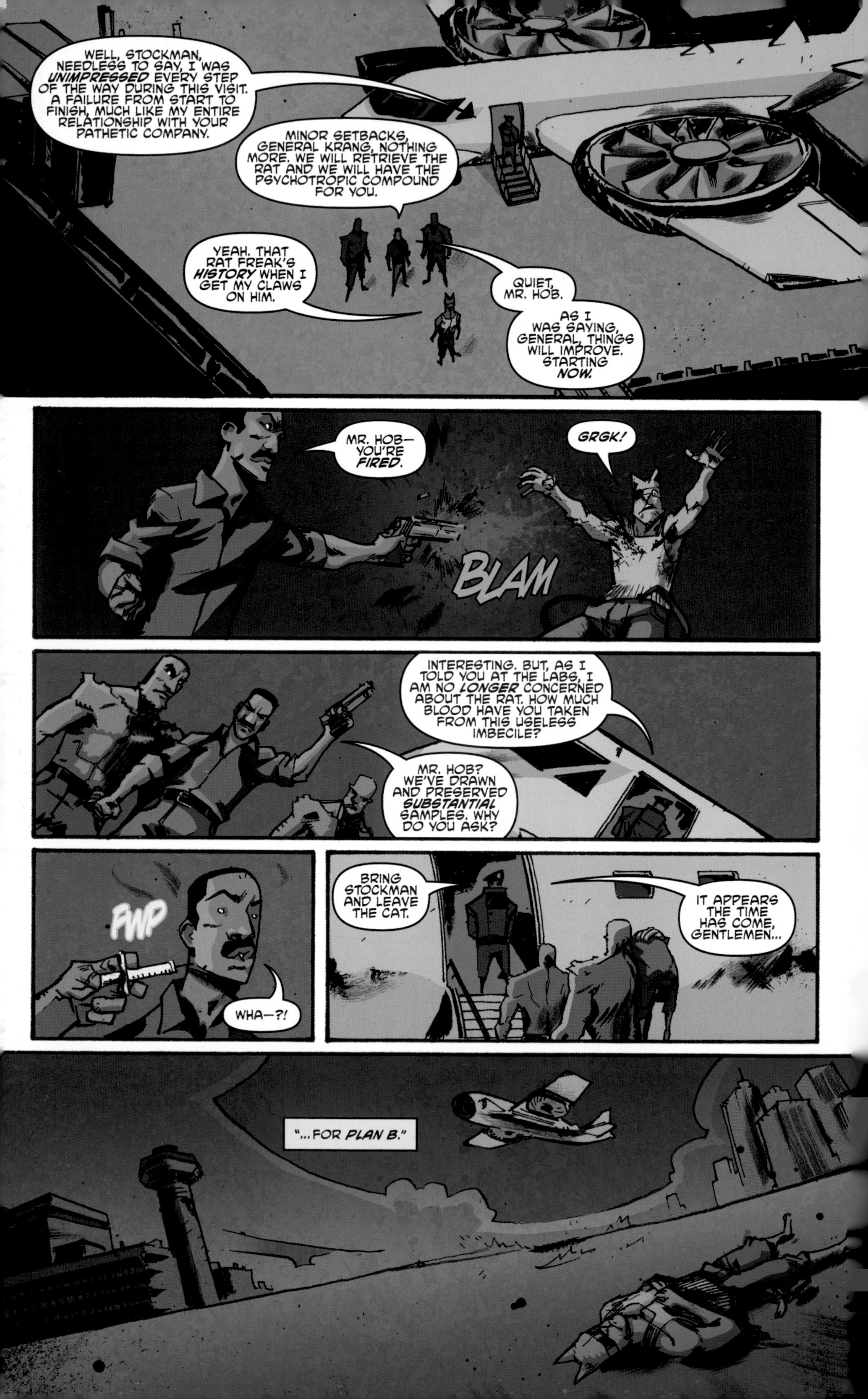
WELL, STOCKMAN, NEEDLESS TO SAY, I WAS UNIMPRESSED EVERY STEP OF THE WAY DURING THIS VISIT. A FAILURE FROM START TO FINISH, MUCH LIKE MY ENTIRE RELATIONSHIP WITH YOUR PATHETIC COMPANY.
MINOR SETBACKS, GENERAL KRANG, NOTHING MORE. WE WILL RETRIEVE THE RAT AND WE WILL HAVE THE PSYCHOTROPIC COMPOUND FOR YOU.
YEAH. THAT RAT FREAK'S HISTORY WHEN I GET MY CLAWS ON HIM.
QUIET, MR. HOB.
AS I WAS SAYING, GENERAL, THINGS WILL IMPROVE. STARTING NOW.
MR. HOB— YOU'RE FIRED.
GRGK!
BLAM
INTERESTING. BUT, AS I TOLD YOU AT THE LABS, I AM NO LONGER CONCERNED ABOUT THE RAT. HOW MUCH BLOOD HAVE YOU TAKEN FROM THIS USELESS IMBECILE?
MR. HOB? WE'VE DRAWN AND PRESERVED SUBSTANTIAL SAMPLES. WHY DO YOU ASK?
FWP
WHA—?!
BRING STOCKMAN AND LEAVE THE CAT.
IT APPEARS THE TIME HAS COME, GENTLEMEN...
"...FOR PLAN B."

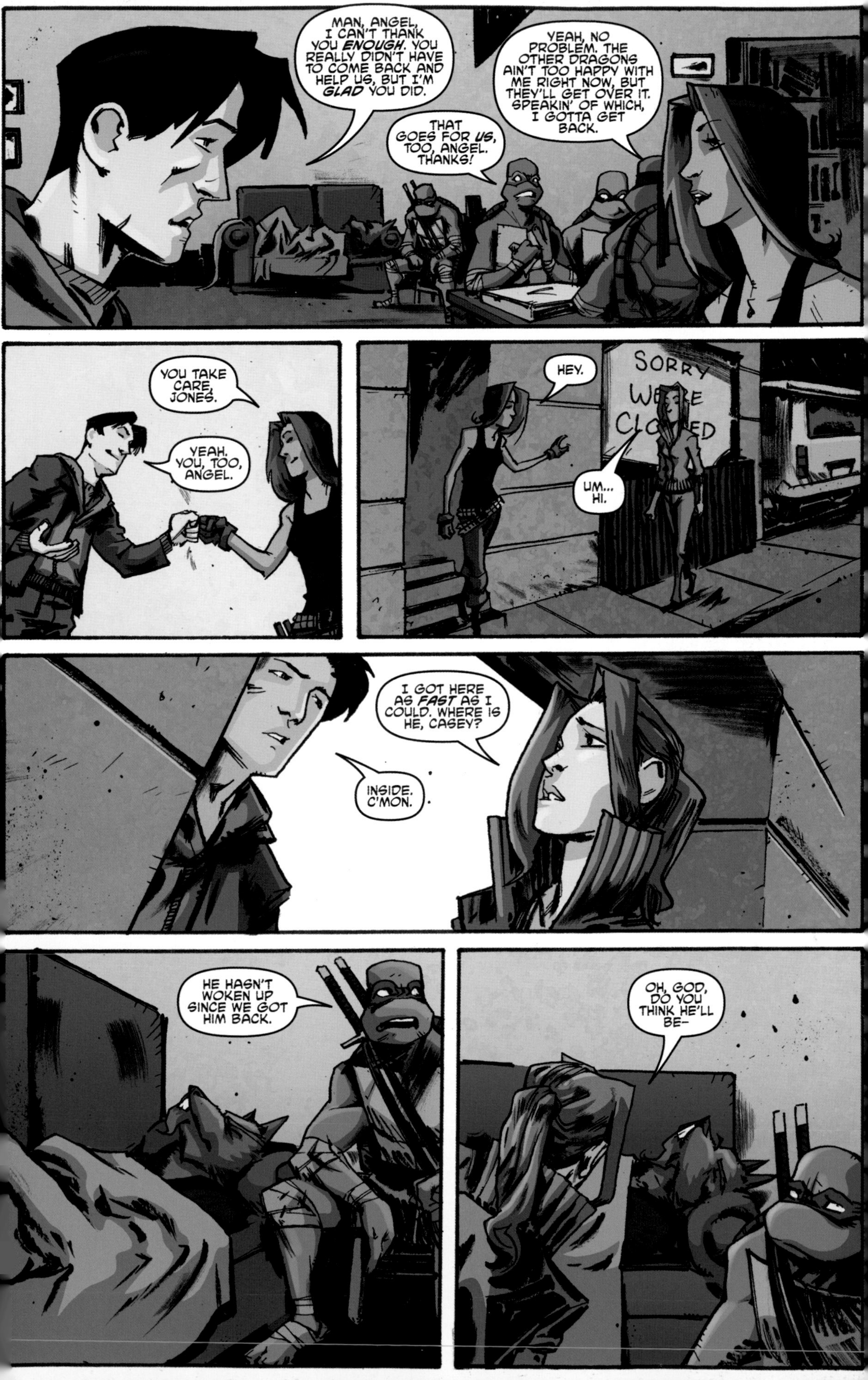
MAN, ANGEL, I CAN'T THANK YOU ENOUGH. YOU REALLY DIDN'T HAVE TO COME BACK AND HELP US, BUT I'M GLAD YOU DID.
THAT GOES FOR US, TOO, ANGEL. THANKS!
YEAH, NO PROBLEM. THE OTHER DRAGONS AIN'T TOO HAPPY WITH ME RIGHT NOW, BUT THEY'LL GET OVER IT. SPEAKIN' OF WHICH, I GOTTA GET BACK.
YOU TAKE CARE, JONES.
YEAH. YOU, TOO, ANGEL.
HEY.
SORRY WE'RE CLOSED
UM... HI.
I GOT HERE AS FAST AS I COULD. WHERE IS HE, CASEY?
INSIDE. C'MON.
HE HASN'T WOKEN UP SINCE WE GOT HIM BACK.
OH, GOD, DO YOU THINK HE'LL BE–

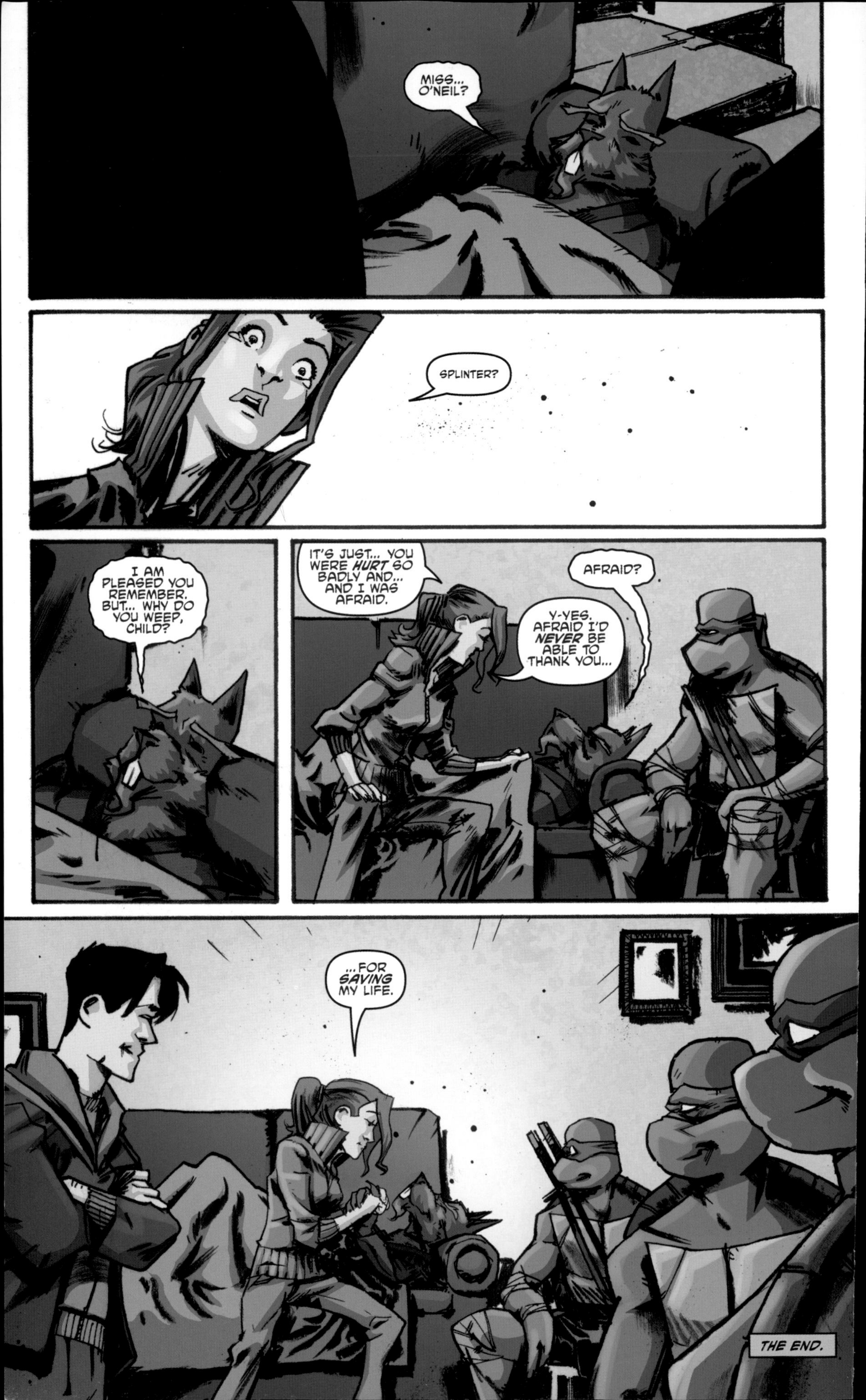
MISS... O'NEIL?
SPLINTER?
I AM PLEASED YOU REMEMBER. BUT... WHY DO YOU WEEP, CHILD?
IT'S JUST... YOU WERE HURT SO BADLY AND... AND I WAS AFRAID.
AFRAID?
Y-YES. AFRAID I'D NEVER BE ABLE TO THANK YOU...
...FOR SAVING MY LIFE.
THE END.

ART GALLERY

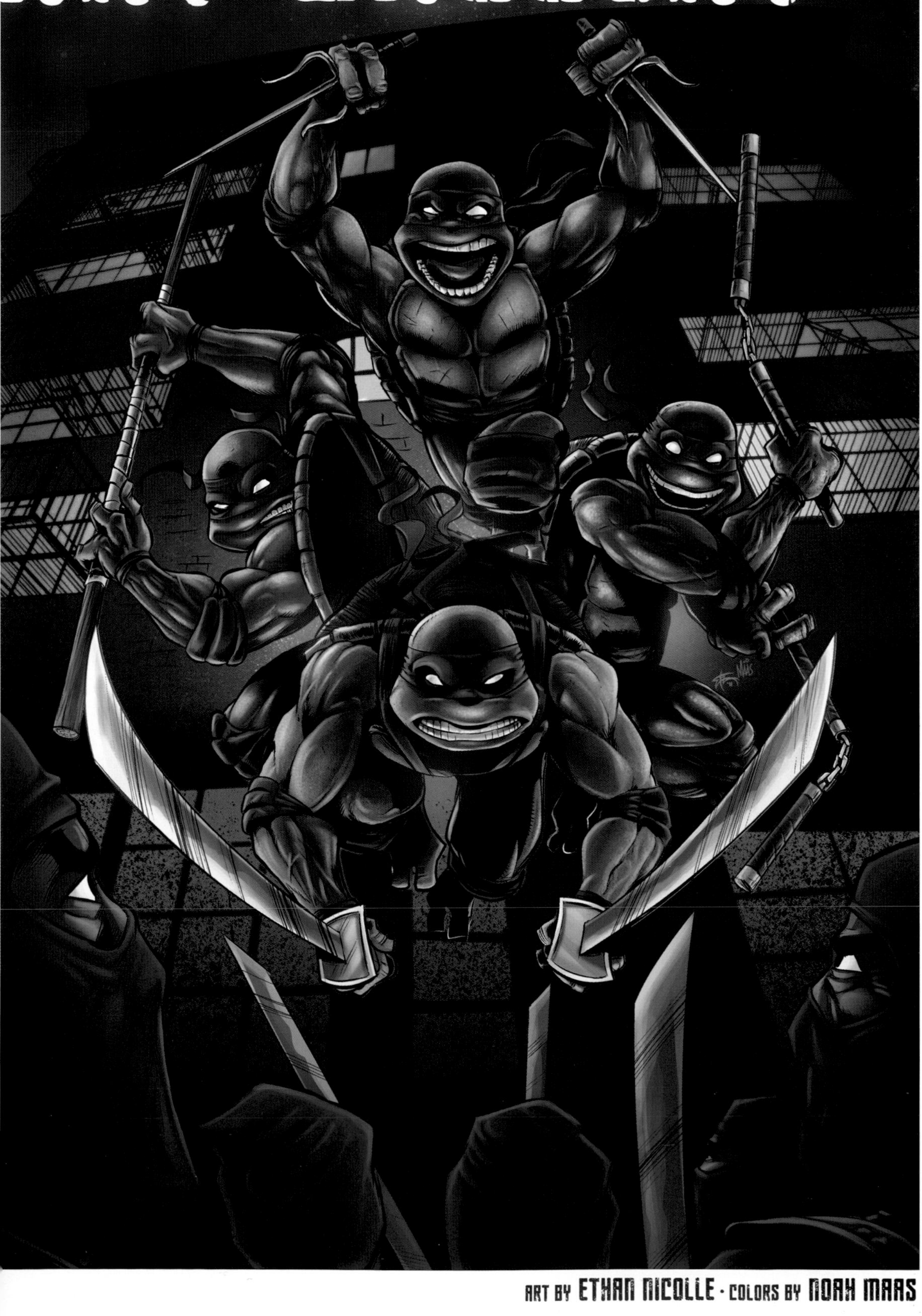

ART BY ETHAN NICOLLE · COLORS BY NOAH MAAS

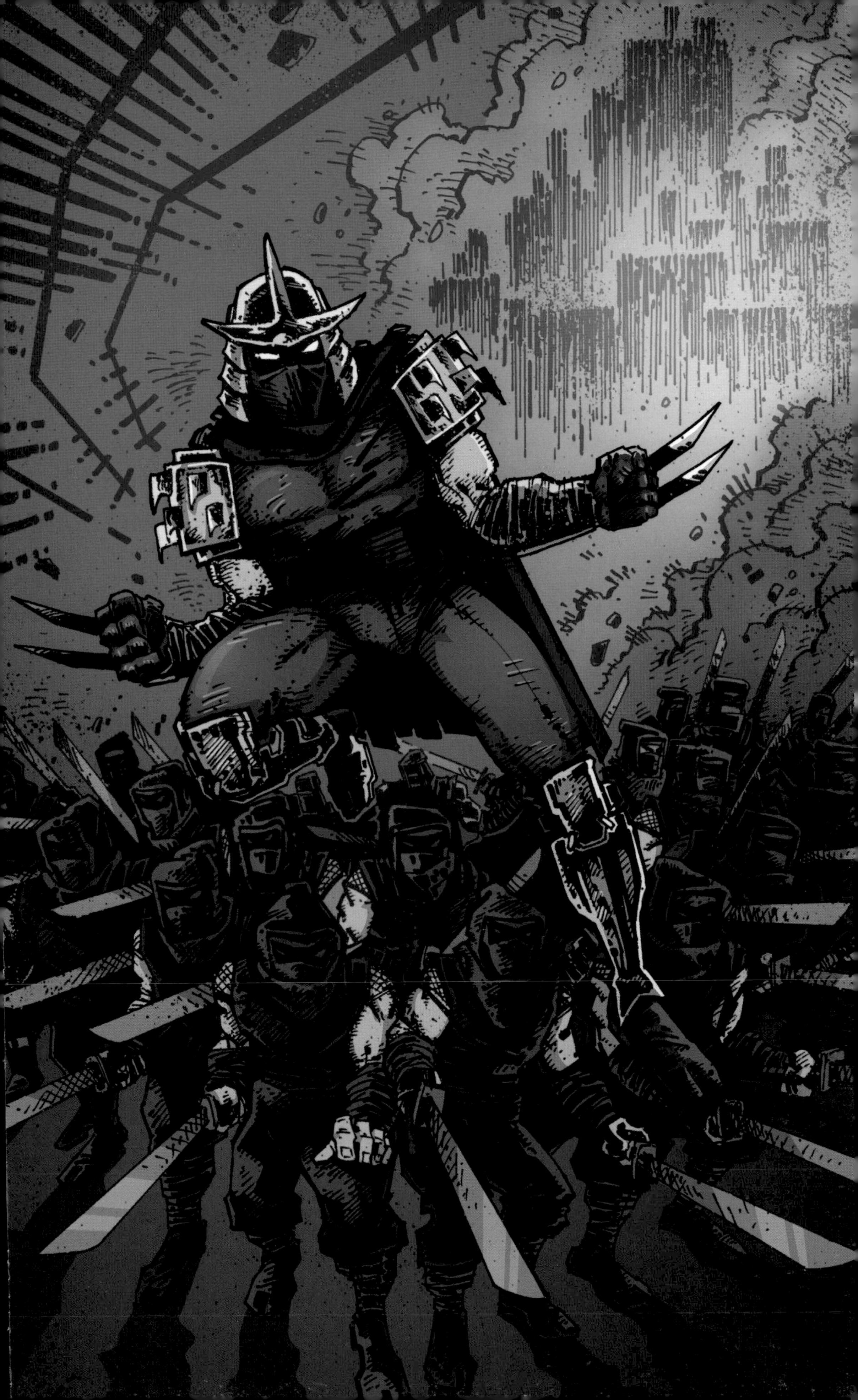

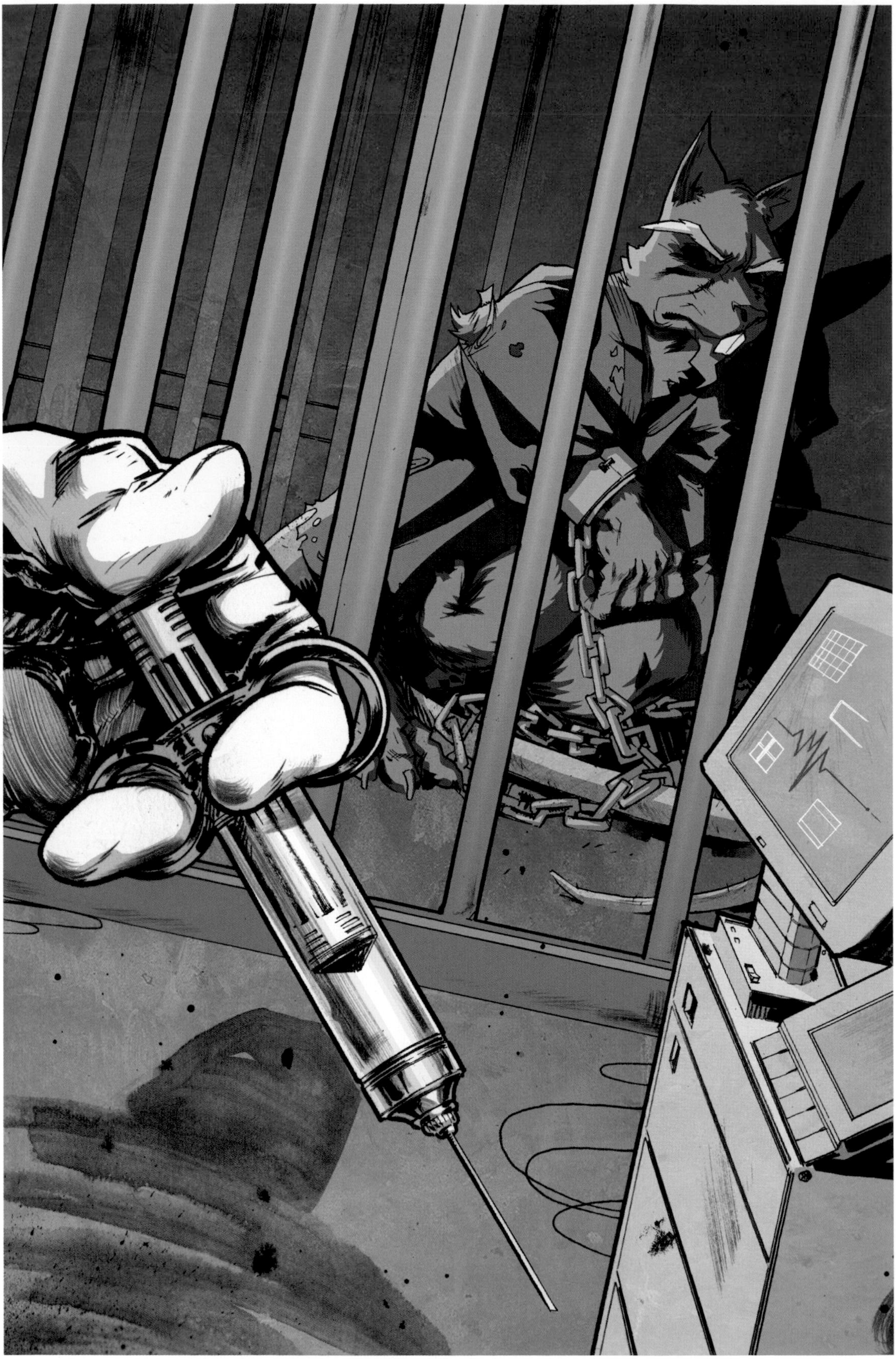

THIS PAGE AND OPPOSITE PAGE: ART BY DAN DUNCAN · COLORS BY RONDA PATTISON

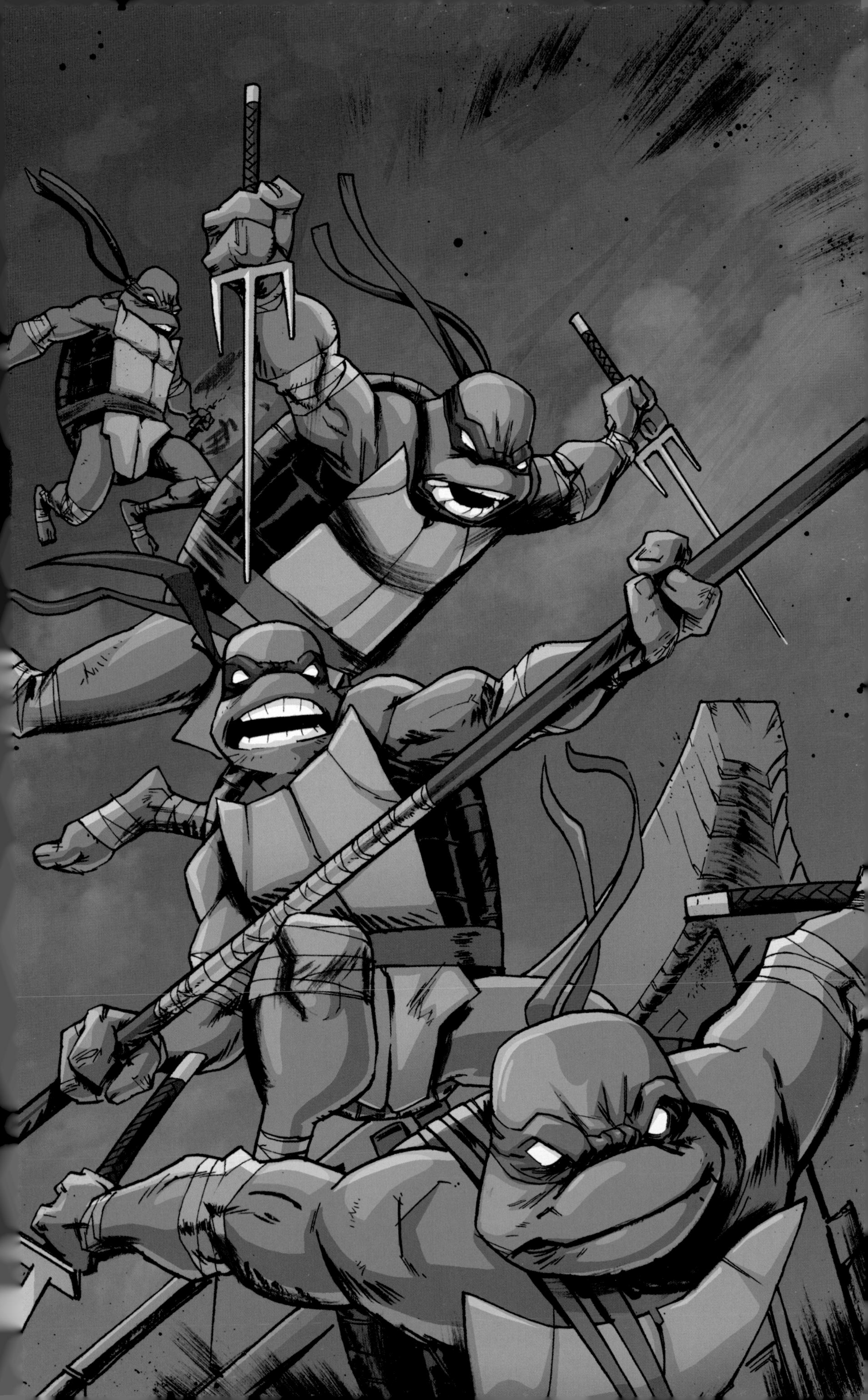

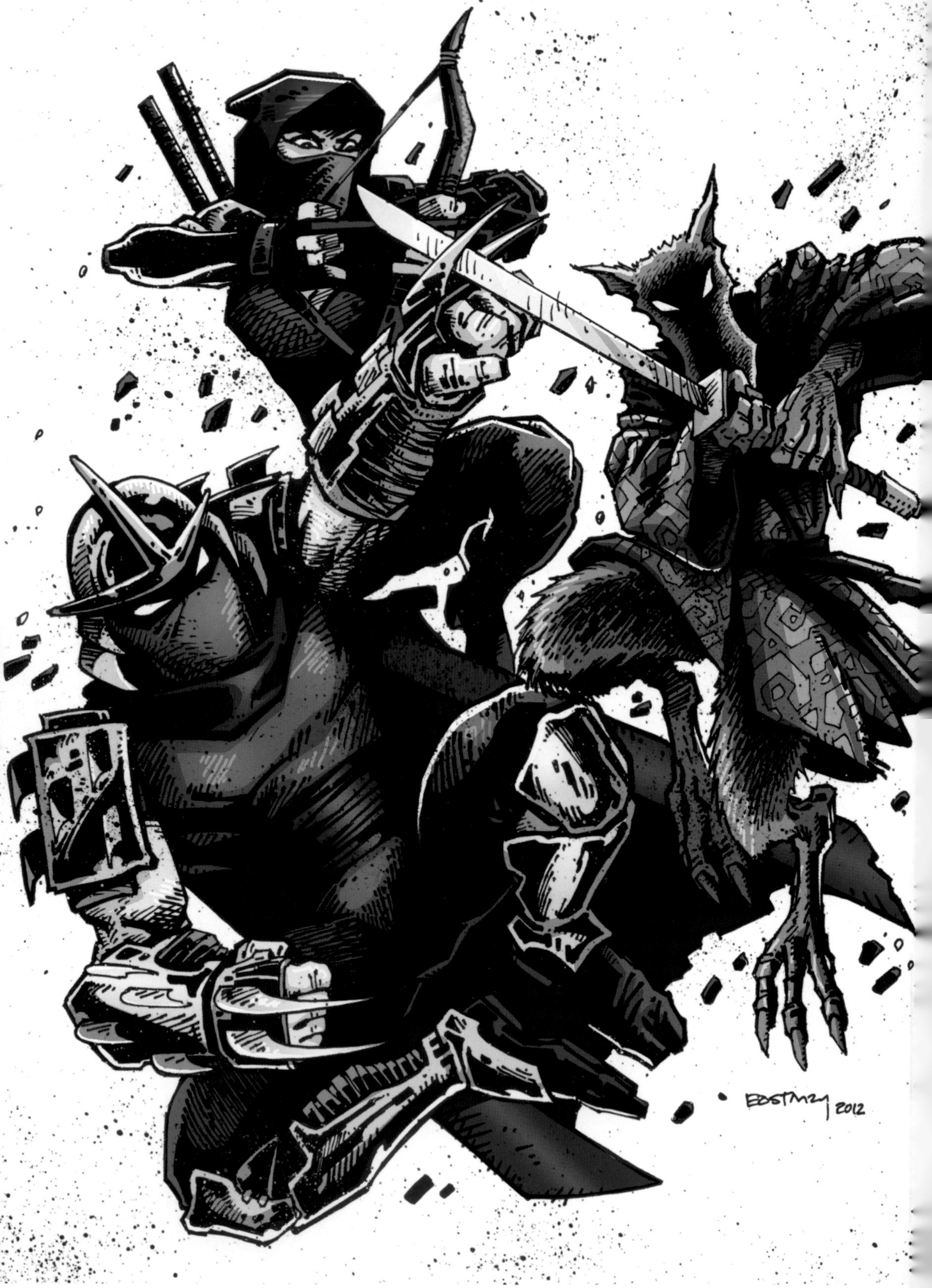
EASTMAN 2012

THIS PAGE AND OPPOSITE PAGE: ART BY KEVIN EASTMAN · COLORS BY RONDA PATTISON

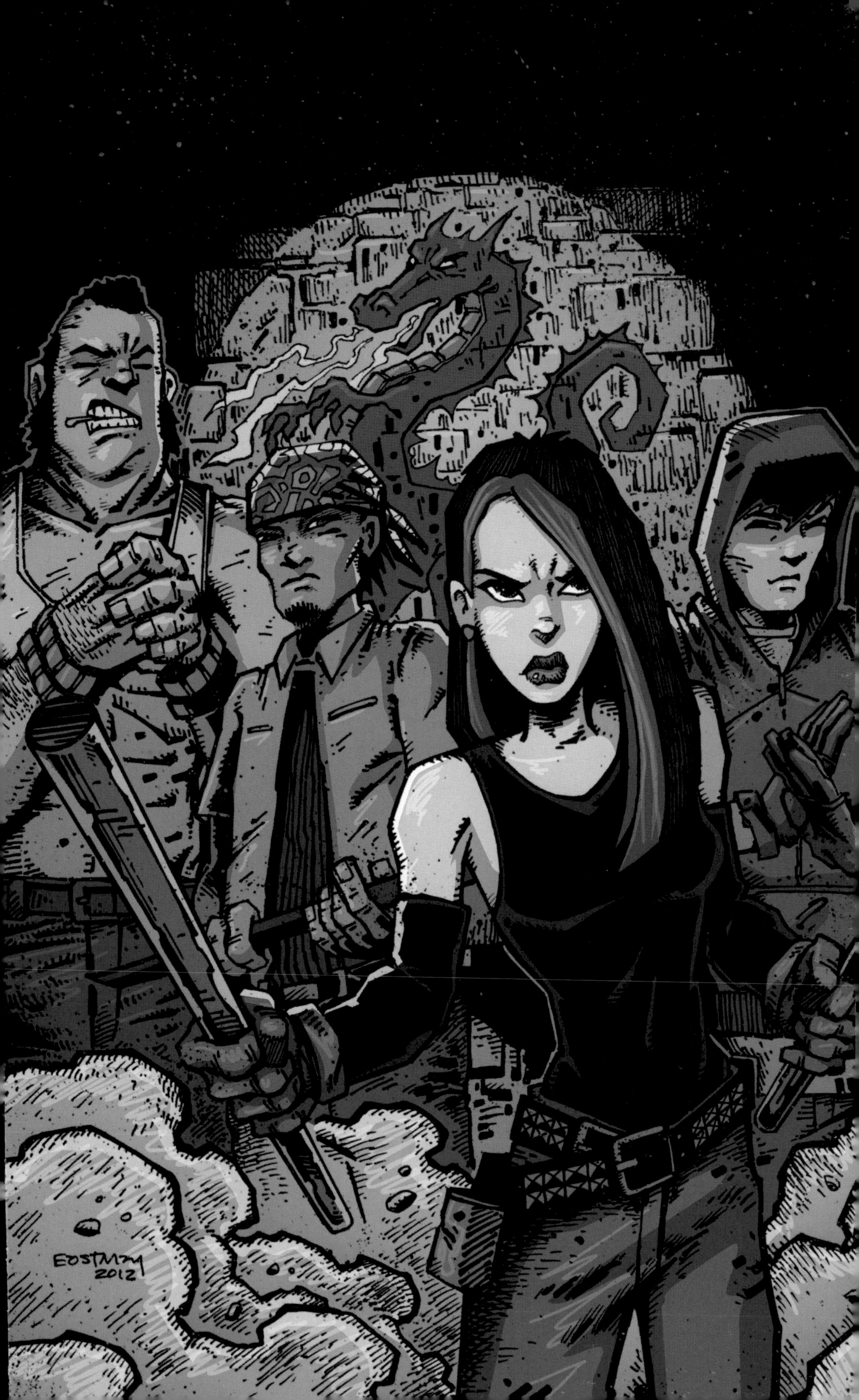
EASTMAN
2012

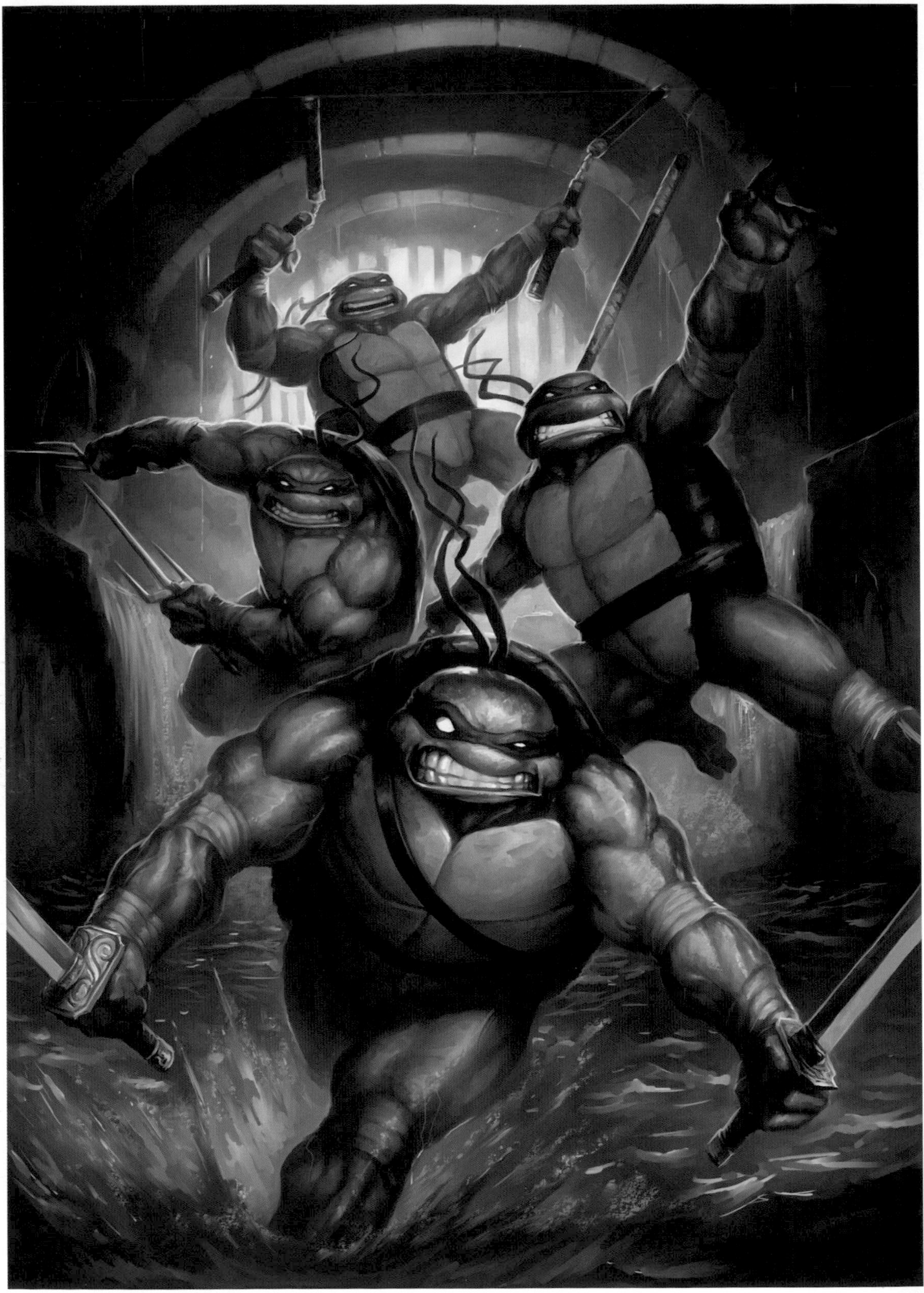

ART BY TYLER WALPOLE

OPPOSITE PAGE: ART BY ZACH HOWARD · COLORS BY NELSON DANIEL

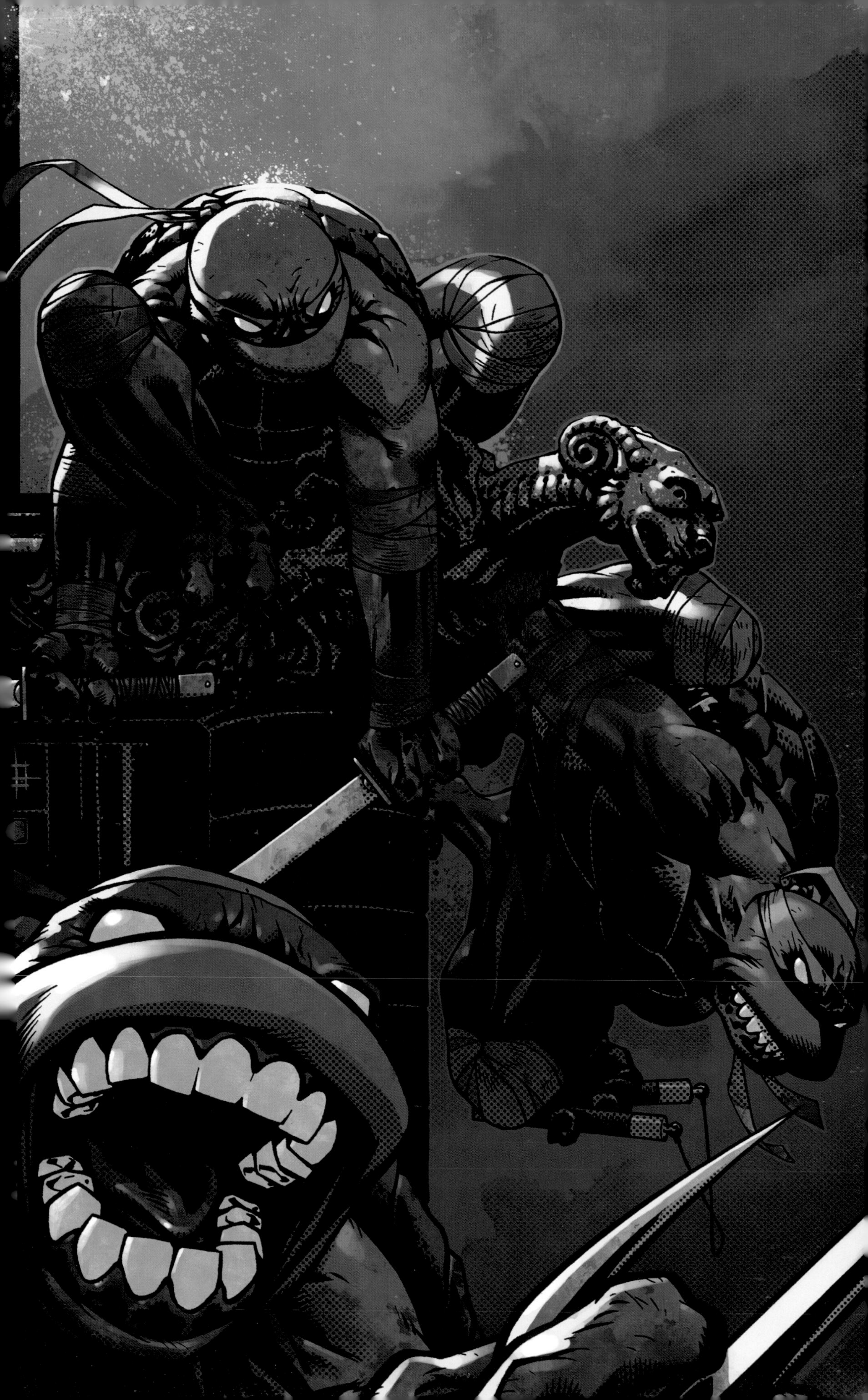

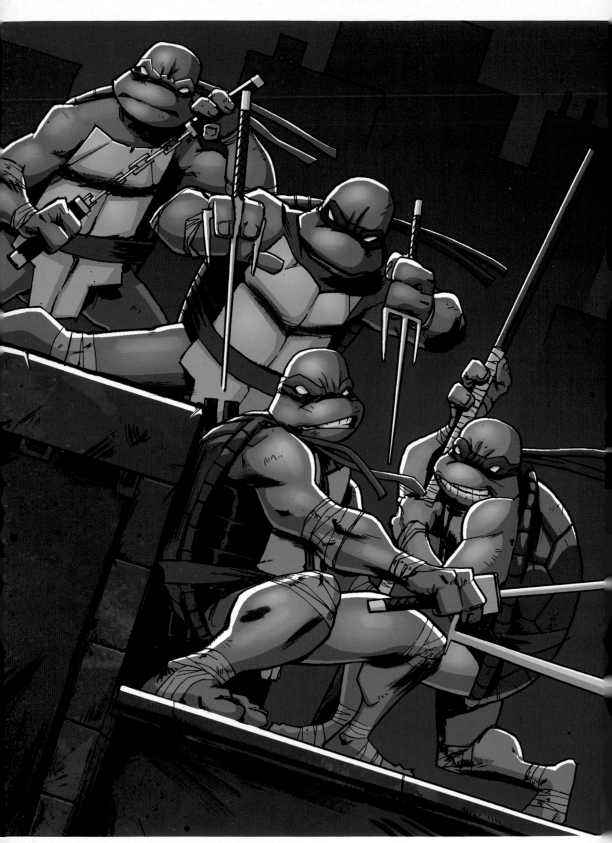

ART BY **DAN DUNCAN** · COLORS BY **RONDA PATTISON**

OPPOSITE PAGE: ART BY **KEVIN EASTMAN** · COLORS BY **RONDA PATTISON**

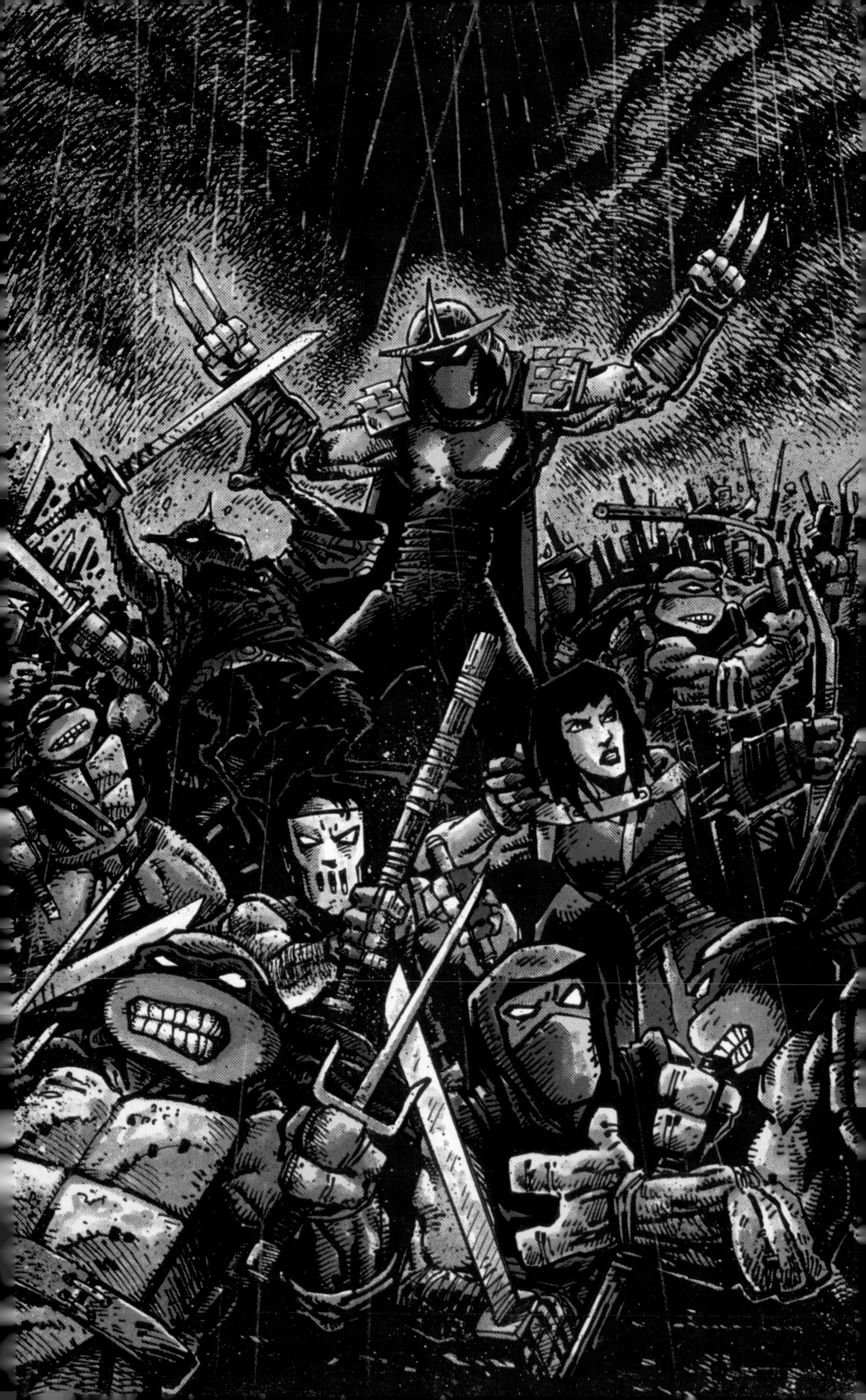

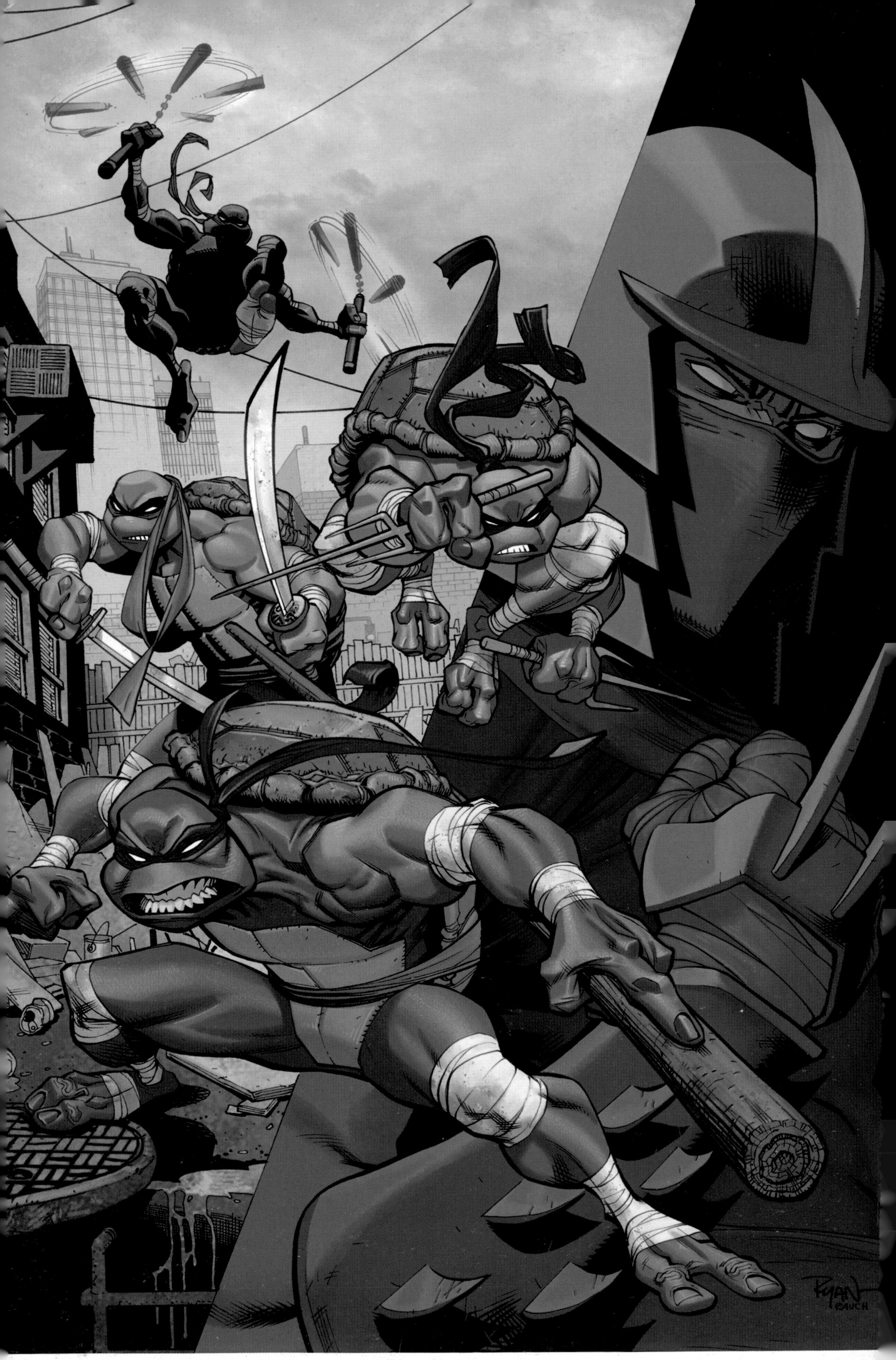

ART BY RYAN OTTLEY · COLORS BY JOHN RAUCH